RAISING LGBTQ ALLIES

RAISING LGBTQ ALLIES

A Parent's Guide to Changing the Messages from the Playground

CHRIS TOMPKINS

ROWMAN & LITTLEFIELD
Lanham • Boulder • New York • London

Published by Rowman & Littlefield
An imprint of The Rowman & Littlefield Publishing Group, Inc.
4501 Forbes Boulevard, Suite 200, Lanham, Maryland 20706
www.rowman.com

86-90 Paul Street, London EC2A 4NE, United Kingdom

Distributed by NATIONAL BOOK NETWORK

British Library Cataloguing in Publication Information Available

Library of Congress Cataloging-in-Publication Data
Names: Tompkins, Chris (LGBTQ advocate), author.
Title: Raising LGBTQ allies : a parent's guide to changing the messages from the playground / Chris Tompkins.
Description: Lanham : Rowman & Littlefield, [2021] | Includes bibliographical references and index.
Identifiers: LCCN 2020052412 (print) | LCCN 2020052413 (ebook) | ISBN 9781538136263 (cloth : alk. paper) | ISBN 9781538192740 (pbk. : alk. paper) | ISBN 9781538136270 (epub)
Subjects: LCSH: Homophobia—Prevention. | Transphobia—Prevention. | Bullying—Prevention. | Parents of sexual minority youth. | Toleration.
Classification: LCC HQ76.4 .T66 2021 (print) | LCC HQ76.4 (ebook) | DDC 306.76/6—dc23
LC record available at https://lccn.loc.gov/2020052412
LC ebook record available at https://lccn.loc.gov/202005241

For my mom.

Thank you for loving me into being.

CONTENTS

ACKNOWLEDGMENTS

Who I am today is not the same as who I was when I began the journey of writing this book. One of the biggest lessons I learned is that so much of writing a book isn't even about writing. For me, it was learning how to manage my thoughts and to ask for help. By asking for help throughout this process, I became more vulnerable. Which both terrified and transformed me.

Working on this book was more challenging than I anticipated, and I absolutely could not have done it without incredible support. It was also the biggest blessing because it brought out the unhealed parts of me that had been dormant for years. The fact that I've even gotten as far as to write an acknowledgment is both a miracle and a gift.

I'd first like to thank my Higher Power. Although challenging, it's been a deeply spiritual experience. One for which I am forever changed.

To my mom, sister, sister-in-law, and brother. Thank you for being there for me throughout this entire journey. It was hard to articulate what writing this book involved, so even just asking me for updates helped cheer me on. Especially to my mom, thank you for encouraging me, praying for me, and constantly showing up despite my unpredictable mood swings. I love you always, and I'm grateful we get to journey this life together.

To my nieces and nephews, thank you for your questions and for always speaking the truth. If I hadn't dedicated this book to Nana, I would have most certainly dedicated it to each of you. I couldn't have written what I wrote without our relationship.

To all the people who ever said anything kind about this project and encouraged me to pursue my dream of writing a book. I especially would like to thank my friends Jose, Griffin, Val (rest in peace), Matt, and Sushant. There aren't enough hours in a year for how much I've talked to you about *Raising LGBTQ Allies*. Thank you for lending your ears for me to talk this through. I look back over the past five or more years, and it's because of our constant conversations that I was given the space to flesh out the ideas in my heart. Thank you for all of our talks. Each of you inspired me to want to keep going.

A huge thank-you to my publisher, Rowman & Littlefield, for giving me the opportunity to share this passion project with the world. Thank you to my editor, Suzanne Staszak-Silva. I appreciate your guidance and help to make each chapter better. Also, thank you for reminding me to use love as my guide.

Another huge thank-you goes to BookEnds Literary Agency. I love being considered a part of your group. Although I don't know all of you personally, what you do and the love you give is felt. Especially to my literary agent, Jessica Alvarez. You have gone above and beyond and I am so very grateful for your time and dedication. I quite literally could not have done this without you. Thank you for seeing the vision of what I hope *Raising LGBTQ Allies* accomplishes and for believing in my ideas, even when I questioned them myself. Your consistency, follow-through, and desire to make the world a better place has helped my dream come true.

I'd specifically like to thank the Allender Center, the Kabbalah Centre, Tilly's Life Center, Al-Anon, and PFLAG. Each group has been integral to helping inform this book's content, intention, and consciousness. Without my relationship and participation with these groups, I couldn't have written the book I wrote.

Another group for whom I'd like to express my gratitude is Toastmasters. I joined the organization to practice public speaking, not realizing I had to write a speech before I gave one. Toastmasters is where I discovered writing.

I'd also like to thank every student I've ever taught. You've been my greatest teachers.

For all the libraries in Los Angeles that gave me a place to lose myself writing, thank you. Writing can be isolating, so being around a lot of books while working on one helped me feel less alone.

To the "angels of AHF," thank you for the years of service and support. I call them angels because I think the staff at AIDS Healthcare Foundation are actual angels.

I would be remiss if I didn't express my sincere gratitude for every person's story I shared and the research I used. So much of what I wrote was made possible because of someone else. I just consider myself a traveler who is simply trying to connect the dots. From the bottom of my heart, thank you. Your lives have impacted mine.

A special shout-out goes to some extraordinary people who have influenced me along the way: Tori, Kiki Spielberg, Melissa, Liz, Ernesto, Steven, TeTe, Louise Hay, Marianne Williamson, and of course, Oprah.

Finally, to LGBTQ generations of the past, the present, and the future:

To those from the past—thank you for your courageous work that's made it possible for me to do mine. To those here right now doing the work—thank you for helping heal the planet by healing yourselves. And to future generations—thank you for carrying the torch and continuing to shine its light.

INTRODUCTION

When most of us think of homophobia or transphobia, we often think of an outward, blatant, and obvious verbal or physical attack. Derogatory language or violence is what usually comes to mind. However, homophobia can also be subtle and multilayered and is deeply insidious. For the past six years, I've been teaching social-emotional learning (SEL) to youth ages ten to twenty-five. Whenever I talk to young people about bullying, and I ask them to tell me what kinds of bullying exist, I can usually count on them to tell me about the more obvious examples, like physical, verbal, and online bullying. However, a form of bullying I often have to bring to their awareness is the silent kind: not talking to someone, ignoring them, or not including others is also a type of bullying. It's more quiet and less obvious, but it usually originates from the belief that a person or group is bad, wrong, or "less than," and its effects are just as harmful and even more pervasive than an outward attack.

In the study of trauma, most professionals classify trauma into two categories, "big T trauma" and "little t trauma." Big T trauma includes domestic violence, sexual assault, death, a natural disaster, or the experience of war. Little t trauma is still a highly distressing event, but it doesn't fall into the big T trauma category; examples are a non-life-threatening injury, verbal abuse, bullying or harassment, and loss of significant relationships. Although this classification of trauma may make big T trauma appear to be more severe than little t, one thing I've come to learn from the study of trauma is to never compare traumas. Research shows the effects of little t trauma, especially if they're ongoing and pervasive, are just as harmful as any big T traumatic event.

I always looked at homophobia, transphobia (including internalized homophobia and transphobia), bullying, and "the closet" through the lens of *shame*; however, it wasn't until I attended a conference for mental health professionals in 2017 that I came to understand how the micro-aggressions LGBTQ youth face on a daily basis, including homophobic bullying, heteronormativity, and not being accepted by family or peers, is itself trauma. And when I say accepted, I mean *truly* accepted. There is a difference between tolerance and true acceptance, which is, in addition to my four goals for *Raising LGBTQ Allies*, something I hope to help schools, mental health professionals, religious leaders, and families understand.

Learning more about trauma, in addition to shame, was the missing link to enable me to convey to parents, caregivers, and teachers why it's so important to not only address the outward, blatant, and obvious forms of hostility or bias toward LGBTQ children but also to show how, now more than ever, the implicit, subconscious, and *silent* forms of homophobia and transphobia are just as damaging. Not addressing the subtle, subconscious, and silent forms of homophobia and transphobia that exist within ourselves, our communities, and our cultures (what I call "messages from the playground" [MFTP]) is like treating only the effects of a disease and not the disease itself.

The four goals I seek to accomplish with *Raising LGBTQ Allies*:

1. To help shine a light on the multifaceted forms of homophobia and transphobia that exist and, although more subtle, are just as pervasive and damaging as any outward, blatant, or obvious attack.
2. To help parents, families, caregivers, and teachers understand that *right now* in our families and classrooms, we have lesbian, gay, bisexual, transgender, and queer (LGBTQ) children. By not acknowledging or recognizing this as a possibility, whether it be our own children or the ones they play with on the playground, we're ignoring it, and our silence still speaks.
3. To help us understand that we *all* play on the same playground. Although we may be affirming and accepting parents, caregivers, or teachers, or we're out and openly gay, lesbian, bisexual, transgender, or queer, we grow up in the same society with the same

religions, watch the same movies, and pick up the same subconscious programming as everyone else. Fragments of external homophobic, transphobic, and heteronormative messaging still seep inside. Left unexplored, these messages can negatively impact our lives, our choices, our communities, and our children.

4. To help prevent bullying, heal queerphobia, and create allies on the playground by encouraging open and authentic conversations within families, and classrooms.

Recently, I asked a classroom of seventh- and eighth-graders, "What if your parents asked you to clean your room?" We were discussing various forms of discrimination and how upset they were with what they've seen and heard on the news lately.

I continued, "You began dusting off the shelves, vacuuming the floor, wiping down the dresser, and picking up dirty clothes. After a little while, your room began to look really clean. But you didn't look under the bed. Underneath your bed there was a thick layer of dust, mold, and fungus. When your parents came to look, they were amazed at how clean your room was. They were so happy to see you'd cleaned your room."

"But is it really clean?" I asked. "On the surface it looks as though you have a really clean room, but with all that dust, mold, and fungus underneath the bed, can you really say you have a clean room?"

They all looked at me in silence, and then one girl yelled out, "Oh, I get it! What's going on in the news is allowing us to look underneath the bed!"

"Exactly!" I said.

I remember after the 2016 election, a friend showed me a video with groups of people verbally attacking one another. He was really upset while showing me the video, and I asked him, "How old are the people in the video?" He said, "I don't know, like thirties, forties, and fifties?" I said, "And they've felt that way for thirty, forty, fifty years. They didn't just all the sudden begin to feel that way this year. Just as strongly as you feel about the things you believe in, they feel just as strongly about the things they believe."

In order for us to truly say our room is clean, we have to look underneath the bed. In this case, I'm inviting readers to look on *the playground.* Until we get in there and clean out the parts of ourselves we haven't seen in a long time or don't want to acknowledge, our rooms, *and playgrounds*, can still be considered dirty. And the way to effectively clean something that's been dirty for a long time is to look at it, acknowledge it, and commit to doing the work to make it shine.

I had always considered myself a good LGBTQ advocate, working hard to create change in the world. It wasn't until I became an uncle that I realized the pervasiveness of homophobia, and that I had to go deeper into my own life to uncover the subtle ways in which it continued to show up in my family.

The common thread among all readers of *Raising LGBTQ Allies* is that they have children, work with children, or have children in their lives they care about. As for parents, these are people who care about the well-being of their children, as well as the world in which they live, and they consciously work to influence their lives in a positive way.

More specifically, this book is for the millennial mother who supports same-sex marriage and has LGBTQ friends, but who doesn't understand the insidiousness of homophobia, transphobia, and heterosexism. It's also for the older mom whose boss is gay and married but is uncomfortable kissing his husband in public. Not knowing about internalized homophobia and how shame affects the lives of gay men, she's curious about why her boss never kisses his husband before he leaves for work-related trips. She intuitively feels his subtle discomfort in demonstrating public affection with his partner and wonders where it could still be coming from.

Raising LGBTQ Allies is for the mother who works at a school and is constantly around youth. She has two children of her own, as well as a lesbian sister, and suddenly realizes she's always told her kids that their aunt's girlfriend is their aunt's *friend*. She's close with her sister and is completely supportive, but wonders why this small truth is something she's kept hidden. She also wonders why her sister hasn't ever said anything otherwise. When she finally does tell her eight-year-old daughter that her aunt's friend is her girlfriend, she's saddened by her daughter's response: "Ewwww, Mom! Girls can't have girlfriends!"

This book is for the father who has a gay brother, but who has avoided talking to his kids about their gay uncle because he's unaware of his subconscious discomfort around what it means to be gay—he associates the word with a sex act.

This book is for the parents of a transgender girl or boy, who don't know much about early childhood development but want to raise their child in an affirming home.

This book is for the teacher who may or may not have an LGBTQ child in their classroom and who often hears their students use the phrase "That's so gay." It suddenly occurs to them that they've never addressed how damaging the phrase can be and wonders why.

This book is for the mother of a gay son who loves him dearly and only wants the absolute best for him, but who shares, at a monthly LGBTQ support meeting, that she still judges her son for "being too effeminate."

This book is for the single gay father who feels uncomfortable introducing his sexuality to his children because he's not aware of his own subconscious internalized homophobia, so he changes the subject when they ask him why he isn't married.

This book is for the best-intentioned adults whose implicit biases affect what they choose to share with the children in their lives.

For the LGBTQ community, this book is for all gay, lesbian, bisexual, transgender, and queer people who have nieces and nephews. They've come out of the closet, and their families are supportive. They are very involved in their nieces' and nephews' lives and pride themselves on being a good aunt or uncle. Nevertheless, they played on the same playground as everyone else and still have some of the negative subconscious beliefs about what it means to be gay, lesbian, bisexual, transgender, or queer. As a result, the subject of their sexuality or who they're dating is kept at a distance from their nieces and nephews. In fact, they may even live in a different state from their family, so their sexuality or gender expression is something they can easily avoid addressing. However, it's never occurred to them that children are more insightful than they realize, and not communicating is *still communicating*.

They also wonder why no one talks about the prevalence of substance abuse in the LGBTQ community nor is bothered by its drinking and drug culture, oftentimes a result of unhealed shame and trauma, which are passed down intergenerationally.

My ultimate goal with *Raising LGBTQ Allies* isn't to change anyone's beliefs; it's to help us understand where our beliefs, both conscious *and subconscious,* come from and how most of them aren't even our own. Unless explored, they can unknowingly control our lives. This is more than a book. It's a peace offering to help heal queerphobia, and it's a way parents, caregivers, educators, mental health professionals, and members of the LGBTQ community can help create a more peaceful planet in a timely, insightful, and instructional way.

Something important to consider is that in my career, I'm fortunate to be able to work with youth of all backgrounds, including lesbian, gay, bisexual, transgender, queer, and questioning youth, as well as with parents of LGBTQ children. I know what it's like to be an ally for sexual and gender minorities; however, my experience is as a gay man. When speaking about other communities, I do so mindfully. I don't have the personal experience of being transgender, intersex, non-binary, bisexual, or a lesbian, so my purpose addressing gender along with sexuality in *Raising LGBTQ Allies* comes from a place of ally-ship.

In the following chapters, you will learn how to effectively and proactively build new playgrounds for future generations. I hope to help parents, caregivers, teachers, and anyone who works with children understand that the argument is no longer around whether being LGBTQ is a choice; the argument is around whether to affirm, embrace, love, and *celebrate* the life of a child.

American mythologist, writer, and lecturer Joseph Campbell, said, "The privilege of a lifetime is being who you are." I believe the privilege of a lifetime is being able to affirm *all children* for who they are.

I

AWARENESS

1

MFTP PART 1: WE ALL PLAY ON THE SAME PLAYGROUND

What We Believe and Why

> The psychology of the individual corresponds to the psychology of the nation. What the nation does is done also by each individual, and so long as the individual does it, the nation also does it. Only the change in the attitude of the individual is the beginning of the change in the psychology of the nation.
>
> —Carl Jung, *The Psychology of the Unconscious Processes*

In 2015, my nephew asked me a question that completely changed the trajectory of my life. I wasn't able to make it home for Christmas that year. So when I was in town visiting a few months later, my mom had all my relatives over, including my childhood best friend, Alyssa. We were in the dining room catching up when my six-year-old nephew, David, ran up to me and whispered, "Uncle Chris, is she your girlfriend?" Now, his version of whispering is talking out loud, so everyone heard and we all started laughing. But it was uncomfortable laughter because everyone knew Alyssa wasn't my girlfriend. I remember turning bright red and feeling this pit in my stomach. I was surprised by David's question and remember looking around for reassurance in the faces of my family. I was even more surprised by how easily everyone was able to dismiss his question and go back to what they were doing.

You know how kids are. Sometimes they have a thought and ask a question, not necessarily consciously wanting an answer. They still learn, though, regardless of what we choose to say or not say.

After everyone left my mom's that night, I started to wonder why David had asked if Alyssa was my girlfriend. I remember looking up at the spinning blades of the ceiling fan before crawling into bed when it suddenly occurred to me, "Oh, he doesn't know I'm gay." Then I had a conversation with myself that went something like this: "Wait, I've been out his entire life and I'm dedicated to LGBTQ advocacy work. How could he not know I'm gay? And how could my family so easily dismiss his interest in whether I had a girlfriend? Oh, his mom, my sister, hasn't talked to him. She must believe something is wrong with being gay."

If my sister's son was in the dark, I wondered about the other kids I knew. I began asking around the next day, and most of the parents I spoke with didn't believe their child was old enough to understand. They seemed uncomfortable addressing the conversation. In fact, when I asked my own loving and supportive mother if my siblings had talked to their kids, ages six to ten, about having a gay uncle, she replied, "Oh Chris, they're not old enough."

Even though same-sex marriage is legally recognized in thirty countries around the world as of 2020,[1] and transgender rights have become an international conversation, we all still play on the same patriarchal playground and grow up in the same heteronormative society. Heteronormativity—the attitude that heterosexuality is the only normal and natural expression of sexuality[2]—perpetuates the closet, and the closet is a hotbed for shame. As children growing up, we pick up the same subconscious programming about what it means to be a man, a woman, gay, or straight.

I love to travel and although I haven't visited nearly the number of places I wish to on my bucket list, I have been fortunate to travel to more than a few. Over the past couple of years, whether it was visiting Bangkok, Thailand, traveling throughout Israel, exploring the seaside city of Barcelona, discovering southern Mexico, taking road trips across the southwest United States, or sightseeing in the Pacific Northwest, no matter where I go, I see playgrounds that look exactly like the ones I played on as a child growing up in Tucson, Arizona, more than thirty-five years ago. To me, they're symbolic and remind me that no matter who we are or where we come from, we all play on the same playground. There are certain collective societal messages we absorb as children, consciously and subconsciously. As a result, we develop certain belief systems that guide our lives.

"Messages from the playground" is an analogy for how I like to describe the subconscious beliefs we *all* pick up from our childhood about what it means to be a boy or a girl, gay or straight, or Black, white, and so on. *Messages* are the dominant societal worldview and *the playground* is our mind or, rather, our consciousness. We can use these terms to describe anything, really, but for the purpose of this book, I will use them as a metaphor to help families understand the complexities of gender and sexuality.

I told my friend over dinner recently, "Homophobia, transphobia, xenophobia, racism, and anti-Semitism can seem like we're fighting a bunch of separate battles. But each is born from the same place: fear." We can all relate to playing on the playground, no matter our background, experience, or beliefs. Using an analogy like messages from the playground unites those of us trying to make the world a safer place for all children. It's something that connects instead of separates.

In order to better understand, or even challenge, our beliefs about people who are LGBTQ, it's important to understand where they come from. When it comes to beliefs, we have to first break a false belief system before we can add a new one—consciously *and subconsciously*. My invitation to you as we begin this journey together is to give yourself permission to consider what I'm saying and be open to what's possible; as I say before each and every class I teach, "We practice nonjudgment here." Try approaching this material without judgment. If you like something I share and find it helpful, great. If not, no worries. Take what you want and leave what you don't.

HOMOSEXUALITY AND THE *DSM*

We've been trained to think of the past in terms of a written historical record. But events don't just get written down; they get recorded and passed on in human bodies.

—Resmaa Menakem

A few months ago, I gave a Messages from the Playground presentation at my alma mater, the University of Arizona. The presentation was part of a speaker series with the university's Institute for LGBT Studies. I began the presentation by playing George Michael's song "Faith." The group was about half students and half faculty and guests, so I asked whether they had ever heard of the song. Most of the audience raised their hands. I then challenged them to tell me what year the song came out. No one raised their hand so I gave them a few hints: it was the same year the shows *21 Jump Street*, *Married with Children*, and *Full House* (the original season) first aired, as well as the year both Kesha and Zac Efron were born, two people popular among a lot of the youth I teach.

Someone from the front row raised a hand and yelled "1987!" I said, "Yes!" Then I continued, "Which was also the same year homosexuality (a sometimes-offensive term I encourage folks to avoid using because of its clinical history used to denigrate gay and lesbian people) completely fell out of the *DSM*." The *DSM* (*Diagnostic and Statistical Manual of Mental Disorders*) is a book used by healthcare professionals in the United States to diagnose mental disorders. It's to healthcare professionals what the Bible is to Christianity. The first edition of the *DSM* was published in 1952 and has since been revised five times. The most current version, the *DSM-5*, was published in 2013.

While most people familiar with the *DSM* and its history of misdiagnosing gay and lesbian people recognize 1973 as the year the American Psychiatric Association (APA) voted to have it removed, *homosexuality* wasn't completely taken out of the *DSM* until 1987.[3] Between 1973 and 1987, it was still considered an ego-dystonic sexual orientation, or a sexual orientation disturbance.[4] In both instances, according to the *DSM*, being gay or lesbian was a malformity of the person.

Following is a detailed timeline of the history of homosexuality in the *DSM*, organized by esteemed psychiatrist and psychoanalyst Jack Drescher, MD, a well-known LGBTQ advocate and spokesperson:[5]

- *DSM-I* (1952): Sociopathic Personality Disturbance
- *DSM-II* (1968): Sexual Deviation
- 1973: Homosexuality per se removed from the *DSM-II* and replaced by "Sexual Orientation Disturbance" (a vote that included almost 10,000 psychiatrists, 5,854 voting to remove homosexuality from the *DSM* and 3,810 to retain it[6])
- *DSM-III* (1980): Ego-dystonic homosexuality (EDH)
- *DSM-III-R* (Revised) (1987): EDH removed
- *DSM-IV* (1994) and *DSM-IV-TR* (Text Revision) (2000): Sexual Disorder NOS

(*NOS* is an abbreviation for "not otherwise specified." When something isn't easy to diagnose, it's a term used by professionals that allows them to show that a person has a treatable illness.)[7]

• *DSM-5* (2013): none

In addition, the ICD-10 (International Classification of Diseases), which is maintained by the World Health Organization (WHO) and is like a globalized version of the *DSM*, didn't remove *homosexuality* from its ICD classification until 1992. Today, it still carries with it the construct of ego-dystonic sexual orientation.[8] Although significant and more LGBTQ-affirming changes have been proposed to the ICD-10 classification of mental and behavioral disorders related to sexuality and gender identity, the ICD-11 with its proposed changes, was only just presented for adoption at the World Health Assembly in May 2019 and won't go into effect until January 2022.

Modern psychology first originated in the late 1800s with the work of Dr. Sigmund Freud. In the grand scheme of things, that isn't a very long time. While I was observing an Introduction to Psychology class last summer at Antioch University, the instructor made a point to share with us how little is actually known about the human brain and how many of the theories that have influenced the mental health field are biased.

For thirty-five years of its almost seventy-year existence, the *DSM* considered being gay or lesbian an actual diagnosable mental illness.

During a recent interview I heard, the late director John Singleton (*Boyz n the Hood*) said, "I'm a product of the last decade, and now I'm out for change."[9] He was speaking about how it's not possible to grow up during a certain time period and not be touched by systemic and dominant cultural belief systems, no matter who we are.

What's so important about the history of the *DSM* in the context of a book for parents, caregivers, teachers, aunts, uncles, and anyone who works with children today is that while the standards of psychotherapy have made advancements, it wasn't that long ago that LGBTQ people were considered mentally unwell. Remnants of misguided beliefs around the mental health of LGBTQ people still exist in the collective consciousness and are connected to many of the stigmas LGBTQ youth face today.

Until we live in a world where the message to young people that being LGBTQ isn't something to fear, LGBTQ youth may experience increased challenges accepting themselves. One of my goals with this book is to make having an LGBTQ child, or knowing one, something to revere.

Most of the parents I know who have a child who is LGBTQ initially questioned why their child is lesbian, gay, bisexual, transgender, or queer. Even the most accepting parents I know once thought there must be a reason or cause for their child's gender or sexuality. Some still question whether it was something they did or didn't do. I don't think I've ever heard a parent question why their child is straight or cisgender (when a person's gender identity matches the sex they were assigned at birth). If we explore what's behind the curiosity about why a child is LGBTQ, we often find misguided beliefs about gender and sexual minorities, which is similar to how the *DSM* was used to misdiagnose LGBTQ people. By digging deep, naming, and cleaning out our consciousness of harmful stigmas, we take their power away.

The point I made during my presentation at the University of Arizona was that if lyrics to a popular song from the 1980s, which is still played on the radio today, and hit shows from thirty years ago are alive in our memories and are only as old as cultural figures like Kesha and Zac Efron, then it's possible that remnants of misguided beliefs about gender and sexuality can still negatively effect modern belief systems, thereby influencing how we parent and subconsciously perceive LGBTQ youth.

Recently, while I was at a lecture with people in their mid-twenties to late sixties (most of whom were parents), the teacher mentioned going to a Bon Jovi concert as something fun to do. I thought, "That's kind of an outdated reference." But then the next morning, during my spin class, before playing "Living on a Prayer," the instructor said, "From 1986, ladies and gentlemen, Bon Jovi—everyone's guilty pleasure!" I thought about what John Singleton said and how it's not possible to compartmentalize what influences society and culture. We are touched by our history—which includes everything from pop culture, food, and trends to psychology, language, religion, and belief systems.

CONVERSION THERAPY—A HARMFUL PRACTICE

Make no mistake: conversion therapy is not about "praying away the gay." It's an emotional torture against our most innocent citizens: our children.

—Gavin Newsom

As of early 2020, conversion therapy, sometimes referred to as "reparative therapy," the harmful and discredited practice aimed at changing an individual's sexual orientation or gender identity, is still legal in thirty-one states. In fact, while doing research for this book, I came across Dr. Joseph Nicolosi's book, *A Parent's Guide to Preventing Homosexuality*, on Amazon. Dr. Nicolosi, considered to be the "father of conversion therapy," was an American clinical psychologist who advocated and practiced reparative therapy for decades in Los Angeles. His book, first published in 2002, was rereleased as a revised edition on March 10, 2017, a few days after his death on March 8, 2017.

Fortunately, in 2019, Amazon removed the controversial book from its site. It's still available, though, on Barnes and Noble's site, as well as in other online bookstores. After finding the book, I began to think about the parents I meet all the time with a child who recently came out—parents who, out of fear, worry, or concern, might google information and accidentally come across Dr. Nicolosi's book or therapists who believe in conversion therapy.

According to studies by the UCLA Williams Institute,[10] around 80,000 LGBTQ youth will experience conversion therapy in coming years, often through the persuasion of well-intentioned but misinformed parents or caretakers. A report from the Williams Institute published June 2019 states: "An estimated 16,000 LGBT youth (ages 13–17) will receive conversion therapy from a licensed health care professional before they reach the age of 18. Also, approximately 57,000 youth will undergo the treatment from a religious or spiritual advisor."[11]

The good news is there are individuals, groups, and organizations working tirelessly to introduce legislation so that all fifty states will have laws banning conversion therapy. What's still concerning, however, is that the laws don't restrict the practice among religious providers, many of whom are fellow members of our communities.

The generational and cultural shifts we need to make, and why this is still an important matter to address, are that there is nothing wrong, bad, or diagnosable about LGBTQ youth. The APA released an official statement in 2013 stating, "No credible evidence exists that any mental health intervention can reliably and safely change sexual orientation; nor, from a mental health perspective does sexual orientation need to be changed."[12]

I personally know three people who have forcibly undergone conversion therapy at the persuasion of their parents. And all three suffered depression and severe anxiety as a result of the harmful treatment. One of the guys I knew was my coworker who eventually had to quit his job because his anxiety was so bad. He became extremely introverted and couldn't be around a lot of people. A report from the American College of Physicians states: "The practice causes more harm, especially to LGBTQ youth and adolescents, including the loss of sexual feeling, depression, anxiety, and suicidality."[13]

What's so devastating about this kind of treatment toward LGBTQ youth is that it continues to happen today in many subtle and seemingly benign ways, even though it's not seen as "conversion therapy," which I share more about in chapters 4 and 7.

Parents seek conversion therapy for an LGBTQ youth because of their misguided beliefs, or fear, about what it means to be LGBTQ. An LGBTQ adult seeks conversion therapy because they haven't addressed their own messages from the playground, or internalized shame, about being LGBTQ, which is a result of not being raised in an LGBTQ-affirming home, learning in an LGBTQ-affirming classroom, or playing on an LGBTQ-affirming playground.

Toward the end of 2019, McKrae Game, who founded one of the largest conversion therapy programs in the United States, came out publicly as gay. After coming out and speaking about the dangers of conversion therapy, he said, "So much of it is trying to change people and fix people. It's a lie and we have harmed generations of people. We've done wrong, we need to admit our wrongs, and do what we can do to stop the wrong from continuing to happen."[14] While Game's acknowledgment isn't a surprise to most allies and members of the LG-

BTQ community, there are still communities that believe in conversion therapy and are fighting to keep it alive.

In January 2019, a lawsuit was filed in Brooklyn, New York, challenging the state's 2017 conversion therapy ban on the basis of free speech and religious freedom. As a result, LGBTQ advocates made a strategic move and asked the New York City Council to repeal its ban. They feared that if the case appeared before the Supreme Court, it could open the door for more lawsuits across the country. Brad Hoylman, the state's only openly gay senator told the *New York Times*, "The legal climate is less favorable at the federal level for the L.G.B.T.Q. community. We crafted the law specifically to pass a legal challenge because we knew this was an area that anti-L.G.B.T. legal forces were exploring."[15] Although the law remains in effect for minors, similar bans are being challenged in other states across the country.

I once attended a lecture, and the speaker shared that even though the Thirteenth Amendment to the U.S. Constitution abolished slavery in 1865, it unfortunately didn't get rid of racism. It's essential that we understand our past in order to create a future in which all children are affirmed and accepted. As in the analogy of cleaning our room, if we don't look under the bed and clean out the deeper layers of dust, we will still technically have a dirty bedroom. The same goes for our consciousness. Until we uncover and name our misguided beliefs about LGBTQ people from not only an individual level, but from a societal one as well, kids today will still be at risk of getting bullied and experiencing queerphobia, the explicit or implicit hostile beliefs about LGBTQ people.[16]

This upcoming generation is set be the first non-white-majority generation. It doesn't mean, though, that we stop talking about racism and xenophobia. When it comes to cultural shifts and new paradigms, we have to take proactive action by helping plant new seeds in the consciousness of new generations.

My goal with this chapter is to have a conversation around the various aspects of queerphobia and shine a light on the work we still have to do to uncover misguided beliefs. Ultimately, my hope is to expand your awareness on the nuanced forms of queerphobia that continue to cause harm in the lives of LGBTQ youth so that we don't pass them on.

HETERONORMATIVITY
AND THE ORIGINS OF QUEERPHOBIA

It is critical to note that our biases against the other are
empowered less by our assumptions of their otherness and
more by our assumptions about our own normality.

—Jamie Arpin-Ricci

My cousin, who recently celebrated her son's second birthday, is a proud
mom. She and twenty of her high school friends have monthly "new
mom" play dates where they all get together, hang out, and watch their
kids play. She posted a picture on Facebook with all the moms holding
their kids, and as I looked at the picture, I thought to myself, "Those moms
absolutely love their children. Each one of them is beaming with joy at
being a mom. I'm sure they would do anything for their child and only
want the best for them and their life." I also thought, statistically speaking,
at least one or two of the children are gay, lesbian, bisexual, or transgender.

An estimated 4.5 percent of Americans identify as gay, lesbian,
bisexual, or transgender, an increase from 3.5 percent in 2012, when
Gallup first started tracking the measure.[17] And this doesn't even take
into account people who aren't out of the closet or who don't identify
as being gay, lesbian, bisexual, or transgender. There's also the "1 in 10"
theory some still refer to, the idea that one in ten people identifies as
having same-sex attraction. Having worked at one of the most popular
bars in the world for ten years, which happens to be a gay bar and an
ideal place to observe human behavior, I would venture to say that the
statistics are even higher. Both gender and sexuality exist on a spectrum.

I began to wonder how many of the moms in the photograph
considered the possibility their child is LGBTQ. I'm not saying they're
queerphobic; what I am addressing, though, is the fact we live in a heteronormative society. We are assumed to be straight upon birth. From
the moment a child is born, they're bombarded with messages of being
straight and cisgender, which creates the closet experience for children
who aren't straight and/or cisgender. It also teaches that LGBTQ youth
are "different" from their straight and cisgender peers.

Although the LGBTQ community has never had more visibility,
we live in a heteronormative world, and among lesbian, gay, bisexual,
transgender, and queer youth, addiction, suicide, and homelessness are

at an all-time high.[18] What's more, beneath heteronormativity is buried homophobia and transphobia. Homophobia and transphobia are multilayered, and each can include conscious *or subconscious* beliefs that someone else or a group of people is inherently wrong. Queerphobia is insidious and more than blatant, in-your-face bullying and name calling. By normalizing for children at a young age something that's otherwise deemed "different" by societal, cultural, and religious standards, we help create allies, prevent bullying, and heal homophobia and transphobia.

My family not talking to their children about me, or worse, thinking they're too young to understand, is a subtle and nuanced form of homophobia. It's also pervasive and harmful. Left unexplored and uncommunicated, implicit messages from what we choose not to share with children can negatively impact their lives, which we'll address more specifically in chapter 5.

As we expand our awareness, I'm going to invite you to begin asking yourself the following questions:

1. Have you ever considered whether your child is LGBTQ? If so, what have your thoughts been? If not, why do you think you haven't considered it?
2. If your child is LGBTQ, what are you doing to create an affirming environment?
3. If your child isn't LGBTQ, what are you doing to help create affirming playgrounds?
4. What messages have the children in your life received, overtly or covertly, about being LGBTQ?
5. What fears, if any, do you have about having an LGBTQ child? Where do they come from?
6. What are you doing to help raise allies?
7. If you have homophobic beliefs, forgive yourself and consider asking, "Where do my beliefs come from?"

These aren't questions you need to answer right now. I'm introducing them here to help open your heart and mind as we delve more deeply into the conversation. Even by considering these questions, we're challenging heteronormativity. They also allow parents and teachers to make the conscious consideration that although they may not have an

LGBTQ child, their child will jump rope or play tag with a child who is LGBTQ on the playground.

We unfortunately live in a world where intolerance of others continues to exist. Children need to be taught how to experience acceptance of others and acceptance of self. By giving parents, family members, and caregivers specific actions to take in their own lives to help navigate conversations, address heteronormativity, and challenge societal beliefs, we help normalize being LGBTQ from a young age.

The journey of this book began originally as a letter I wrote my own family to address a conversation that wasn't taking place. I have twenty-nine cousins, as well as five nieces and nephews. Statistically speaking, there are LGBTQ youth in my family.[19] The purpose of my letter, and impetus for this book, was to help prevent homophobia from being unintentionally passed on by my family to the next generation. That letter has since become:

- an article published on nine different media platforms around the world;
- a presentation at Los Angeles's Central Juvenile Hall, at the University of Arizona, for therapists and mental health professionals across LA County, at Los Angeles's largest LGBTQ youth conference, and for PFLAG Los Angeles;
- a guide for parents and caregivers to use with youth ages six to twenty-four;
- a 2017 TEDx talk, "What Children Learn from the Things They Aren't Told";
- a translation into Portuguese featured on a popular parenting site in Brazil, Papai Educa; and
- a book to help parents, families, caregivers, and teachers unlearn fear.

UNLEARNING FEAR

Love is what we are born with. Fear is what we learn.

—Marianne Williamson

When it comes to gender and sexuality, people often think of the subject matter as something "to understand." I propose that you approach the content of this book not as something to understand but, rather, to consider it as a "process of unlearning." When I first began to explore meditation and spirituality, the common theme among all the books I read and lectures I listened to was that personal and spiritual development aren't so much about trying to understand as they are about unlearning. As you engage each chapter, I invite you to think of this as an experience of unlearning a thought system based on fear and relearning a thought system based on acceptance.

Ultimately, behind homophobia and transphobia is fear. The word *homophobia* itself can be misleading because most people who have homophobic beliefs aren't afraid of gay people. They fear what's outside of societal norms. The intersections of religion, gender policing, and heterosexism must be taken into consideration, which we will explore more. But what it really boils down to is the fear of what will happen if we question long-held societal beliefs—the fear of a world in which the dominant heteronormative patriarchal worldview is challenged. And we, both consciously and subconsciously, assume that what we're unfamiliar with is harmful. We also fear the associations we have, consciously or subconsciously, with words like *gay*.

According to Chapman University's 2018 Survey of American Fears,[20] death and illness are the top fears. Also included on the list are things like pollution, global warming, government corruption, and financial instability. If you look beneath the surface of each of these fears, however, you'll find the truth behind all fear: the unknown. What we really fear most as humans is not knowing. Fear of the unknown is where homophobia, transphobia, xenophobia, anti–Semitism, and racism all stem from.

In an interview I watched of Shonda Rhimes, creator of shows like *Grey's Anatomy* and *Scandal*, she was asked about racism and why she thinks it exists. She said it's because of fear, and the only way to beat racism is to address it, talk about it, have the conversations, and confront it. I once had a fear of public speaking. After my nephew asked me the question that helped inspire this book, I joined Toastmasters, an organization that teaches public speaking and communication skills. The only way I was going to be able to share my message with others was by confronting my fear. I know in my own life, whenever I confront a fear, it usually brings with it a blessing. Confronting fear releases us from the grips of its control. After a year of speaking at Toastmasters, the blessing

I received was the opportunity to give a TEDx Talk. The more we face queerphobia and the nuanced ways it can show up, the more we will release the next generation from its control.

A friend recently said something that captures the essence of *Raising LGBTQ Allies*. He said, "The best tool to expand consciousness is to ask questions. Asking questions helps to increase our level of awareness and broaden our belief system." In the following pages, I'm going to ask you questions in order to broaden your belief system and unlearn fear. On the deepest level, my purpose is to help expand your consciousness.

AWARENESS, WILLINGNESS, CHANGE

Awareness is the greatest agent for change.

—Eckhart Tolle

It takes courage to create change, whether it's within ourselves or in the world. It also takes awareness. Once we're aware, we cannot become unaware. We can choose to ignore what we've been made aware of, but we truly cannot become unaware of something once it's in our consciousness. We may not always like what comes into our awareness, and sometimes it's the very thing we'd rather ignore. But what I've learned from my own life is that nothing is ever brought into my awareness that I'm not ready to either change or help change. I've also found that the longer I ignore making the change, the louder it eventually becomes.

When it comes to engaging matters of the heart, it isn't very easy, not because it's hard but because often we resist what's most important for us to do. There is a reason you're reading this book. It's been brought into your awareness because you have been called to help create change in the lives of LGBTQ youth.

I've intentionally organized the chapters of this book into three parts: "Awareness," "Willingness," and "Change." Just as on any serious personal-development path, once we have awareness, all we need is our willingness to make change. In order to create true and lasting change out in the world, though, we must first begin within. As you read this book, you're going to go within in order to learn specific ways to help raise allies and prevent queerphobia in the world.

Before we conclude the first chapter, I invite you to consider holding two perspectives as true throughout this book:

1. **The LGBTQ community has made tremendous progress.**
2. **There is still more work to do.**

In the following chapters, I'm going to share examples from my own life, as well as from the lives of those who have impacted me. And while it's important for me to hold in my heart the change that has occurred, it's also my desire to lovingly name the work we still have to do with regard to affirming, empowering, and celebrating LGBTQ youth.

In the next chapter, we're going to explore the power of words and how the labels we still use can cause harm in the lives of young people.

Before we go, I'm leaving you with a "Messages from the Playground Proclamation" to help you connect more fully with the purpose we are here for: to make a positive contribution on the planet for the sake of the next generation.

MESSAGES FROM THE PLAYGROUND PROCLAMATION

I am willing to change my beliefs. I am willing to change my thinking. It is easy for me to embrace new beliefs, and I welcome a new way of thinking. My new thoughts and my new beliefs are supportive and loving. I view all children as deserving and worthy of love, and it's up to me to let them know. I forgive myself for unloving thoughts and unsupportive beliefs. I am willing to forgive myself for any beliefs I have that may cause a young person harm. I now choose to think in a new way. My new beliefs make me feel good about myself and others. I feel free. My mind is free. My heart is free. I am open and accepting. I have an open mind. I am open to new possibilities. I help create new playgrounds for new generations. I choose to pass on love and acceptance. I am continuing to grow. I bless the past and honor the future. I create a new world with my new thoughts. I create new playgrounds with my new beliefs. All children are safe and supported in the new world I hold in my heart. It is safe for me to create change. And so it is.

2

MFTP PART 2:
LANGUAGE MATTERS

The Meaning Behind Our Words

The subconscious doesn't distinguish sarcasm and jokes.
It just accepts what it hears. That's the power of words.

—India Arie

Chances are, if you're reading this book and were born within the past hundred years, you've been influenced by homophobia and transphobia. We are shaped by our families, our cultures, and our environments. It's not possible to have grown up in modern civilization and not have picked up, either consciously or subconsciously, fear-based beliefs about gender and sexuality.

Specifically as it pertains to being gay, the word *gay* often has a sexualized or negative association, which is one of many reasons why some parents can have a subconscious aversion to speaking to their children about sexuality or considering the possibility their child might be LGBTQ. Some think sex and sexuality are the same, but sexuality is about much more. Our sexuality is also about love, relationships, and family, not only about sex.

One of the things I've learned from giving Messages from the Playground presentations is that most of us, especially when we're around other people, won't openly admit or acknowledge homophobic or transphobic biases. Similarly, with racism, most people don't want to accept that they may have racist beliefs, yet we know racism unfortunately still exists in our country and around the world. In the article "Implicit Racial Bias," author Bailey Maryfield says, "Everyone possesses implicit biases, even people with avowed commitments to impartiality. Moreover, the implicit associations we hold do not necessarily align with our declared beliefs or even reflect stances we would explicitly endorse."[1]

Not long ago, a parent shared with me how shocked they were to realize their own level of subconscious racism. They've never considered themselves racist and told me they have many African American friends. It wasn't until they considered the possibility their child might date someone Black did they come into touch with their internal and subconscious racial bias. I asked what they discovered when they took an honest look within themselves, and they told me they feared how society would treat their child. They also worried about what their child's life would look like and the challenges they could face being in an interracial relationship. The fears this parent shared about the possibility of having a child in an interracial relationship are the exact same, almost verbatim, fears I often hear from parents with regard to having a child who is LGBTQ.

For example, I recently watched a video where an openly gay celebrity father said he would prefer it if his five-year-old son wasn't gay because he worried about him getting bullied and picked on at school. Hearing a parent, especially a gay parent, say they prefer their child be a certain way makes me sad and frustrated. It also reminds me that just because we're LGBTQ, or an ally of the community, doesn't mean we can't be homophobic or pass along homophobic beliefs. Being an ally or a gay parent doesn't automatically exclude us from teaching homophobia, just like saying we have African American friends but fear our child being in an interracial relationship doesn't make it any less racist.

Growing up in a heteronormative society, it's not possible to completely escape homophobic beliefs that exist in the world from influencing us. That's the conscious inner work I'm inviting us to do: to look within our own life and see where it's possible we're teaching homophobia through our choice of words and language, which ultimately reflects our beliefs.

As an uncle, someone who works with youth, and also a gay man who has worked to heal his own homophobia, I want to further explore why I think it's harmful for adults to prefer children be a certain way. Especially when it comes to having a preference over a child's gender and sexuality, it can be particularly harmful.

The first reason is that it implies that being LGBTQ is a choice. Being LGBTQ is no more a choice or trend than being right- or left-handed. Some people are born right-handed and some left-handed, but it's neither a choice nor a trend. In fact, if we were to try and remember how we made the choice to start using our dominant hand, we couldn't. It's just something inherent in us.

The second is that it doesn't address the root of the concern. I understand not wanting a child to experience hardship or challenge, but when we prefer our child to be straight because we're afraid of how the world will treat them, blame is placed on LGBTQ children and does nothing to change why they're statistically more at risk for bullying and abuse.

The third and most damaging reason I think it's problematic for anyone to prefer their child not be gay, lesbian, or transgender is that it sends the message that being LGBTQ is "less than." It also teaches queerphobia. Preferring a child to not be gay reinforces the closet—and the closet is a hotbed for shame (which we will explore in chapter 6).

What's more, it's quite common for a lot of parents to see their children as only straight and cisgender, an example of heterosexism. If we want to be a part of the solution and help create a world where all children are normal and natural, we have to challenge the dominant heteronormative worldview and not make assumptions about children's identities. By having preferences over our children's gender and sexuality, we send the subtle message that being straight and cisgender is somehow superior to being LGBTQ.

When we prefer a child to be a certain way, we're automatically making the ones who aren't that way wrong. A more empowering and inclusive parenting approach would be to explore why we have certain preferences and whether we're willing to challenge them before they're passed down intergenerationally.

As we work to create a world in which all children are affirmed and accepted, it's important for each of us to heal any queerphobia within ourselves so that we don't teach it in our families—including what words we use, or *don't use*, to talk about our LGBTQ loved ones.

In this chapter, we're going to explore how language matters and how behind each word we use are subconscious beliefs, that is, messages from the playground, about people, places, and things. For example, in addition to the word *preference*, other common words I often hear, read, or see associated with LGBTQ people include: *issues, lifestyle, choice, different, trend,* and *transition*.

Oftentimes, when it comes to language, we may not even be aware of the words we use and how they eventually stick to us like labels. The late literary icon Toni Morrison passed away in 2019, and I recently read one of her quotes about language that struck me. She said, "We die. That may be the meaning of life. But we do language. That may be the measure of our lives."

To the extent we are unaware of how queerphobic beliefs can infiltrate language, we will teach them to youth. This chapter is a continuation of the previous, and in it, we're going to explore how labels, especially, keep queerphobia alive, even in the most accepting spaces. When it comes to addressing queerphobia, or anything that has to do with societal, cultural, and familial harm, it's important we approach it holistically as a system—from all angles.

When my cousin's husband was diagnosed with cancer in 2018, he wasn't automatically given radiation. Instead, he met with an oncologist to address not only the disease but also its prevention, diagnosis, and various forms of treatment. I look at healing queerphobia in the same way. Just like cancer, queerphobia is a disease. Not only do we need to consider where it comes from, but we also need to look at all the ways in which it manifests itself in families, societies, and cultures—which includes the language and labels we use when we speak, read, and write about LGBTQ people.

THE POWER OF WORDS:
LGBTQ + *ISSUES, PREFERENCE, LIFESTYLE,*
CHOICE, DIFFERENT, TREND, TRANSITION . . .

Language reveals one's consciousness.

—Niruka

In 2018, I had a series of articles published on one of the largest online parenting sites. While I was grateful to have articles related to gender and sexuality published on such a large platform, what was eye-opening to me in being published by a site specifically dedicated to parenting was that the very familial matters I was addressing manifested themselves in the publishing process.

When I was notified that my first piece had been published, I saw that the title they used included the word *homosexuality*. As I shared in the previous chapter, using the term *homosexuality* outside of a clinical context is often discouraged and actually restricted by the *Washington Post*, the *New York Times*, and the Associated Press because of its negative history of putting down gay and lesbian people. I was surprised they chose to include it in their title.

I emailed them to change the title, and they were extremely helpful and immediately updated it to be more inclusive. The second title they used, though, included the expression *LGBTQ+Issues*—again, something that appears to be harmless. However, in the article, I specifically address the subconscious forms of homophobia that perpetuate shame within our culture. Using *LGBTQ+Issues* can have negative connotations in the way it's subconsciously interpreted.

It's an example of subconscious residue left over from psychology's history of labeling LGBTQ people as mentally ill. The subconscious mind is powerful and absorbs everything. What, consciously, may not seem like anything harmful is subconsciously informing our beliefs.

In fact, while writing this chapter, I did a Google search using "LGBTQ+Issues," and it returned 73,400,000 results. Some of the results were from LGBTQ-affirming organizations and websites, using "LGBTQ Issues" to talk about matters pertaining to the LGBTQ community. There's even an entire section on Time.com, which generates 35.6 million unique US visitors, dedicated to "LGBTQ Issues." It's not that these websites or groups are intentionally trying to cause harm, but what I'm addressing in this chapter is the meaning behind our words.

Words matter, and each carries with it an entire world of meaning. One of my favorite teachers, *New York Times* bestselling author and spiritual teacher Caroline Myss, says, "Every word is a universe unto itself." Caroline often uses an exercise during her workshops to demonstrate the power of words. To emphasize her point, she asks people to give her a word they can never use again. Along with the word, she says, "I get to have everything that comes with that word. Everything." She explains, "If you choose the word blue, as an example, you'll never see blue again. Or if you give up zebra, you'd never see a zebra, or everything that goes with it, again." Caroline says, with regard to the power of our thoughts and our words, "When someone says your thoughts and your words are not powerful, go to this exercise and come in through this door and then construct the words that you say to another person, word by word. How powerful is every word now?"[2]

Difference versus Different

I've lost count of the times I've stood alongside supportive and loving family members speaking about their LGBTQ children as being "different" from others. I often hear it from members of the LGBTQ community themselves when they share their coming-out story with me. And every time I hear someone use *different* to describe a person who is LGBTQ, I think about young children in the room. Children who may or may not be LGBTQ themselves, but who are listening and internalizing each and every word we use. As an adult, I have a strong enough sense of self to look past the word, but subconsciously, each of us fears being "othered."

Everything is energy, including the words we use. When we use words, we're injecting energy, and that energy can be uplifting or it can separate. Words can inspire. They can also bring down. Consider the following headline examples:

- "Parents Figure Out Child Is Different and Now Tolerate LG-BTQ Issues"
- "Matters Pertaining to the LGBTQ Community Are Important for Families Who Affirm LGBTQ Children"

Which sounds more uplifting to you?

It's human nature to want to be a part of something. We're a community-oriented species born with an innate desire to belong. Especially as children, all we want to do is to be seen and feel like we are part of the family, class, or community. Placing an emphasis on how LGBTQ people are "different" from their straight peers perpetuates the closet, teaches heteronormativity, and continues to keep LGBTQ people in the margins of society. It's okay to recognize differences in ourselves and others. Raising children to understand differences rather than to see LGBTQ youth as different is a much more unifying parenting approach.

My nephew and his father, my brother-in-law, share a first name: David. When David Jr. was younger, my family used to refer to him as "Little David" to distinguish him from his father. David Jr. also happened to be shorter than a lot of other kids his age. I remember having a conversation with my family about how I didn't think we should refer to him as "Little David" because we were helping contribute to the complex he was beginning to develop about feeling small. I told them we have the ability to help make him feel stronger and bigger than he does, and constantly referring to him as "Little David" was only helping make him feel just that—little.

This isn't about making youth hypervigilant about differences; it's about instilling in them a sense of awareness and helping all kids feel affirmed for who they are. There's a fine line between awareness and hypervigilance. Helping raise allies; preventing homophobia, suicide, and addiction; and creating safe playgrounds for all children happens when we acknowledge differences without treating one another as different.

So what can we do? The answer is simple. I would like to invite you to *consciously use a better word*. Instead of *issues* use *matters*. For example, you can say, "Matters pertaining to the LGBTQ community" rather than "LGBTQ issues." Also, I recommend using *LGBTQ+matters* because LGBTQ people matter and quite frankly, *matters* is a more uplifting word than *issues*. When it comes to *different*, use *new normal*. I went to a play my friend produced recently, and in it he talked about how he and the mother of his four-year-old son aren't together, but they have a loving relationship where they co-parent their child—something he refers to as a "new normal." For a four-year-old child, hearing his family describe themselves as "new normal" and not "different from other families" will positively impact his sense of belonging.

Earlier this year, while at a transgender awareness training at an LGBTQ-affirming organization given by a transgender person, the word *lifestyle* was used. The instructor said "transgender lifestyle" in talking about transgender people. It was an example of the messages from the playground we all carry—including members of the LGBTQ community—about people who are LGBTQ. With regard to *issues, lifestyle, different*, and *trend*, being LGBTQ is none of these. Each one is connected to the outdated narrative that says being LGBTQ is a choice. The most important choice we can make when it comes to LGBTQ youth is whether we choose to love and affirm them. Which includes being more mindful of how we speak about people who are LGBTQ.

BE MINDFUL OF WHO IS IN THE ROOM

> Every word, facial expression, gesture, or action on the part of a parent gives the child some message about self-worth. It is sad that so many parents don't realize what messages they are sending.
>
> —Virginia Satir

In February 2019, I wrote a letter to the editor that appeared in the *Arizona Daily Star* titled "Repealing ARS 15-716 Matters, but So Does How We Talk about It." It was a response to an article in the newspaper about the repeal of ARS 15-716, which until July 2019, was considered Arizona's "No Homo Promo" law. The Arizona law was officially repealed in 2019, but similar laws still remain in six US states: Alabama, Louisiana, Mississippi, Oklahoma, South Carolina, and Texas. Section C of ARS 15-716 stated, "No district shall include in its course of study instruction which: 1. Promotes a homosexual life-style; 2. Portrays homosexuality as a positive alternative life-style; 3. Suggests that some methods of sex are safe methods of homosexual sex."[3]

The law itself was being challenged by Arizona's new superintendent of public instruction, Kathy Hoffman, who did wonderful work getting it overturned. My article, though, was in response to how the story was covered by the *Arizona Daily Star*—including their title "New School Chief Seeks Repeal of Law about Gay Lifestyle." Although the article showed that Hoffman was seeking to accomplish something positive, *gay lifestyle* was in the headline—a similar title to the one I referenced earlier, *LGBTQ+Issues*, from the popular parenting site. These titles are problematic and send a conflicting message. In fact, when my mom sent me the *Arizona Daily Star* article, I had to read it a few times to determine whether or not it was an LGBTQ-affirming article.

Ultimately, what I addressed in my letter to the editor, and what I want you to consider, is that the youth referenced in articles and reports are actual people. They're fellow human beings who read the stories we write and hear the words we use to describe them.

For every youth who is out, there are more in the closet who think they are different or fear being themselves. My hope in bringing words and language to your awareness is to help you become more mindful of who is in our homes, classrooms, and churches.

A few weeks ago, I was part of a gender support group organized by Gender Spectrum, a wonderful organization dedicated to creating a gender-inclusive world for all children and youth. The executive director, Joel Baum, emphasized how important word choice is when it comes to youth. He shared a story of a young transgender man who inspired the organization to stop using the word *transition* in speaking about people who are transgender. When someone asked the young man when he transitioned, he replied, "You don't get it. I didn't transition. I've always been here. It's all of you who have had to make the transition of getting to know *me*." Gender Spectrum now uses "change of status" instead of "transition."

My purpose isn't to condemn anyone for using the wrong word. Each of us is learning. Rather, it's to help bring further awareness to the importance of language and to consider how each word not only carries with it meaning, but if we look beneath the surface, also comes from a belief. A Course in Miracles says, "There are no idle thoughts. All thinking produces form at some level."[4]

For example, if you stop reading for a moment and look down at the outfit you're wearing right now, what you have on was a thought. And the design of your outfit was once a thought in the mind of its designer. Each and every thought we have is creative. Especially when it comes to helping normalize being LGBTQ among new generations, everything we say matters.

USE A BETTER WORD

Whoever controls the media, controls the mind.

—Jim Morrison

In this section, I'm going to share with you a few examples of how our language can subconsciously keep some of the stigmas about the

LGBTQ community alive in the collective consciousness, thereby still negatively impacting the lives of young people today.

One of my friends sent me an image from an LGBTQ-affirming organization during Pride month this year, and it read, "If your parents aren't accepting of your identity, I'm your mom now. Drink some water. Take your meds. Make sure you eat. I love you." My friend sent me the post with the question, "Thoughts?" My first thought was, "Why does it say meds and not vitamins?" When I asked my friend what he meant and the reason he sent it to me, he, too, questioned the statement, "Take your meds." He said, "It's not even an HIV-related post, so what does that even mean? Every gay kid has HIV?" The post is a perfect example of how easy it can be to unknowingly perpetuate beliefs that have been passed down intergenerationally about the LGBTQ community, that is, messages from the playground.

It reflects a misguided subconscious belief from the *DSM* that LGBTQ youth have mental illness or, as my friend thought, HIV. In this instance, LGBTQ youth need to take medication instead of vitamins. And medication is usually taken for a sickness or to treat an illness, whereas vitamins are for staying healthy. The message also speaks to the most common fear I still hear from parents when their child comes out as gay: that they may get HIV. My goal addressing our subconscious beliefs, or messages from the playground, is that they inform our lives, and we influence others based on what we believe about them.

In a 2019 article published in the *Atlantic*, the author asserts that hypersexualized images of women and girls have contributed to a culture of sexual abuse. Regarding marketing and advertising the author says, "If we believe in the power of words and images to shape our minds and our lives, then we must also believe in the power of advertising, the power of the assumptions and messages of that advertising, to inform our behaviors."[5]

Recently, while driving through West Hollywood, which is considered Los Angeles's gay neighborhood, I read an advertising sign that said, "Being gay is like glitter. It never goes away." Although light-hearted and fun, the message has a subtle connotation that being gay is something you contract and is another example of how sophisticated misguided beliefs can be. I don't think I've ever heard of someone referring to being straight as something that never goes away. Or how about gender? I'd never say, "Being a boy just never goes away."

When it comes to advertisements like these, as adults we have the wherewithal to intellectually challenge their meaning. However, most of these advertisements I referenced cater to children, and children are like sponges and absorb everything.

I used to work for an LGBTQ advertising agency, and companies would hire us to market their products and services to the LGBTQ community. Having behind-the-scenes experience creating ads for corporations, what I came to discover is that every advertisement, billboard, and marketing slogan is an idea thought up by a person—a person who has beliefs, some of which are biased.

For example, in 2018, Heineken aired a thirty-second advertisement for its light beer.[6] The commercial showed a bartender sliding a bottle past three people, all of whom were African American. The beer arrived in front of a light-skinned woman, with the slogan, "Sometimes lighter is better." If we unpack how the ad came about, it probably went something like this: Heineken hires a marketing/advertising agency responsible for creating ads. The agency has a few people who work on each account and brainstorm ideas. Someone comes up with an idea, and they present it to a group. It's signed off, approved by a manager, and then presented to the client. All of the people involved are individuals with biases and subconscious beliefs, most of which have been formulated from dominant societal and cultural norms. If we don't explore our biases, we can sometimes unknowingly send harmful messages through the words and language we use. The ad from Heineken was eventually pulled because of its cultural insensitivity and racist undertones.

Another example is a billboard for Corona beer that pops up every year during Pride month right in the heart of West Hollywood. On display in the middle of the street greeting people as they drive into West Hollywood is their ad "Tops off. Bottoms up." The background is a beach with a sign that says, "Nude Beach." Again, a seemingly minor example, but the use of sexual positions and referencing a nude beach in an advertisement is quite commonplace for anything marketed to the LGBTQ community. It speaks to the greater sexualization society has of people who are LGBTQ. Sex and sexuality are not the same. The oversexualization of LGBTQ people that exists within the collective consciousness is what prevents us from considering sexuality outside societal standards as a part of a child's normal and natural development.

Unless we understand and acknowledge how words create labels, we won't be able to dismantle fear-based belief systems from individuals or institutions. After all, institutions, societies, and cultures are just a collection of individual beliefs.

BELIEFS INFLUENCE WORDS, AND WORDS CREATE LABELS: INSTITUTIONALIZED HOMOPHOBIA

> Martin Luther King Jr. emphasized that societal transformation does not take place by keeping injustice and corruption hidden, but only by bringing them into the light and confronting them with the power of love.
>
> —Gender Reconciliation International

A 2016 article published on the *Huffington Post* stated: "Lesbian, gay, bisexual and transgender people are disproportionately jailed in federal and state prisons."[7] The article referenced a report released by the Movement Advancement Project,[8] an independent, nonprofit think tank, and spoke specifically about the unfair treatment LGBTQ people receive within the system.

My mom sent me the article right before I was going to give a Messages from the Playground presentation to the Mental Health Department at Los Angeles County's Central Juvenile Hall. I was invited to speak and address the concerns they had around the abuse and discrimination LGBTQ youth face on a daily basis while incarcerated.

I had met a gentleman from Juvenile Hall at a conference earlier in the year whom I had approached after hearing a story he shared about a Catholic priest who visited the youth in "juvie." Upon finding out one of the youths was a transgender female, the priest walked up to the young girl, took her hand and placed it at her heart and said, "You need an exorcism, may God be with you."

After he shared the story with the entire room, I approached him to introduce myself and ask how I could help. The next week I had my appointment with the Los Angeles County Probation Department to get my VISTO (Volunteers in Service to Others) clearance to begin my almost two years of work at Juvenile Hall.

Whether it's individuals or institutions, when it comes to homophobia, transphobia, or something that we don't understand, projecting our fears onto a human being is never the answer. Questioning our beliefs and the labels we give people is. When children's lives are in the balance, we have to address our biases, including the labels we assign to LGBTQ youth with our words, language, and judgments.

A study from the Williams Institute shows that in the Los Angeles County child welfare system, 19 percent of youth identify as gay or lesbian and 17 percent identify as transgender. Some of the other findings show "LGBTQ youth have a higher average number of foster care placements and are more likely to be living in a group home. They also reported being treated less well by the child welfare system, were more likely to have been hospitalized for emotional reasons at some point in their lifetime, and were more likely to have been homeless at some point in their life." In addition to incarcerated youth, according to the William's Institute, 40 percent of homeless youth nationwide are LGBTQ.[9]

A few years ago, I mentored a young man for two years while he was in high school. His name was Mike, and he was also exactly who I just described. He had been living in a group home since age fifteen because of the emotional and physical abuse he experienced in his childhood as a result of his sexuality. He had a few attempted foster care placements, but nothing permanent. Whenever I would pick Mike up from his group home, I thought about all the other Mikes out there who would graduate from high school, get jobs, and live in our communities.

All youth, including the Mikes and 40 percent of homeless youth, are the future. Regardless of their treatment or our beliefs about them, they are members of society. They make decisions and will make decisions that affect our lives in ways we may never realize.

The number-one goal for any child in foster care is permanency. One of the key findings from an LA County Child Welfare System study was that "improving permanency outcomes for LGBT youth requires a multi-pronged approach that examines how oppressions operate at structural and institutional levels."[10]

One of the ways to do this, according to the report, is to "address the roles that racism, heterosexism, and anti-trans-bias play in creating disparities for LGBT youth in foster care"—in other words, to address institutionalized queerphobia.

For us to improve any outcome, we have to address the cause. But before we can make any changes within ourselves, our lives, or our communities, we first need awareness.

The blanket percentages I'm sharing from reports done by researchers to emphasize a point are the lives of children who are being discarded and disowned from families and institutions because they're gay, lesbian, or transgender. They're the lives of people we may see on the street, interact with at the grocery store, or talk to at a restaurant in our own neighborhood. They're the lives of our friend's family members. They're the lives of human beings.

I still keep in touch with Mike, and he recently told me about his new job at a local amusement park. I wondered how many people know about his circumstances. How many people he has smiled at have any idea that he was once removed from his home because it was unsafe for him to be himself? The same person who was hired, takes their order, rings it up, and tells them to have a nice day was at one time being abused for being just that . . . himself.

This is a call to us all to really explore our own biases and our own beliefs. When you see LGBTQ youth, do you have a bias about who they are, how they act, or what they wear? Do you think the messages you heard growing up about someone's gender or sexuality have impacted how you treat them? If so, how? If not, I'd encourage you to look a little deeper. Not only do our biases affect the labels we stick to the people we see, but they contribute to our actions.

Something interesting I learned from a study around racism and homophobia is that showing images of African American people doing positive deeds in a positive way helped to combat racism—it actually helped shift an individual's racist beliefs. However, showing images of LGBTQ people doing positive deeds and in a positive way didn't help to change homophobic beliefs. The only way to change a person's homophobia was for them to get to know someone personally.

Since we live on this planet together—billions of people coexisting—we have to realize the life of one is the life of all.

NEW WORDS, NEW LABELS, NEW BELIEFS

Repairing ruptures is the most essential thing in parenting. And a child will pick up your intention to do good
by them.

—Dr. Dan Siegel

When I first came out to my dad, I was living in a cute little townhouse
with my cousin in Tucson, Arizona. It was in the middle of town off of
a busy road near the University of Arizona. Immediately behind us was
a strip mall with a few restaurants, a Laundromat, and an adult bookstore. After coming out and telling my dad I was gay, he looked in our
backyard and saw a lawn chair near the fence we shared with the strip
mall's parking lot. He accused me of using the chair to stand on and solicit sex from people at the adult bookstore. All of a sudden, a chair that
had been there every time my dad visited me became something sexual
in nature after I told him I was gay. Not only that, but in a matter of
moments I became a sexual deviant in my father's eyes—a projection of
the misguided beliefs he developed from his childhood about gay men.

I understand some queerphobia, like my dad's, runs deep and isn't
going to be resolved by reading a book. I do believe, however, by having conversations addressing the words and labels we associate with LG-
BTQ youth, we can prevent future generational effects of homophobia
and transphobia. Misguided beliefs are passed down. They inform the
language we use to say the words that become labels we assign, whether
they have to do with money, race, gender, or sexuality.

It's said that in nature, "the antidote grows next to the poison." Exploring our subconscious biases, or messages from the playground, with
regard to gender and sexuality is what will help us prevent homophobia,
transphobia, and bullying. It will also help us change the narrative the
next generation will tell, which we'll explore more in chapter 3.

Now that we understand a little bit more about where some of our
misguided beliefs about LGBTQ people come from and why our words
and language matter, where do we go from here?

The next chapter will conclude the first section of this book,
"Awareness." I'm going to share with you a powerful exercise that you
can use on yourself and with youth, and that you can share with others.

It's something I use in my Messages from the Playground presentations that can help turn a negative misguided belief into one that's more affirming.

Before we finish this chapter, it's time for a pause and reflection. I invite you to ask yourself:

1. How have my biases affected my thoughts, words, and beliefs about people who are LGBTQ?
2. What beliefs do I have that are heart-full and hurtful?
3. What am I teaching the young people in my life through my conscious *and subconscious* beliefs?
4. What messages from the playground am I passing on?

3

MFTP PART 3: CHANGE OUR BELIEFS, CHANGE THEIR STORY

It is true if you believe it to be true.

—Louise L. Hay

In 2013, while waiting for a friend at the library, I discovered the book *You Can Heal Your Life* by Louise L. Hay. The tattered, worn, and colorful book cover caught my attention. When I picked it up off the shelf, it seemed really old, which confused me because when I happened to flip through and read a section about gay men, it was as though she was talking about modern times. I turned to the front of the book to see when it was written and when I saw the date, I felt this sudden rush of awareness. The book was first published in 1984, yet Louise Hay described experiences relevant to gay men today.

I'm not sure if you've ever had one of those moments when everything changes. Like becoming a parent: life before the moment and then life afterward. It confirmed for me that although the LGBTQ community has made tremendous progress, there remains healing that LGBTQ people still need. I thought, "If I could bring Louise's philosophy of self-love to LGBTQ youth, it could prevent shame and a low self-concept from taking shape at an early age."

A few months later, I joined thousands of others across the world and became a licensed Heal Your Life Teacher, based on the teachings found in Louise Hay's bestselling book. I wanted to share the information I learned about self-love with the LGBTQ community as a means of achieving *inner* equality. Since then, I've been teaching and working with agencies, institutions, parents, and groups on matters ranging from homophobia to spirituality. I've taught with organizations like:

- Los Angeles Central Juvenile Hall
- Models of Pride
- LA's LGBT Center's Youth Center
- Positive Images
- University of Arizona's Institute for LGBT Studies
- Penny Lane Centers
- Strength United
- Tilly's Life Center

One of the organizations where I teach, Tilly's Life Center, uses social-emotional learning, as well as Louise Hay's self-love methodology. And for the past six years, one of the classes I've been teaching is called "Who AM I." Students participate in an exercise where we ask them to tell us what they believe about things like boys, girls, school, life, family, money, and so on. The purpose of the exercise is to uncover negative beliefs and replace them with something positive.

During the class, I often pick money as a topic to discuss because (a) everyone has a specific belief about money, and (b) the subject is usually pretty charged. No matter where I teach or what age level the class is, there are always a few students who raise their hand and share the cliché "Money is the root of all evil."

This might even be something you've heard yourself. I'm not sure if you're aware of this, but it's a New Testament reference, and this is not even the full passage. The full passage is "For the love of money is the root of all evil: which while some coveted after, they have erred from faith, and pierced themselves through many sorrows." If we unpack the passage, we see it's about selfishness and not about money. Money itself is not evil; selfishly putting it before everything else is.

It's an example of how misinterpreted biblical passages become collective societal beliefs that are unknowingly passed along generation after generation, causing harm in young people's lives. The purpose of this chapter is to explore our individual and collective beliefs and why exploring them matters.

WHY OUR BELIEFS MATTER

"If you do not run your subconscious mind yourself, someone else will run it for you."

—Florence Scovel Shinn

One summer, I taught the "Who AM I" class to a group of fourth-graders. This particular group was the youngest class I've explored belief systems with. After they completed their journaling exercise, I asked a few of them to share with me their belief about money. A young boy, age nine, immediately flung his arm in the air. When I called on him, he said loudly and with conviction, "Money is the root of all evil!" I was shocked to hear someone so young have such a strong belief about money.

I was pretty certain he didn't have a job, so I asked whether the belief was his or was something he had heard. With further conviction he exclaimed, "It's my belief!"

Now, if someone believes money is the root of all evil, chances are, even if they consciously recognize its value and the importance of using it to get the things they want, like a house or a car, they'll subconsciously get rid of money anytime they have some. For example, they might have a difficult time saving money. Whenever they receive money, like a paycheck, they'll immediately find ways to spend it. Consciously, they can tell you the importance of money. But subconsciously, they have a negative association with money. It's the, "root of evil" and who wants to hold onto anything evil?

So I asked the young boy in my class if he had a job or received an allowance. To which he replied, "No."

"Well if you don't have a job and you don't actually receive money, how did you learn it was the 'root of all evil,'" I asked.

"Well, it's something my mom says a lot," he replied.

That's the thing with beliefs. Most of them aren't our own. As children, we pick them up from the adults around us.

I asked the class if they wanted to have a car when they got older. The entire group shouted, "Yes!"

I continued to ask the class if they wanted a house when they're older, maybe a pet, or to buy things they enjoyed. They all said, "Yeeeeesss, Mr. Chris!"

Having a subconscious negative association with something, whether money or being LGBTQ, can cause us to resist the very thing we support or recognize as important. Even if we consciously see it as good.

In addition to the analogy of a dirty room, today while hiking, I thought about how the process of uncovering beliefs is similar to gardening. Getting rid of negative beliefs around gender and sexuality is like ridding our garden of weeds. Some of the weeds are easier to dig out than others, however. Similarly, some of our beliefs are easier to get rid of because we have less of an attachment to them. As with surface-level weeds, we barely have to put our hands in the soil, and we can effortlessly pluck them out. But there are the weeds with thicker, longer, and deeper roots. They require a lot of digging to dredge up. They can also sometimes cause more harm than good at first because after we pull them out, we realize how interconnected their roots were in the foundation of the garden. After they're removed, the area around them might collapse, leaving a big hole.

I view homophobia and transphobia like the deeper roots. We have to dig deep in order to prevent them from growing in the minds of future generations. But once we do, once we dig them out, we get to grow a new garden filled with affirming and uplifting new beliefs of our own.

Whenever I teach a class or give a presentation, I find that people are more apprehensive about acknowledging their negative beliefs than they are about sharing positive ones. Once, I gave a presentation to a group of fifty therapists—people who pride themselves on being open and honest. I did an exercise where I invited a volunteer to stand in the middle of the room. I passed around blank labels and asked everyone to take a few minutes to write the messages they've either heard or believe about people who are lesbian, gay, bisexual, and transgender. After they finished writing, I asked each person to walk up to the front of the room and stick the label onto the volunteer. It was supposed to be an exercise used to show how we can sometimes project our misguided beliefs about gender and sexuality onto people who are LGBTQ.

When I began to peel the labels off and read them out loud in front of the group, demonstrating the purpose of the exercise, most of the words were politically correct, like "gay is friendly and nice" or "trans is beautiful." And while both of these statements are true, they unfortunately aren't the primary messages most LGBTQ youth experience growing up. Our society is homophobic and transphobic, and we can't change what we aren't willing to see. An old Alcoholics Anonymous adage says, "You're only as sick as your secrets."

It's not possible to grow up in a homophobic and transphobic society and not be touched, or somehow influenced, by either. Acknowledging our personal biases and misguided beliefs helps to heal them within ourselves and prevent them from occurring in the belief systems of youth.

Also, as we discussed in chapter 1, the word *homophobia* can be misleading. A phobia is a pretty serious condition stored in the fight, flight, and freeze part of our brain, otherwise known as the "lizard brain" or amygdala. Phobias are often anxiety producing and can feel like a life-or-death moment when experienced. According to Harvard Health, "A phobia is a persistent, excessive, unrealistic fear of an object, person, animal, activity or situation. It is a type of anxiety disorder. A person with a phobia either tries to avoid the thing that triggers the fear, or endures it with great anxiety and distress."[1]

Harvard places phobias into three categories: specific phobias, social anxiety disorder (formerly "social phobia"), and agoraphobia (fear of places and situations). I once had a friend who had a specific phobia of clowns. He would break out in sweat, have shortness of breath, and begin to shake if he saw one in person. His specific phobia prevented him from going to amusement parks or being in public during Halloween. The effects of his phobia were uncontrollable before he sought professional help.

Often, people have specific phobias of doctors, dentists, and clowns. In fact, on Harvard's list "Phobias from A to Z,"[2] homophobia and transphobia aren't included.

Using *homophobic* to describe a parent who has conscious or subconscious negative beliefs about people who are gay or lesbian isn't entirely accurate. Doing this can actually prevent us from uncovering and acknowledging the misguided beliefs we have about people who are gay and lesbian because beliefs and opinions are housed in a completely different part of the brain from the amygdala. Our thoughts, beliefs, and consciousness live inside the cerebral cortex, otherwise known as the rational part of the human brain.

Therefore, when it comes to "homophobia," or having negative opinions of people who are gay or lesbian, we aren't actually addressing an anxiety-producing or specific phobia. We're addressing misguided thoughts, words, and beliefs, which we can actually control and, through inquiry, change.

What's more, the same part of our brain that houses our consciousness and thinking also holds our courage. In his book *What Happy People Know*, author Dr. Dan Baker states, "You can't rise above fear without courage, because fear is hardwired into your neural circuitry. If fear is eternally programmed into your brain, though, so is courage. It comes from the neocortex and is a product of the spirit, the intellect, and the higher emotions of love and generosity."[3]

It's through courage that we develop an increased awareness of what we need to change within ourselves and our communities. Changing the story for the next generation begins with us, but the outdated beliefs we don't name will remain the same. Dr. Baker continues, "The neocortex is also the physical site of the human spirit, the entity that links the intellect with intuition and the subconscious."[4]

When I give a Messages from the Playground workshop today, I offer a visualization beforehand. The visualization acts as a sort of meditation and helps access the subconscious mind. Most of our life operates from the subconscious. An easy way to distinguish between the conscious and subconscious is that the conscious mind is what's telling you to read this book or when to go to bed. Our subconscious mind works behind the scenes. It's the real driver of the ship and is what controls our breathing and digestion and houses our belief system. Together, our conscious mind, subconscious mind, and belief system make up our consciousness. A simple formula is: **beliefs + thoughts = consciousness around a particular subject**.

To help demonstrate my point, I'd like you to consider Google as the "collective consciousness." Whatever we Google, whether it's *bird, dog, tree, God,* or *gay,* the most common image will result, and it typically tends to be what most people have in their conscious or subconscious mind about that particular subject. Go ahead and try it for yourself. Google a particular word and see if the results match what you learned or heard growing up and then ask yourself these two questions:

1. Does this support what I personally believe?
2. Is this true 100 percent of the time?

For example, I once gave a presentation about reestablishing a relationship with a higher power. To demonstrate my point that Google acts as the collective conscious, I printed out the four most popular images of God. After I asked the group to write down what they learned God looked like growing up, I showed the group the life-size images I made. They all matched the description each person gave in the class: an angry older man with a beard on a cloud in the sky—which is connected to a lot of the fear-based beliefs we carry, consciously *and subconsciously*, about God and religion.

The purpose of the exercise was to encourage participants to consider an expanded view of what a higher power could look like and is something we're going to explore further in the next section.

REESTABLISHING A
RELATIONSHIP WITH A HIGHER POWER

My trust in a higher power that wants me to survive and
have love in my life, is what keeps me moving forward.

—Kenny Loggins

In chapter 1, we looked at the connection between misguided beliefs around LGBTQ people and the mental health field. In this section, I'd like to have a conversation about God. This can be a sensitive subject, especially if we've been hurt by religion. As a gay man, I didn't think God was available for me growing up. But whether I call the higher power *God, love, universe, Divine,* or *nature,* reestablishing a relationship with my version of a higher power and cultivating a spiritual connection was one of the best decisions I ever made.

Whether or not we grew up with religion, our lives have been influenced by religious beliefs. The United States was founded on Puritan values that still course through the veins of many North Americans today. Part of unlearning a thought system based on fear is by reexamining our beliefs, especially as they pertain to outdated and misinterpreted religious concepts that create harm in the lives of LGBTQ youth or any human being.

In 2018, I took a trip to Spain and Israel. Visiting Israel inspired me to learn more about Judaism, and so when I returned home, I signed up to meet with a rabbi who holds weekly classes at his home in Los Angeles. I wasn't converting, but one of the things I love learning about from other religious and spiritual traditions is that no matter the faith, there are deeper teachings relevant to us all, regardless of our backgrounds or beliefs. Being gay and raised Christian, part of my coming-out story includes spiritual harm by the church. And part of my healing has involved exploring lots of spiritual and religious teachings to understand where certain misguided beliefs about people who are LGBTQ come from and what we can do help create change.

The topic of the classes I attended at the rabbi's house was the Ten Commandments. He wanted to clear up some of the misinterpretations there are about them and explain to us their deeper meaning. I remember after the first class calling my mom while walking to my car because what I learned completely blew me away. "Out of all the commandments," the rabbi shared, "the third commandment is the one most imperative of which to not break: 'Thou shalt not take the name of the Lord thy God in vain.'" He said it's the one people confuse the most, but that it's the most important one to understand. He asked us, "How many of you think this means to not swear or say something like 'God dammit?'" Most of the room, including me, raised their hand. In fact, it's the reason I called my mom because it's what I was told growing up. To this day, even if I say, "I swear to God," my mom corrects me and says, "Don't take God's name in vain!"

The rabbi shared that the true meaning of the commandment is to not use God as a means of causing another human being harm. He said, "Simply put, the 3rd Commandment is telling us to not ever use God to justify harming another person, whether it's with our words, judgments, or fists." When I told my mom what I learned, as a Christian of more than forty years, she was speechless. She told me she had never heard it put that way and wanted to call her Christian friends to share with them what the rabbi said. Part of my mom's journey of being a devout Christian with a gay son has been reconciling her relationship with God, the church, her unsupportive friends, and her religion.

I understand this can be a hot-button topic, but I don't think I can write a book about uncovering misguided beliefs about LGBTQ people without at least addressing religion. The purpose of this chapter, and in particular, this section, isn't to explore religion. There are many LGBTQ-affirming religious books out there. I do think, though, it's important to invite those of us who have had an experience with religion to consider, for the sake of our journey together, reestablishing a relationship with a higher power that is affirming and supportive of all youth. Someone asked me the other day how I'm able to do the work I do. I told them, "Honestly, I don't know if I could have hope for a world where all children are affirmed and accepted without a higher power to lean on."

Even if we don't believe in God or we weren't raised with religion, both influence our beliefs. As I shared earlier in this chapter, in the six years I've been exploring belief systems while teaching social-emotional learning throughout Los Angeles County, I haven't come across a single class where at least one young person hasn't had a belief that reflects misinterpreted religious doctrine. And what I've learned working with LGBTQ youth is that the most important journey a person who is LGBTQ can make is to heal shame and trauma, including internalized queerphobia. Healing our relationship with ourselves helps us to heal our relationship with a higher power, which is what ultimately connects us with our purpose and why we are here.

For years, certain religious groups have failed to accept gay, lesbian, bisexual, and, transgender people. And for that reason, the LGBTQ community has had to create alternative spaces to gather, connect, celebrate, and, essentially, worship. After almost seven years of sobriety and ten years working at a gay bar, what I share with others from my experience is that what people do at a bar and what they do at church are ultimately the same: the pursuit of a connection with something beyond the realm of this world. It's just that one source is sustainable, and one isn't.

Making amends where there's been harm is part of the healing process. The more we can recognize, repent, and repair religious harm, the more we can prevent future generations from experiencing not only shame but also trauma. And the more we can make space for a young person to cultivate a meaningful spiritual connection and teach them an inner sense of self-acceptance from an early age—which includes feeling welcome, celebrated, and affirmed—the more we will be able to repair.

According to Native American tradition, when we heal, we heal seven generations before us and seven generations after. Doing the work to repair, now, both individually and collectively, will not only heal our past, but by doing it with love, it will also help heal the future.

WITH LOVE

> Our blessing stems from the fact that we have had to over-
> come huge obstacles in order to know love. We must now
> love deeply, passionately, compassionately, completely and
> selflessly. It is our calling as a people. It is our calling as
> human beings.
>
> —Christian de la Huerta

Recently, while attending a health and wellness event with various spiritual leaders from the Los Angeles community, one of the meditation teachers said to the audience as he looked around the entire room, "All of this, all of what we're here to learn. All of it is to get to a place of 'Love thy neighbor as thyself.'" I thought it was a beautiful reminder that whatever our spiritual or religious beliefs are, getting to a place of "love thy neighbor" is really what affirming, accepting, and loving LGBTQ youth is all about.

It also reminded me of something the mother of a transgender little girl said on a panel I recently spoke with. She said, "As someone raised in a Catholic family, I've had many fights with family members over my daughter. In the beginning, I didn't know how I was going to do it. Then I had the realization, I can do it with love. Love is the only way I can keep fighting for my daughter's rights."

A few years ago, I was invited to speak to a group of high school students and tell my coming-out story. The school told me I could share whatever part of my story I wanted, but that I only had ten minutes. For most gay men, our coming-out story is something we're used to sharing. It's typically the conversation we have on our first or second date. A lot of the stories I hear involve hardship, challenge, and, sometimes, family rejection. I was pretty comfortable sharing my story individually, but didn't quite know what I was going to say publicly.

What astonished me was that I wound up telling a love story. Out of all the things I could have shared, the story I told was about when I met my first boyfriend and fell in love. After I reflected on my talk, it occurred to me the reason I came out was for love. Each of us is on a journey of love; whether it's self-love, love of a higher power, love of a partner, or love of our children, love is the common denominator that unites us all.

Whatever our faith background, when we explore what we believe, we open up our hearts and minds to an entirely new world. At the end of this chapter, there is an exercise you can use to further explore your own beliefs. The benefits of bringing them into your consciousness, whether they have to do with race, religion, gender, or sexuality, is that you become a conscious creator. You get to let go of the ones that no longer serve you and your life.

Once you uncover a negative word or belief, ask yourself:

1. Is this true?
2. Where might this belief come from?
3. Is it my own?
4. Is this a belief I want to continue believing?
5. Does this word imply something positive or negative?

LET'S MEET WHERE YOU'RE AT

Sometimes, all we need is someone to believe in us in order for us to believe in ourselves.

—Karen Berg

The other day I taught a class called "I AM Happy." Most of the youth in the class had been in foster care since they were children and had been in and out of Juvenile Hall as adolescents. When I sat down and started to talk to them about happiness, I wondered if this conversation was even something helpful for them to be having during our first class together. I believe each of us desires to be happy, but I also believe meeting people where they are is necessary when engaging in any type of discussion.

After I asked, "What makes you most happy?" A young girl replied, "Being able to see my brothers makes me happy." Then one of the boys said, "Going home makes me happy." I realized speaking to them about happiness without first considering their specific circumstance could actually do more harm than good. Not thinking about their living situation and life experience was inconsiderate.

Needless to say, we completely missed the mark with the group, and it wound up being a very difficult class to instruct. The youth were resistant and checked-out, which only afterward, I realized, made perfect sense. On the drive home, I thought about how, if I went to the chiropractor with a shoulder injury, it might take six months to be able to move my arm fully. Doing exercises on the first day that are normally reserved for someone who has been in physical therapy for a long time could further damage an already-injured arm.

The same can be said for changing our beliefs around anything, whether happiness or gender and sexuality. Being willing to meet people where they're at, in learning anything new, is part of the healing journey. Especially when it comes to biases and beliefs, people will sacrifice their lives defending what they believe. Speaking to someone's potential while meeting them where they are at is the most powerful approach we can take when navigating complex conversations. During a presentation organized by Gender Spectrum, the facilitator encouraged parents to do a short exercise before meeting with school administrators. They were giving tips on what parents and allies can do when facing a nonsupportive or unaware loved one, and they suggested before any meeting to close our eyes and ask ourselves, "If I imagine this going perfectly, what would it look like?"

It's a beautiful example of how not only is it important to meet people where they're at, but holding in our hearts and minds a vision of what we're hoping to create is a vital part of creating lasting change. What we believe about our process matters just as much as the process itself.

WHAT DO YOU BELIEVE?

If I accept you as you are, I will make you worse; however, if I treat you as though you are what you are capable
of becoming, I help you become that.

—Johann Wolfgang Von Goethe

After reading Louise Hay's book *You Can Heal Your Life*, my life completely changed. For the first time, I was introduced to the notion that
our thoughts create our life. I was like, "What?!" If our thoughts create
our life I was going to have to pay more attention to what I was thinking. The thing is, though, it's not really our thinking that creates our
life. It's our beliefs about our thoughts that do. I believed what I read,
which is why my life changed.

The past few weeks I've been watching various documentaries on
old Hollywood actresses, like Sophia Loren, Natalie Wood, and Audrey
Hepburn. What's fascinated me about each documentary is that while
they've been about completely different people, the women's childhoods had so much in common—including a belief instilled in them
by their mothers at a very young age that they would be actresses or
entertainers. It got me thinking about the messages we pick up as young
children and how, just as for these women, they help formulate our
beliefs, whether we're conscious of them or not.

In one of the documentaries, I was astonished to learn that Natalie
Wood almost drowned as a young girl on a movie set and so she had
a specific phobia of big bodies of water. I had known about her death,
but I never knew that during her entire life, she believed she'd die from
drowning. As I watched her story, I kept thinking about the power of
our beliefs. It's one thing to understand how our thoughts create our
experience, but it's our beliefs about ourselves and our lives that really
have power.

Our beliefs tell our story. They can also tell the story of those to
whom we pass them along. My invitation to you as we continue this
journey together is to become aware of the beliefs you're helping to pass
down to the youth in your life.

We're going to conclude this chapter with an experiential exercise.
As we move from "Awareness," we'll take what we've learned in the

first section of this book into the second section, "Willingness," which will help us examine the effects of shame, learn more about trauma, and understand why it's so important to have early conversations with children about matters pertaining to LGBTQ youth.

MESSAGES FROM THE PLAYGROUND VISUALIZATION

Get into a comfortable position. Close your eyes and take a deep breath . . . now gently exhale. Imagine you're in an open field lying under a tree. The view is of a hillside overlooking an ocean. This is a calm and peaceful place. A place that is safe and welcoming. Take another deep breath in . . . now gently exhale. You can come here anytime you want to collect your thoughts and to feel at peace. Begin now to visualize yourself relaxing. You can feel the warmth of the sun gently embracing your skin. You can hear the waves of the ocean in the distance softly lapping the sand. You can feel a smooth breeze brush against your face, making you feel even more relaxed and calm. You are completely alone and feel completely open. You allow any tension in your body to melt away. All cares and worries of your day are gradually melting away. Take a slow deep breath in and gently exhale. Visualize in your mind any place you may be holding tension in your body, any aches or pains, gradually softening and releasing.

You are completely open. You feel completely serene and at peace under this tree. I want you to notice a shiny green envelope that is lying next to you. You reach down and pick up the envelope. As you hold the envelope in your hand, you notice there is a note inside. You open the shiny green envelope and reach in with your fingers to pull out the piece of paper. You unfold the paper and read written in blue ink the word: *gay*.

What *immediately* comes to mind? Is there a feeling or a sensation in your body you experience when seeing the word?

Take a slow deep breath in and gently exhale. You notice another piece of paper in the envelope. You pull it out and written on the paper in the same blue ink is a question, "What have you heard about being gay?" What words come to mind? Any feeling or sensation in your body?

Take another slow deep breath . . . and gently exhale. What messages did you hear growing up about boys? What messages did you hear growing up about girls?

Take a slow deep breath in and gently exhale. When you hear the word *homophobia*, what comes to mind? Notice any feeling or sensation in your body.

What is the first memory you have of knowing about someone gay? What's the first thing that comes to mind?

Take a slow deep breath and gently exhale. I'd like you to imagine you're on a playground. You may see yourself as a young child or you might just be observing a group of kids playing. You're aware that one of the kids in the group is transgender. What do you see? What is the image you have? What words do you hear? How do you react? How do the other children act? Become aware your thoughts. It's safe to be honest and okay to share.

It is now time to leave this visualization. When you feel ready, gently bring your awareness back to your body and to the room. Begin to feel where your hands are placed and become aware of your feet planted on the ground. You can give your fingers and toes a wiggle, and when you're ready, gently open your eyes.

MESSAGES FROM THE PLAYGROUND EXERCISE: UNCOVERING MISGUIDED BELIEFS ABOUT GENDER AND SEXUALITY

After the visualization, I'd like you to take out a journal or a sheet of paper and complete the sentences below. Be as honest as you can with your answers. It's best if you can recall the first word or image that came to mind during the visualization exercise.

GAY IS:

BEING GAY IS:

MESSAGES I'VE HEARD:

Note:

- Messages from the playground are the subconscious beliefs we all pick up from our childhood about everything, including gender, sexuality, religion, and race. They formulate our belief systems, and our belief systems control the way we live our lives.

- Subconscious—of or concerning the part of the mind of which one is not fully aware but which influences one's actions and feelings.[5]
- Other words you can do this with: *boys, girls, gender, sexuality, transgender, masculine, feminine.*

Once you've written a few words or phrases for each topic, please circle any negative word or belief. If you haven't uncovered a negative word or belief, I'd like you to consider what words or beliefs you've heard used, either from headlines in the news, on television, in movies, from social media, or even from your childhood on the playground. The goal with this exercise isn't to be politically correct and avoid saying something you might judge as offensive. The purpose is to explore our subconscious mind and uncover our blind spots.

By exploring our subconscious mind and shining a light on the hidden beliefs about what it means to be LGBTQ, we're helping to clean up the collective consciousness. As you do this exercise, be kind to yourself if you uncover unkind beliefs.

After you've circled the negative word or belief, I'd like you to seriously contemplate this question: Would I do this, say this, or think this way if I knew my child was gay, lesbian, bisexual, or transgender?

Every negative belief you uncover about being gay (or from one of the other words listed above), you can now replace with a positive new one. To help, ask yourself whether you think your belief is heart-full or hurtful. Does it uplift or separate?

After you've uncovered old misguided messages and have replaced them with something new, use the following statement to help ground your new beliefs:

I am safe. I see all young people through eyes of acceptance. Each child matters, and I am open and accepting. It is easy for me to affirm all identities. All kids are the future, and it's important for me to affirm and acknowledge each one for who they are. I create a safe space wherever I am. I surrender beliefs that no longer serve me. I am willing to see, hear, and speak with an open heart. I am here to be truly helpful. My new thoughts and my new beliefs help create a new world. And so it is.

I invite you to visit my website (www.aroadtriptolove.com) to hear a recording of the visualization and complete the worksheet in the privacy of your home. It's also an exercise you can do with your own kids, friends, and anyone else you think it can be of benefit to.

II

WILLINGNESS

4

GENDER, SEXUALITY, AND SANTA CLAUS

An Easy Approach

Our gender journey is influenced by many things, including our families, cultural backgrounds, where we grew up,
and, for some, faith. All of the unique experiences we have
impact our gender.

—Lisa Kenney

Gloria realized her daughter Michelle was transgender one night
while consoling her after a panic attack. She said Michelle began
getting really bad panic attacks before bed when she was around seven
years old. On this particular night, while Gloria was rocking her in her
arms, Michelle asked a question. Since Michelle hadn't been raised in a
particular religion, Gloria was shocked at what she asked.

Through her tears, Michelle asked, "Mom, you wouldn't lie to me,
would you? If I asked you something, you wouldn't lie?"

Gloria said, "Of course not, honey. You can ask me anything."

Michelle continued, "Mom, if I die, God won't make me do this
again, will he? If I die, I won't have to come back and do this again?"

Michelle had heard about reincarnation somewhere and was asking
her mom, if she died, would she have to come back again in a boy's body.
If so, she couldn't do it again. It wasn't something she'd be able to handle.

The very next day Gloria googled "I think my child is transgender." Since then, she's been sharing the journey of her daughter's
change-of-gender status, as she did with a class of seventh-graders during
an LGBTQ panel I was part of in 2018.

While she was sharing Michelle's story, I looked around the room
and saw twenty twelve-year-olds listening. They listened with intent,
and they heard everything she said.

I was amazed at the questions they asked, the insights they had, and the experiences they shared from their own lives.

One girl raised her hand and said she liked wearing "boy's clothes" ever since she could remember. So when her grandfather, who always asks why she wears boy's clothes, gave her a blouse for her birthday, she told us it made her feel sad. She wondered how someone who knew her so well would purposefully get her something he knew she wouldn't like.

While shopping in the boy's section for a shirt to wear to a friend's birthday celebration, that same little girl told us a sales lady told her she was in the wrong section. The little girl wanted to know our advice on what she could have done.

She said, "I knew I was in the right section, but based on the sales lady's reaction, I didn't know how to respond. I just let her walk me to the section she thought I belonged in."

Gloria, whose story was one of the most moving I've had the privilege hearing, was able to answer the little girl's question in a heartfelt way. She told the entire class she was there to share with them her daughter's experience.

She began to tell them that when she gave birth and the doctor told her it was a boy, she chose a typical boy's name. Gloria didn't know much about gender and sexuality but knew something was going on with her child at a very young age.

Ever since Michelle could walk, she always wanted to play with "girl's toys." She would even wear dolls' clothes and loved anything to do with princesses. When she was about five or six, Michelle wanted to dress as a princess for Halloween two years in a row. In their house, toys didn't have gender restrictions, so it wasn't much of a concern.

It wasn't until Michelle started kindergarten that Gloria really began to pay attention. Like a lot of stay-at-home moms I know, she volunteered at her daughter's school and noticed the difference in how Michelle acted in class from when they were at home. The thing she noticed most was how Michelle began to lie. "She would lie about the toys she liked and what games she wanted to play at school," Gloria said.

It appeared Michelle had observed what the little boys in her class liked. So she tried to model her behavior on what they did and not behave the way Gloria knew Michelle did *naturally*.

My eyes welled up with tears when she described a memory of Michelle's kindergarten teacher asking her about her favorite color. Gloria knew her favorite color was purple, so when she overheard Michelle say it was the same color as the boys who answered, she couldn't believe she had lied.

Most of us don't realize how insightful children are. Not only are they aware of their surroundings, they're so aware that they'll even pretend to be someone they're not, just to fit in.

What I saw that day gave me so much hope for the future. I saw a group of young children asking really powerful questions and challenging the norm. I saw a group of critical thinkers. I saw a group of human minds open and available to learn.

I also saw that children will learn anything we teach them. They can learn acceptance just as easily as intolerance. All it requires is the space to have the conversations and a willingness to be open.

In a study about language and its impact on the brain, researchers show that when a child learns a second language early on, it's stored in a different part of the brain than when we're older—it's more natural and becomes a part of who we are.[1] There's a reason why they say teaching language to children at an early age can help them become more fluent. When we learn a second language as adults, we don't store it in the same part of the brain as when we're young.

In this chapter, we're going to take a similar approach with gender and sexuality. My intention is to help you see the benefits of talking about gender and sexuality with children at an early age. Also, this isn't a one-time or one-size-fits-all conversation. It's a dialogue for all families, but each family is as unique as each child. What's important is that the conversation is happening, has boundaries, and feels safe.

CHILDREN ARE MORE INSIGHTFUL THAN WE THINK

You were a child once, too.

—Mr. Rogers

Earlier this year, I was with my nieces and nephews at a restaurant, and a young transgender man took our order at the counter. It made me grateful to see someone trans working at a local restaurant in my home-town. Later that same day, while showing my five nieces and nephews something on my phone, an email notification from LA's LGBT Center popped up on the screen. My youngest nephew asked, "What does LGBT mean?"

After I defined each letter, they asked me what *transgender* meant. I told them, and then as a reference, I mentioned there was a transgender person at the restaurant earlier that day. Without skipping a beat, they all said at the same time, "Oh, Bobby!" I asked if they knew him, but to my surprise, they said, "No." They knew what being transgender meant, though. I just gave them a word to define something they *already* understood.

In 2014, Occidental College cognitive scientist Andrew Shtulman published a study about how children come to disbelieve in Santa Claus. The study found that a child's developing intellect is what causes them to stop believing in Santa Claus, even if a parent tries to keep this myth alive.[2] The same thing that helped my nieces and nephews understand Bobby is what tells a child Santa can't be real.

As you move through this chapter, consider thinking about how a child's developing intellect helps them understand gender and sexuality similarly to the way they learn and naturally unlearn traditions like Santa Claus. It's not because gender and sexuality are necessarily easy subjects to talk about; gender and sexuality are complex. Because each of us has these qualities, children can intuitively learn about them. Regardless of whether children are gay, lesbian, bisexual, straight, transgender, questioning, or queer, all humans have a SOGIE (sexual orientation gender identity and expression).

One of my favorite lines from Mr. Rogers in the 2019 movie *It's a Beautiful Day in the Neighborhood* is "Anything human is mentionable. Anything mentionable is manageable." If most children are taught about a man who flies around the world on a sled pulled by reindeer, deliver-ing toys to all the children in the world on a single night, and we give them clever answers for when they begin to naturally challenge us about him, then I believe parents and caregivers have the capacity to approach gender and sexuality with a similar level of open-mindedness.

After my nephew asked me whether I had a girlfriend, I began ask-ing parents and my LGBTQ friends if they talk to their kids, or nieces and nephews, about being LGBTQ. Most parents, aunts, and uncles told me they hadn't, which was interesting to me because I remember knowing I was gay even as a young child. In fact, I was becoming aware of traditions like Santa Claus around the same time.

One parent of eight- and ten-year-olds said she didn't know what to say or how to bring it up. She told me it was something she thought about, but didn't know at what age it was appropriate. I told her, "If children are old enough to know what a girlfriend is, they're old enough to understand why I wouldn't have one."

A letter addressed to the parents of infants and toddlers from Rady Children's Hospital, the largest children's hospital in California, says, "Sexual development begins in a child's very first years. Infants, toddlers, preschoolers, and young school-aged kids develop an emotional and physical foundation for sexuality in many subtle ways as they grow."[3]

According to the Center on the Developing Child at Harvard University, "Children are born with the capacity to focus attention and retain information in memory, but their experiences lay a foundation for how well these and other executive function skills develop."[4] In other words, learning comes from more than what children think. It comes from what they feel, sense, and experience in their environments, including what they learn to believe from the things they aren't told.

Studies on KidsHealth,[5] run by Nemours Children's Health System, show that by age two or three, children start to develop a sense of being male or female, otherwise known as *gender identity*. By age three to five, most kids have a strong sense of being a boy or a girl. Three to five is also the age children will learn important sexual attitudes from their parents. Around six to ten, kids are interested in things like pregnancy and gender roles, and you'll hear questions like "Where do babies come from?" or "Is she your girlfriend?" This is also the age where their outside world begins to influence sexual attitudes, that is, messages from the playground.

The ages at which gender identity and sexual orientation are established aren't the same with every child. "Gender identity for some children may be fairly firm when they are as young as two or three years old," says *Healthy Gender Development and Young Children: A Guide for Early Childhood Programs and Professionals.*[6] For other children, gender identity may be fluid until adolescence and sometimes even later. The window for sexual orientation development, on the other hand, is more varied and can emerge during childhood, adolescence, or adulthood. An important consideration to make is that sexual orientation emergence is different from sexual behavior.

When some children are young, they can have a fixed way of thinking—which is why jokes and "white lies" can be confusing for them. Child development experts refer to this stage as the most "rigid" period of gender identity, and it usually occurs at around five to six years of age.[7] For example, I live next door to a preschool, and one day I was getting ready to leave my house. I used to have long hair and was going through the "man bun" phase (please don't judge). As I was walking to my car, a little girl from the preschool ran up to the fence and yelled, "Hi!"

"Hi! How are you?" I replied.

"My name is Vanessa," she said.

"Nice to meet you, Vanessa. My name is Chris," I answered.

With her head slightly tilted to one side, as if confused, she asked me, "Are you a boy?"

"Why yes, I am," I said with a smile. Then her friends came over and they continued playing on the playground.

I can almost guarantee Vanessa's parents never sat her down and said, "Vanessa, boys *only* have short hair and girls *only* have long hair." Her question, though, reflects what her four- or five-year-old mind has absorbed about what it means to be a man and a woman. She saw what appeared to be the body of a man (gender), but with long hair and a bun (gender expression), so like my nephew David, she asked the question based on what she's already learned (subconscious beliefs or messages from the playground).

While walking by the same preschool this week, I overheard another little girl say, "Eww, Mommy, two girls can't kiss." She was responding to a conversation a group of adults nearby were having. Both Vanessa's and this girl's reactions were from a fixed way of seeing gender and sexuality combined with what they've picked up from their surroundings.

In the next section, we're going to explore how biological sex, sexual orientation, gender identity, and gender expression aren't the same. My hope is to continue encouraging you to not view children as only straight or cisgender and to consider LGBTQ as a new normal. It's also to help all children learn how they can better support their LGBTQ friends so that they don't think it's not okay that two girls kiss.

GENDER AND SEXUALITY ARE NOT THE SAME

> Sexuality is who you want to be with. Gender identity is who you want to be in the world.
>
> —Hari Nef

One of the most important distinctions for us to make with youth is understanding that gender and sexuality are not the same. There are plenty of online resources and books regarding gender and sexuality. My goal isn't to tell you anything that isn't already out there; it's to meet you where you're at and offer an easy approach.

Some of you may already be familiar with terms, and some may need a little more information. For the sake of the conversations I hope this chapter inspires at home, and to support beginners and professionals alike, I'm going to touch on a few:

Queer

Over the past few years, many young people from the LGBTQ community have reclaimed the term "queer." In the past, it was used in a derogatory way. Now, it's become more popular to use. It's considered an "in-group" term, however. Someone from the community may refer to themselves as queer, but a person from outside the LGBTQ community wouldn't because it could be considered offensive. *Queer* can't be defined like *gay* or *transgender*. Its meaning is specific to each person who considers themselves queer. For example, a lesbian woman can consider herself queer, but not all queer people are lesbian women.

Sexual Orientation versus Sexual Behavior

Sexual orientation is not a choice or a trend; it's a normal part of human development. Sexual orientation for most humans naturally develops between the ages of five to twenty-five, so attuning to a child's natural sexual development as early as five isn't too young. Considering the possibility we might have a gay, lesbian, or bisexual child, or that our child will at least have a friend who is, helps us anticipate their needs, prevent bullying, and heal homophobia.

Gender Identity versus "Sex" or "Assigned Gender"

Gender identity is not a decision, choice, or trend and develops naturally, just like sexual orientation. When a baby is born, they are immediately assigned a gender, or sex, based on their outward physical appearance. Gender identity is different from sex in that it's an internal sense of how someone views themselves. This could be as male, female, somewhere in between, a combination of both or neither.[8] The GLMA (Health Professionals Advancing LGBTQ Equality) says, "Reducing gender to an unchangeable, binary construct determined by one's genitalia at birth is contradictory to the prevailing view of healthcare providers and their professional societies that have reviewed the science and medicine."[9]

According to the American Academy of Pediatrics (AAP), gender identity develops in stages:[10]

1. Around age two: Children become conscious of the physical differences between boys and girls.
2. Before their third birthday: Most children can easily label themselves as either a boy or a girl.
3. By age four: Most children have a stable sense of their gender identity.

Gender Expression

Gender expression is an outward way of expressing how we feel about our inner sense of gender identity. How we dress, the style and length of our hair, or whether we wear makeup or have a man bun are examples of how each of us expresses outwardly what we feel internally.

Gender versus Sexual Orientation

Gender is personal and sexual orientation is interpersonal. Gender has to do with how we view ourselves, and sexual orientation involves how we feel about another person—what makes our heart skip a beat, our palms sweat, or our face blush.

Gender Spectrum says, "Our society's conflation of gender and sexual orientation can also interfere with a young person's ability to understand and articulate aspects of their own gender. For example, it's not uncommon for a transgender or non-binary youth to wonder if they are gay or lesbian (or any sexual orientation other than heterosexual) before coming to a fuller realization of their gender identity. How we come to understand our gender and our sexual orientation—and the choices we make to disclose and express these parts of ourselves—are distinct paths."[11]

Figure 4.1 is from Trans Student Educational Resources. I love sharing it with parents because it emphasizes that the heart is what's

Figure 4.1. The Gender Unicorn
Graphic by TSER (Trans Student Educational Resources) and designed by Landyn Pan & Anna Moore.

involved when it comes to physical and emotional attraction. Showing how our heart is connected to who we're attracted to and not what's between our legs softens the hypersexualization of the LGBTQ community. It also most accurately captures our SOGIE. And what's great about using the term SOGIE is that it's inclusive of everyone.

One afternoon, shortly after I had come out to a few family members, I went to visit my grandmother. While sitting in the living room watching TV, she turned, looked at me, and asked, "So, Chris, your uncle tells me you're gay. How do you have sex?" Startled by her question and that someone had already told her, I turned bright red and said, "Grandma! I'm not going to have that discussion with you!" My grandmother was a very blunt woman and never shied away from personal conversations. Her question, though, didn't respect boundaries—a necessary part of any person's gender and sexuality.

It's also an example of what many parents automatically think of regarding LGBTQ people. My grandmother didn't ask me about dating, whether I was in a relationship, or what it was like to be gay; what she wanted to know was about sex. She automatically associated being gay only with a sex act.

There are more affirming ways to engage youth about gender and sexuality. Projecting adult constructs of gender and sexuality onto young people makes assumptions about how they view gender and sexuality. One of my intentions for *Raising LGBTQ Allies* is to separate the two in order to keep LGBTQ children out of the closet—which is a hotbed for shame and the focus of chapters 6 and 7.

In a recent "Ask Amy" column titled "Gay Daughter Presents Sleepover Dilemma for Her Parents,"[12] a parent wrote in to ask how she should handle sleepovers with her eleven-year-old daughter. The daughter recently came out and now the mother is concerned about sleepovers. Columnist Amy Dickinson replied, "My point is that gay people have platonic friends, both straight and gay. Just as many straight teens manage to participate in group 'lock-ins,' overnight trips and retreats, gay kids should also be granted the same opportunities, with the same assumptions: Sometimes they behave as the adults would wish, and sometimes they don't. Trust, but verify."

Raising LGBTQ children shouldn't be approached any differently from raising straight children. Having early childhood conversations supports all children, regardless of gender or sexuality. With our increased willingness, we can more affirmatively read children's lives.

My mom called me recently to tell me about a conversation she had with a friend she hadn't talked to in more than thirty years. A woman my mom knew from when I was a child, and had lost touch with after my parent's divorce, found her on Facebook. My mom told me they spoke for more than an hour on the phone, reminiscing about the past. She also told me that when Jan asked her about me and my brother, my mom mentioned, among other things, that I was gay. Jan said, "Beth, I intuitively knew when Chris was four that he was gay."

As my mom shared Jan's insight with me she began to cry. She said, "How could I have not known? She knew you were gay even as a four-year-old little boy. I was so blind." The conversation was healing for my mom in a lot of ways. It also made me think about how even parents who love their children dearly sometimes still misread who they are. When we set aside expectations of who we want children to be, we can see them more clearly.

As prepared as we may try to be, raising or caring for children isn't easy. We will make mistakes. The purpose of the next section is to help parents and caregivers become more aware of their children's naturally developing lives. Gaining new information won't make us perfect, but it helps prevent queerphobia, bullying, and gender policing.

POLICE BELIEFS, NOT GENDER

Toys are children's words and play is their language.

—Garry L. Landreth

During a recent class check-in, I asked students to tell me something they wanted to work on. One boy jokingly said he wanted to make one of his male friends "cry like a little girl" from beating him at *Fortnite* (a popular online video game that I'm sure you're familiar with). The class errupted in laughter, so I asked him, "Can you please explain what you meant by 'cry like a little girl'?" The room got quiet and he replied, "I don't know, that he'd cry because he was upset for losing." I asked him if telling a boy that he'd make him cry like a girl was supposed to be an insult. He said, "Yes." Then, looking at the girls in the room, I asked, "Were you offended by his comment?"

One of the girls said, "It sounds like he's saying girls are weak." I asked, "And how does that make you feel?" She replied, "It makes me upset that just because I'm a girl I'm considered weak."

Through our open discussion, I was able to convey to the class, and particularly to the young boys, how saying something like that isn't only hurtful to girls and women, but how crying is a healthy form of emotional expression.

It was a powerful teachable moment where we could speak openly about sexism, gender policing, and their lasting effects. Fortunately, this was an after-school program, and we were able to take time to have the conversation. Far too often, comments like these aren't immediately addressed. Left unaddressed, misguided beliefs remain intact and grow inside a young person's belief system. Like weeds, unless we catch them early and pluck them out, they can take over entire playgrounds.

Recently, a friend shared with me how sometimes when she babysits her family's children, the kids play dress-up. One of the children is an eight-year-old boy who likes to put on my friend's earrings and wear her high heels. He always makes it a point beforehand to say, "Please don't tell my dad because he would get upset." The young boy loves sports and acts like any high-functioning, rambunctious eight-year-old. And sometimes he likes to dress in women's clothes when he plays dress-up.

How children play and which toys they use are not indicators of gender or sexuality. Sometimes, when boys play with toys associated with girls, there's a belief the child might be gay. Also, some parents fear that if a little boy plays with toys associated with girls, he will somehow be less of a man when he gets older. This is an example of gender policing and not only hurts LGBTQ children but also all children.

Not long ago, an older straight man shared with me how badly he was treated as a young boy because he didn't play sports or dress like the other boys. He specifically recalled a memory of how his father looked at him disappointedly one day when he wore a Mouseketeer costume in public. He was only about eight years old and can still recall the disdain in his father's eyes. Later that afternoon, he threw the favorite costume away, along with his creativity. With tear-filled eyes, he said, "I traded innocent creative expression with shame and self-contempt."

A study in the *American Journal for Men's Health*, reported by the National Center for Biotechnology Information, states, "Hegemonic masculinities (i.e., sets of socially accepted masculine behaviors and beliefs within a given time and culture designed to legitimate [*sic*] male domination) has received increasing attention in the public health literature given its association with numerous risk behaviors across the life course."[13]

The study further asserts, "Gender policing during childhood and adolescence may have long-lasting effects into adulthood . . . researchers reported that participants who recalled gender atypical behaviors in childhood were more likely to exhibit a greater number of current depression and anxiety symptoms. Moreover, researchers have noted that sexual minority young adult men may rely on alcohol, tobacco, and other drugs as a coping strategy to offset psychological distress." Gender policing is a harmful social construct rooted in queerphobia, and it informs how many well-meaning parents raise children.

Both my brother and stepbrother were athletic and played on the same baseball teams growing up. My stepdad also played baseball, so he was very involved in their lives and was even their coach. My gender expression as a young boy and disinterest in sports wasn't something my stepfather, who was a "stereotypical macho man," could relate to. I have many memories of my mom trying to encourage my stepdad to interact with me. I knew she meant well, but it was only salt to the wound as far as I was concerned. Knowing my stepfather didn't enjoy spending time with me was one thing, but hearing my mom try to convince him to show me attention only made me feel worse.

I remember one afternoon my mom asked my stepdad to try and teach me how to throw a baseball. Although she was trying to be helpful, no one asked me if it was something I even wanted to learn. I didn't like baseball. The idea of playing sports or having to throw a ball didn't feel natural. Even though my stepdad was a baseball coach, intuitively, it felt more like judgment and less of coaching. After a few attempts at throwing the ball, I tossed the ball back one last time and ran into the house with an even worse feeling about playing sports than I had before.

Even as an adult, I was still self-conscious throwing a ball. In fact, I can vividly remember the first time one of my nephews asked me to go outside with him and play catch. I actually got nervous. I didn't want to ever withhold an experience from my nieces and nephews because of my unresolved childhood shame. As silly as it may sound, I had to work on myself so that I could play something as simple as catch. Gender policing children limits the potential of who they can be and how they see themselves.

I love cycling and have been doing hot room spinning for about a year. One of the benefits of living in Los Angeles is unconventional fitness trends. During a class I took the other day, the instructor told us that out of all the workouts she's ever done, hot room spinning has been the most challenging. She kept referring to us as athletes. I suddenly thought, "Wait a second, I *am* an athlete." I've enjoyed physical exercise for as long as I can remember, but because of the roles imposed on my gender as a young boy, sports and athleticism were reserved for things like baseball, basketball, and hunting, none of which I ever enjoyed.

When I left spin class that day, I thought about all the young boys and girls who enjoy doing activities outside of what's considered "normal" for their gender. I also thought about young kids, including members of my own family, who participate in activities because they think it's what they're supposed to do. We may unknowingly impose expectations on children without considering whether they might be interested in something outside their gender's "norm." A valuable question for parents, teachers, and caregivers to ask themselves is, "How well do I support, encourage, or celebrate children's activities that aren't traditionally associated with their gender?"

Boys Dance and Girls Play Basketball . . . Really Well

I once taught a group of seventh- and eighth-grade girls who happened to all play basketball. During their final class project at the end of the year, they got to film a public service announcement. For this group's PSA, they wanted to talk about gender roles and how, despite their basketball team playing really well, parents don't attend girls' games as often as they do the boys'. They complained about how vacant the stands were during their basketball games, but how they filled up for the boys'.

Not showing up for girls' activities the way we do for boys' sends an implicit message and is an example of how we unintentionally gender police children's activities. It subconsciously feeds misogyny, sexism, and misguided beliefs about gender. It can also negatively affect a young person's self-esteem.

One of the things I've learned in working with youth is how much unspoken feelings influence behavior at home and performance at school. A lot of the young people I work with tell me that it isn't easy to tell their parents how they really feel. Unless we're consciously keeping our eyes, ears, minds, and hearts open, we might not realize how oppressive and limiting our gender bias feels to a young person, even in the most unassuming ways.

In fact, while working on this chapter, a friend shared with me a video of Lara Spencer from *Good Morning America* laughing about Prince George taking ballet. She seemed to find it funny that a little boy liked to dance. What was so damaging to me about the clip is how normalized gender policing is and how easy it can be to let it happen.

I'm sure there was at least one person in the audience who thought, "Hmm, I don't think laughing at whether or not a little boy likes to dance is appropriate." This is how easy it is for bullying to occur. There isn't just the bully; there are bystanders as well. Hearing everyone's laughter in the video made my stomach sink. Unless we speak up and name something for what it is, it will continue.

In the study in the *American Journal for Men's Health*, researchers show the most common form of gender policing among young men includes being told by a parent or caregiver to "correct behavior so as to not appear feminine."[14] Unless we become more aware of when, where, and how gender policing shows up, it will perpetuate a culture of bullying—in families, at schools, and on playgrounds.

After the *Good Morning America* clip was shared on social media, there was an outpouring of support for Prince George. People from all over the world defended boys who like to dance. I read comments like "How could she think something like that?" The fact is, gender policing happens all the time, everywhere. I gender-police myself. To this day, I sometimes notice my voice deepens depending on who I'm talking to and the environment I'm in. It's subconscious residue from when I was younger and tried to pass as a straight person.

One of the best ways we can be allies for all children is to take action in support of the new playgrounds we want to build. Being willing to have gender and sexuality conversations and challenge gender policing shifts the collective consciousness for generations to come.

LOVE IS MORE THAN LOVE

Love is an action, never simply a feeling.

—bell hooks

Earlier this week, my aunt sent me a meme with two men kissing in front of a little kid and his father. A woman in the cartoon was upset and said to the father, "How will you explain this to your child?" The dad replied, "I'm not sure." Then he asked his son, "Do you know what you just saw?" The little boy, looking at the two men kissing, said, "Love." Then, looking at the woman, "Bigotry."

It was a cute cartoon with an affirming "love is love" message. While I agree, love *is* love and is an aspiration many of us desire at our core, we aren't entirely there yet. Using the utopian phrase without true regard for what it means isn't enough. It can be easy to hide biases behind catchphrases because we don't actually have to unpack why we're using them in the first place.

Similarly, someone using the phrase, "I don't see color," to hide discomfort around racism and privilege, sometimes using statements like "love is love," allows us to bypass personal discomfort about gender and sexuality. When it comes to raising allies and affirming the identities of LGBTQ loved ones, memes or catchphrases don't replace personal conversations and doing the inner work to transform fear-based belief systems.

This isn't about blame or shame; it's about bringing more awareness to our willingness to create change. Having conversations about gender and sexuality with children versus replying only on memes, catchphrases, or rainbow flags helps to not only transform misguided belief systems, but it helps us to transcend them.

In 1992, *The Oprah Winfrey Show* aired a well-known special about racism with antiracism activist and teacher Jane Elliott. Unbeknownst to them, Jane separated audience members into two groups: blue-eyed people and brown-eyed people. The exercise is actually called the "blue eye and brown eye" exercise. According to, Jane, it labels participants as inferior or superior based solely upon the color of their eyes, exposing them to the experience of being a minority.[15]

After the experiment, Jane appeared on stage to discuss the exercise and talk about how all white people are raised with *some* racist beliefs. During the discussion, she had a young African American man stand beside her. She asked members of the audience to name the differences between her and the young man. One by one, audience members raised their hands and mentioned things like, age, height, and gender. After each observation, she asked the young man whether it was an important characteristic to him. For example, she asked, "Is your height important to you?" To which he replied, "Yes."

Finally, she exclaimed, "Nobody wants to say the 'c' word. Color." Then she asked him, "Is your color important to you?" And the young man said, "Yes." The point Jane so powerfully made was that when we say we don't see color, we're saying we don't see the person. She continued, "It's important to acknowledge differences because differences matter."

Although racism and queerphobia aren't the same, Jane's message can still be applied. A friend of mine, who is transgender and works with national youth-serving organizations, also shares Jane's work whenever she gives presentations to emphasize the importance of addressing LG-BTQ bias when working with youth. If some families say they don't think gender or sexuality is necessary to talk about with youth, what they say with their silence is that gender and sexuality outside societal norms are "less than."

A few weeks ago, I watched a lecture given by a well-known motivational speaker and teacher. She's an advocate for mental health, has written numerous bestselling books, and is considered a thought leader for the next generation. During the lecture, she commented on gender and said, "Can we just get rid of gender by now? I mean, we're spiritual beings having a human experience!"

While audience members applauded her and I certainly agree, the entire lecture was gendered—from multiple references she made about her skirt, makeup, and hair, to referring to her husband as a "manly man," and her baby boy as liking typically male things like "muscle tees." Now, I'm not saying any of that is bad. What I would like us to pay attention to is how easy it is to make comments without examining the ways in which we contribute to behavior.

There are differences in children's genders, gender expressions, and sexualities, just as there are cultural differences among the human race. However, because we live in a predominately straight and cisgender world, it requires a concerted effort on our part, especially as parents and caregivers, to be aware of how we pass on outdated social constructs. Gender is something that I do believe will eventually be something of the past, but making blanket statements without seeing how gender and sexuality still impact our lived lives today isn't effective.

Love *is* love. More importantly, to demonstrate love is to challenge negative messages from the playground around gender and sexuality and have proactive conversations with young people. In the next chapter, we're going to explore how not communicating something *still* communicates something. I don't ever recall needing to be told Santa Claus isn't real, but I do remember being aware of my gender and sexuality from an early age.

5

BENIGN NEGLECT

Not Communicating Is Still Communicating

> One of the many interesting and surprising experiences of
> the beginner in child analysis is to find in even very young
> children a capacity for insight which is often far greater
> than that of adults.
>
> —Melanie Klein

This weekend was LGBTQ Pride here in Los Angeles. As I drove around town a few weeks before, I noticed rainbow flags in stores where I hadn't ever seen them before. It got me thinking about Pride and how the increase of public support from when I was a child is incredible. While it shows progress, queerphobia still exists, and its nuances are subtle and can be seemingly benign.

What's so damaging about unrecognized queerphobia is that it continues to grow in the crevasses of society. My goal with this chapter is to show that just because something is benign, it doesn't mean it isn't harmful. I also want to specifically address how silence is perceived when it comes to not having conversations around gender and sexuality. Sometimes, waiving a rainbow flag can unknowingly disguise cultural, religious, and familial queerphobia. Having a rainbow flag in a storefront doesn't replace having authentic conversations at home or in school to challenge misguided beliefs about people who are LGBTQ.

After I gave my TEDx Talk, one of my friends from college sent me a private message on Facebook. He said my talk reminded him of when his son was about four years old and asked why some people have darker skin than other people. He told me his son's question made him realize the importance of having proactive conversations with children about differences. Whether we have an LGBTQ child or not, our chil-

73

dren will jump rope or play tag with a child who is LGBTQ on the playground. Having conversations with youth about race, gender, and sexuality prepares them for the diverse world in which they live.

One of my favorite teachings from the Kabbalah Centre, a place I go to for spiritual nourishment here in Los Angeles, talks about the difference between proactive behavior and reactive behavior. Put simply, when we're spiritually, emotionally, and mentally prepared before we enter a situation, we'll be less reactive if it doesn't go our way. The concept makes sense for matters pertaining to life, work, and relationships. But what about how we engage children? When it comes to proactive parenting and talking to our kids about gender and sexuality, it's important that we explore the reasons why we choose, consciously or not, to avoid certain conversations. Oftentimes, the topics we don't like to talk about are the ones we don't understand, are uncomfortable bringing up, or avoid having. Hidden in our avoidance is an aversive belief, shame, bias, or fear, including the fear of offending and the fear of failure.

Currently, there are only four states requiring public schools to teach LGBTQ history (with a fifth state's legislation taking effect in July 2020). If we're not proactively having conversations with youth at home or in classrooms, they are limited to learning about LGBTQ people from the media, online, or on the playground. In addition to what we say, children learn from our inaction and the conversations we choose not to have at home.

I recently read an article on CNN.com about the discovery of a Hitler-owned book detailing his plans for a North American Holocaust.[1] A representative from the Holocaust Education Trust, who expressed shock in learning that such a book even existed, said, "It reminds us of the need to remain resolute in standing up to anti-Semitism, defending historical truth, and educating the next generation."

Furthermore, Steven Wilson, chief executive of the UK's United Synagogue, shared in the article: "This is a reminder of the continued importance of the fight against anti-Semitism and the ongoing importance of Holocaust education, particularly for younger generations." As I read the article, I thought about the importance of standing up to fear in all of its forms, including queerphobia. Relying on Pride flags to demonstrate our acceptance can only go so far. Passive social support unfortunately isn't enough. When it comes to fear-based ideology and misguided beliefs about people who are LGBTQ, we have to go further. To prevent queerphobia from occurring in future generations, it's important to have proactive conversations now.

A friend recently shared a story from the book *Tribal Leadership*. He described a well-known hospital that specializes in cancer treatment and research. When asked about their success and whom they considered to be competition, the hospital said their competition wasn't other hospitals; it was cancer. I feel the same way about all forms of queerphobia. It's easy to look around at the corporatization of Pride and the rainbow section in Target and see the world as LGBTQ affirming. Until children are no longer bullied and queerphobia no longer exists, there's still work for each of us to do. When we have open and honest conversations with children about gender and sexuality, we help youth learn how to value themselves, their identity, and their community.

WORDS CAN HURT; SOMETIMES, SILENCE HURTS MORE

A person may cause evil to others not only by his actions but by his inaction, and in either case he is justly accountable to them for the injury.

—John Stuart Mill

I happened to catch the end of an interview on the radio about racism in the United States while driving to the library last week. The woman interviewed was a professor at Harvard University. She shared how we don't talk to children about race or racism in this country early enough and how harmful our silence can be.

It reminded me of a conversation I had with a good friend one night. We were discussing the prevalence of racism inside the LGBTQ community, and my friend, Anthony, who is Black, shared with me that as a young boy his father sat him down to give him "the talk." I asked, "What do you mean, 'the talk'?" Anthony proceeded to tell me that, as children, most African American boys are told about racism by their families and given rules to prevent them from being in harm's way. His father warned him to take care whenever he was out in public, especially if there was a situation involving police. For example, he learned to place his hands on the dashboard and to never move too quickly if a cop were to pull him over.

As he shared "the talk" with me, my heart dropped into my stomach. The shock and disbelief of my friend's experience came from the privilege I have as a white person living in a country with a long history of racism. Until we can understand the experiences of marginalized groups by having open and honest conversations, we can't heal from systemic fear-based social structures.

During a lecture I once attended, author and politician Marianne Williamson asked the African American guests in her audience to stand. She then led the entire room in a prayer and asked the white audience members to recite an apology for the harm our ancestors may have caused to the ancestors of the Black audience members. There wasn't a dry eye in the room. Tears streamed down white audience members' faces as we said *sorry* with our words, as well as with our hearts. She continued to talk about how after the Holocaust, one of the things Germany did right was to acknowledge, atone for, and make amends for the harm they caused Jewish people.

Being able to discuss gender and sexuality with our children at a young age is a sort of modern mea culpa for the years we've forced LGBTQ youth to develop in the closet. It helps to remove societal, cultural, familial, and religious shame, as well as transform misguided beliefs about people who are LGBTQ. Author and activist, Adrian Pei, author of the book *The Minority Experience*, says, "Leading change isn't just about transforming individual behavior, but about addressing broader systemic issues."[2]

A common misconception from parents is that talking to children at a young age about gender and sexuality will result in experimentation—which research shows is untrue. Having conversations with children at a young age helps them to see gender and sexuality as sacred. It teaches them to respect, honor, and value their gender and sexuality. Regardless of our beliefs or opinions on the matter, each and every human being on the planet has a gender and sexuality. By talking about them, we take away the shame each of us carries about gender and sexuality—gay, straight, transgender, male, female, or non-binary.

Benign Neglect

The *Merriam-Webster's Dictionary*'s definition of *benign neglect* is "an attitude or policy of ignoring an often delicate or undesirable situation that one is held to be responsible for dealing with."[3] *Benign neglect* was a policy proposed in 1969 by Daniel Patrick Moynihan, President Nixon's urban affairs advisor.[4] At that time, Moynihan sent the president a controversial memo, stating: "The time may have come when the issue of race could benefit from a period of 'benign neglect.'"

It's been suggested that benign neglect and racism in the United States are directly correlated to events like the deaths of Trayvon Martin in Florida and Michael Brown in Ferguson, Missouri. Not communicating something still communicates something. One of the biggest reasons I continue to hear from parents about why they don't discuss gender and sexuality with their children is, "They're too young to understand."

When families don't have proactive conversations with their children about an LGBTQ family member, it communicates something. After my nephew asked me if my friend Alyssa was my girlfriend, I realized there was unrecognized fear in my family's silence about my being gay. Some friends and family members told me they didn't think it was necessary for my sister to say anything. After all, I live out of state and I'm single. He hasn't had the opportunity to see me with a boyfriend yet, so why bring it up now?

Choosing not to share something with a child because we don't think it's necessary and avoiding the conversation because of fear, shame, or bias are two distinctly different reasons. Through open and honest conversations with my family, we discovered benign homophobia living inside of their silence. An article addressing race, published by the National Alliance on Mental Illness (NAMI), stated, "Address race in therapy sessions. If your client is from another race and ethnicity, it is wise to address that in the first sessions. Making believe that we are all just one human race does not align with how our society actually views race."[5] The same is true for why it's important to be able to talk about gender and sexuality with youth. When we don't have conversations, our silence still speaks.

Children are truth detectors and they pick up on subtleties. Often, when I'm giving a workshop or presentation, I ask participants of the group to think of a time in their childhood when their parents hid something from them. What did they learn? What did their parents' silence teach them?

When I was a young child, I intuitively knew something wasn't right with my father. No one in my family ever talked to me about his drug use, though. Everyone acted as if I wasn't aware of his unpredictable behavior and avoided bringing it up. It made me frustrated with the adults in my life because I knew they were keeping something hidden from me. It also made me question myself.

When a good friend of mine got caught up in his own addiction a few years ago, I began observing how his children started to behave. Everyone complained about how difficult his children were and how they had started acting out. I told a friend, "Tim's kids aren't acting out because they're troubled or bad; they're acting out because they don't feel safe. They intuitively know what's going on in their family, but no one is giving them the language to express how they're feeling on the inside."

Telling the truth, even with children at a young age, gives them a sense of safety. It also helps them develop their intuition, which is one of the most powerful tools we can help a child learn to use.

For my birthday this year, my nieces and nephews sent me a "Best Uncle" t-shirt. When I was in town visiting a few months ago, my niece asked me if I had worn the shirt yet. Her question caught me off guard, and so I replied, "Oh, yes, the shirt! Yes, I have worn it!"—which wasn't the truth. I hadn't worn it yet.

The moment I said yes, I wondered if she knew I lied. Everyone knows everything on a subconscious level, so even if she consciously didn't pick up on my little "white lie," she intuitively knew. When we don't tell children the truth, even if it's about something benign, we still communicate, and we:

1. teach them that lying is okay, even if it's a little "white lie";
2. discourage them from trusting themselves;
3. fracture their sense of safety, both consciously and subconsciously;
4. miss an opportunity to be vulnerable, strengthening our relationship;

5. deter them from asking us questions, knowing they may or may not get the truth;
6. prevent them from being open, authentic, and vulnerable;
7. create frustration and resentment with the adults in their life; and
8. demonstrate avoidance.

My sister not having a conversation with her kids about their gay uncle communicated she was uncomfortable with the conversation, which was inadvertently teaching her children being gay is different, further perpetuating guilt, shame, and the closet. As a gay child, this is what I picked up from my surroundings—the benign neglect. Silence about developing gender and sexuality is what feeds shame, or for LG-BTQ youth, internalized queerphobia (which we will learn more about in the next chapter).

NO TIME FOR SILENCE

> You cannot hide your fights. You cannot hide the dissension in your marriage. You cannot hide your infidelity from the spirituality that kids feel.
>
> —David Ghiyam

Earlier today, I called my niece to make amends for lying to her about wearing the shirt she got me for my birthday. I also asked if she knew I wasn't telling the truth. She said, "To be honest, I wondered why you didn't send us a picture with it on if you had worn it." I asked her if she knew what intuition was and she said, "Yes, it's a feeling you get about something." I said, "Yes, exactly! So did your intuition tell you something about my response?" She confirmed what I thought. She intuitively knew I wasn't being truthful. I told her it's important to be able to trust her intuition and that it's her super power. I also told her that sometimes adults don't know how to respond to a question, so we end up changing the subject or telling a white lie. "A white lie," I said, "doesn't make the truth we're hiding any less important to tell."

I asked her what a white lie was, and she told me it was a "little lie." I told her I don't believe in white lies, especially if we use them to replace being vulnerable through having honest and open conversations. I want her to feel comfortable enough to question my response when her intuition is telling her otherwise. We even role-played a scenario so she can confront someone in a nonaccusatory way if she feels as though what they're telling her isn't the complete truth.

My response to not wearing her shirt may seem benign or insignificant, but as parents and adults, where do we draw the line between a little lie and a big lie? Children will ask questions that catch us off guard, and they might even require us to filter our response. The point I would like more parents, caregivers, and educators to consider, though, is that children are intuitive and more capable of handling the truth than we often give them credit for.

When it comes to answering unpredictable questions or shielding the feelings of another person, a thoughtful parent I know said they always use love as their guide. When it comes to commenting on a child's actions or responding to them about a gift, what I've since learned is that there are ways of praising their efforts without lying to them about a result.

Silence, especially with regard to identity, is loud and often deafening. By withholding information from young people about entire groups of people, we send a message. Sometimes, we think we choose not to tell the truth because children are too young. If we're honest with ourselves, we see that it's because of our own discomfort. And children can sense fear. In the following sections, we're going to explore a form of language everyone knows and is especially pronounced in young children: intuition. We're also going to learn more about authentic communication and how to authentically communicate with youth.

A NEW GENERATION: EVERYTHING IS ENERGY

> Intuition is the soul's language. The more we are able to tune into it, the better we know ourselves.
>
> —James Van Praagh

While I was in Venice Beach recently, someone stole my phone. After I got an ice cream cone and looked for a spot to sit, I walked to an open area to enjoy my ice cream and to people watch. The moment I sat down something inside told me I wasn't safe. I thought, "I'm fine, there are plenty of people around, and it's the middle of the day." I set my phone down to my right because the ice cream was beginning to melt. After about the two minutes it took to hurriedly finish, I turned to get my phone, and it was gone. Someone must have watched me sit down and quietly snagged my phone while I was busy eating. It was a huge lesson of remembering to trust the small, still voice within.

Intuition is something each of us has. For gender and sexual minorities, our intuition is something we use to safely navigate life. From an early age, most LGBTQ youth have relied on their intuition to keep them from harm. The degree to which a child has been in the closet is the degree to which they've used their intuition.

When I was younger and still in the closet, keeping my identity hidden was my number one priority. I relied on my intuition to tell me who was safe. I also relied on nonverbal communication to tell me if anyone suspected I was gay. A quick shift of the eye or subtle glance could sound the alarm that someone was onto me. I was so good at reading faces and picking up on nonverbal social cues that I could tell from your handshake and eye contact if you were trustworthy.

I recently watched a video of the late American writer Toni Morrison where she asked, "Does your face light up when your kid walks in the room?" She was talking about the importance of helping a child feel our approval by how we look at them. All children can read faces and intuitively feel if we approve of them or not. LGBTQ youth, who may or may not be in the closet, are searching for any sort of recognition that who they are is okay. The purpose of this chapter, and really, the essence of this book, is to help children feel affirmed from not only our words and faces, but from our energy as well.

Before the holidays, I was driving with my mom, and she mentioned that she could feel fall in the air. I was in Arizona visiting and remember thinking, "Arizona only has two seasons: hot and kinda hot." But even in the desert, there's a subtle change in the air you feel—an unexplainable change of season you can sense.

I shared this with my class of sixth- and seventh-graders after I returned home. We were talking about energy, and I asked if they could tell when their parents were in a good or bad mood based on how they felt when they were around them. They all responded, "Yesss!" I said, "When I open the door and walk into the room, you've already felt my energy before I've even said anything." I continued, "The same way my mom can subtly feel the change of season in Arizona is the same way each of us feels and experiences energy."

Last summer, I joined my brother's family during their annual trip to Disneyland. While waiting to go on a ride, we noticed a young father holding his crying baby. The father seemed upset and attempted to quiet his child by rocking it up and down faster than normal. The baby's cry was getting so loud, it began to attract attention from everyone nearby. As we watched, questioning if one of us should say something, my sister-in-law said, "Well, of course the baby is crying; she's responding to his energy. He needs to rock her calmer." Energy is something each of us is always using and responding to whether we realize it or not. In this situation, the baby sensed its father's frustration, and as he calmed down, the baby eventually did as well.

Energy and intuition go hand in hand. In my experience working with youth, feeling energy is part of how I'm able to effectively instruct the lesson I'm there to teach. If a class has too much energy, it can be disruptive. If the group I'm teaching doesn't have enough energy, they've typically tuned me out. Being able to intuitively read the energy of the room also helps me hone in on whether a student is having an off day.

When I began giving classes at LA's LGBT Center's Homeless Youth Shelter, the first thing I noticed was how responsive the youth were to my energy. From the moment I walked into the room, I could sense their level of sensitivity. I often thought about what it must be like to live on the streets. Relying on nonphysical senses, like intuition and energy, is what keeps homeless youth alive. From closets or the streets, I quickly learned how aware of their nonphysical senses LGBTQ homeless youth were.

Once, a girl named Robyn told me she was able to navigate living on the streets by being able to see auras. Relying on how she felt and the energy she saw when she met someone kept her safe. She said she could see my aura, and it helped her know she could trust me.

Whether she could see auras isn't the point. The point is how well LGBTQ youth can intuit energy and read facial expressions. I can say

I accept my LGBTQ family member, but if my face or energy doesn't match my words, there's a subconscious disconnect. Everything has a vibration and energy frequency, including our thoughts, words, and beliefs. What's more, we can energetically interpret silence from the conversations we don't have. If you've ever been around a group of kids, and all the sudden they've gone silent, you know they're either up to something or that something is wrong. Understanding how energy impacts a young person's learning can help us move from tolerating LGBTQ youth to being able to celebrate their lives.

PHASES OF ACCEPTANCE: FROM TOLERANCE TO CELEBRATION

World Peace will be achieved when humanity moves beyond tolerance and even acceptance and begins celebrating each other's differences.

—Karen Berg

Being gay and growing up in a religious household, I still wonder to what degree my sexuality is celebrated, accepted, or tolerated whenever I'm in religious spaces. One weekend a few years ago, I attended an event with one of my best friends at a local synagogue in Los Angeles. My friend is a conscious gay man and someone committed to his personal and spiritual development. After the service, we were in the lobby enjoying some refreshments. A nice woman walked up to us and asked how we enjoyed the service. We told her it was our first time attending services at a synagogue and she said, "Well, if you come back, I'll have to introduce you two to a few nice Jewish women."

Her statement caught me off guard. I thought to myself, "Didn't she know we were gay?" My friend and I looked at each other and then uncomfortably changed the subject. I wanted to tell her I was gay, but I chose not to say anything because I didn't want to risk ruining the evening. I also didn't want to disappoint her heteronormative assumption. Instead, I complemented the service and her delicious snacks.

Later that night, my friend and I went to dinner. After we both sat down at our table, I asked, "What happened earlier?" He knew exactly what I was talking about. Two conscious gay men working to heal homophobia who, in fact, were both part of a spiritual community in Los Angeles specifically for LGBTQ people, faced a situation where we chose not to be authentic.

Some might say, "Well, it's not anyone's business," or "You don't have to come out to everyone you meet." And while I agree, coming out to every single person throughout the day would be exhausting and unnecessary. There is a reason behind every choice we make, including the times we choose silence over telling the truth. Code-switching, the practice of acting differently depending on the social context, is something a lot of gay men do. It's a term often used with regard to race but can also apply to people who are LGBTQ. In the LGBTQ community, code-switching satisfies heteronormativity and is born from fear, shame, and trauma.

The situation with my friend reminded me how easy it can be to code-switch and that just because we're gay or lesbian, it doesn't mean we can't perpetuate homophobia.

Earlier this week I was at a Starbucks in West Hollywood, often referred to as "gay Starbucks" because it's located in the middle of what's considered to be LA's gay neighborhood. While I was waiting for my coffee, a young man on his phone sat down next to me. I could tell by his conversation that he was talking to a guy. I even happened to catch a glimpse of his phone because he was sitting so close, and the person on the other end had a traditionally male name. Before ending the call with his friend, he said, "Okay girl, I'm gonna let you go to get back to work. Love you, beyotch." As soon as he hung up, a male Starbucks employee walked over to greet him, and the guy who was just on his phone said, "Oh hey bro, I didn't know you still worked here." Going from "girl" and "beyotch" to "bro" in a matter of seconds is an example of code-switching and a sometimes subconscious form of internalized homophobia.

One of my writing mentors is an older gay man who's married with two children. He and his husband are active LGBTQ advocates and do a lot of work to support members of the community. They've both been instrumental in my personal, professional, and spiritual growth. I credit them with helping me get to where I am today. My mentor and I used to meet at the same "gay Starbucks" for brainstorming sessions.

Every time I met with him, his voice would lower to almost a whisper whenever he said "gay." In the middle of West Hollywood, at the "gay Starbucks," a married gay man with two children would unconsciously lower his voice when he said "gay."

Our subconscious beliefs are powerful. Developing an increased awareness of them can help us understand what's behind the conversations we don't have or the words we lower our voice for when we say them in public. When I look back on my childhood, I energetically knew what my parents were trying to hide. If I didn't know, I assumed what they tried to keep from me was bad because why else didn't they want me to know? As children, most of what we learn isn't from what we think. It's from what we unconsciously learn to believe from the subtleties in our surroundings. In his bestselling book *People of the Lie*, Dr. M. Scott Peck says, "When we are adults, the greater part of our 'thought life' proceeds on an unconscious level. For children and young adolescents, almost all mental activity is unconscious."[6]

The next time you tell a white lie, change the subject, or lower your voice to use a certain word, check in with your body. If it feels tight or tense or, for example, you have a knot in your stomach, it's because you intuitively already know the choice you're making isn't the choice of your heart. When I pay close enough attention to how I feel, I can usually feel a tightness in my stomach if I make a choice out of alignment with my truth. My heart knows when it isn't aligned with my highest good.

Once, I sent one of my teachers from the Kabbalah Centre an email asking them a question. I've been taking classes at the Kabbalah Centre for over a year. It's a wonderfully diverse community of people from all backgrounds and religious beliefs. Still, because of my personal experience, I am sensitive to the degree with which religious spaces are LGBTQ affirming.

In the email to my teacher, I included a published article I wrote about a topic we had discussed in class. The article also happened to mention that I'm gay. After I sent my teacher the email, I wondered if he already knew. If not, I wondered how he was going to respond. The community members have welcomed me during my time at the Centre, but the fear of rejection in religious spaces can sometimes still reappear. Normally, my teacher is very responsive and replies by the next day. So, when I hadn't received a return message in a week, I wondered if he was homophobic.

His silence was loud and reminded me of my past. A few days later, my teacher sent me a text message asking if I had a moment to talk. I thought, "Okay, here we go. He's going to confirm my biggest fear." When I answered his call, he greeted me with the same warm and friendly voice I was used to. Then he asked if I was interested in speaking at an upcoming event for about 150 people. He said he'd love to highlight me as a valued member of the community.

I replied, "Daniel, I'm going to be really vulnerable with you right now, but the story playing in my head is that you didn't reply to my email because you're homophobic." I continued, "You're normally very responsive, so I thought your silence was because of the contents in my article." He said, "Oh my gosh, Chris. I am so sorry. I got your email, yes, but I forgot to reply. It's been a crazy week and I haven't had the chance to read your article."

I was relieved and told him how part of my story includes religious harm. While I loved being a member of the Centre, I hadn't been able to tell how LGBTQ affirming members are—do they tolerate people who are LGBTQ or do they celebrate us? Tears welled up in my eyes when he said, "Chris, I hope you know how appreciated you are here. Not only that you know, but you feel it." It ended up being a wonderful experience that not only brought us closer but also helped heal my heart a little more. Daniel also realized the importance of affirming the identities of LGBTQ community members and recently invited me to be a guest on his international podcast to talk about *Raising LGBTQ Allies*.

During a trip to San Francisco last summer, I noticed every church I saw had a sign outside that read, "All are welcome here." Considering that I had walked thirty-five miles in two days, I walked by a lot of churches. I thought about LGBTQ youth church members who see the signs and feel affirmed. I thought about the conversations the churches had as religious institutions choosing to display the signs. I also thought how valuable it is for parents and families to talk about why there's even the need for signs in the first place. Having a sign without including LGBTQ people in conversations is only part of the equation. Inside families and religious communities, it can be easy for LGBTQ youth to confuse silence with intolerance or even tolerance. It reminded me of why it's meaningful to proactively affirm LGBTQ identities, especially in spaces where historically there has been harm.

I view celebration as the ultimate standard by which we should treat all youth. Going from LGBTQ tolerance to celebration can be a journey and may come in stages. In my experience, the phases include tolerance, acceptance, embracing, appreciation, and celebration. The journey between phases isn't linear, nor is it complete. We can be in different phases, as well as go back and forth, depending on the situation.

It's common to hear "LGBTQ acceptance," or tolerance. What I want us to consider is that to even have acceptance means there's something we must give up. Accepting an LGBTQ person's identity still implies there's something different about them for us to accept. My hope is that we can move beyond acceptance and learn how to celebrate the lives of LGBTQ youth.

Creating allies and a world where closets don't exist happens one child at a time. And it begins with each of us and what we say, as much as what we choose not to say. If the thought has ever crossed your mind of whether or not your child is LGBTQ, be open to talking about it. Not communicating something still communicates something. As parents and caregivers, we have the potential to change the trajectory of a child's life by being patient, supportive, and vulnerable. There are many resources, professional groups, and individuals out there. If you don't know, ask for guidance, follow your heart, and let's continue being the parents and caregivers we're capable of being.

The opposite of benign neglect is authentic communication. Authentic communication is like a muscle. The more we use it in our lives, the stronger it becomes. It also proactively prevents guilt and shame. What children hear from us can be very different from what we actually say, so here are a few questions you can use to help align your thoughts and beliefs with your energy and words.

HOW TO AUTHENTICALLY COMMUNICATE

1. How does my body feel with my response or lack of response?
2. Am I avoiding telling the truth because of fear or because I don't know how to respond? Is it truly something not worth addressing?

3. If I'm being completely honest with myself, what is behind my reason to avoid having this conversation, and what does my silence say?
4. Will my response (including silence) help or hurt?
5. Does this require vulnerability, and if so, how can I create the space to share my truth, even if I don't know the answer?
6. What am I teaching?
7. What do I fear from having this conversation?
8. Do I fear offending or failing?
9. Am I aligned with love?

In the next chapter, we're going to learn more about the harmful effects of silence around matters pertaining to gender and sexuality. In this section of the book, we're continuing to develop our willingness to create change in the lives of LGBTQ youth.

6

SHAME

Prevention versus Treatment

The less we talk about shame, the more control it has over
our lives.

—Dr. Brené Brown

In 2019, I attended a workplace sexual harassment training. California
had introduced a new law that required all companies to ensure their
employees complete a training by 2020. When the organization with
which I teach first announced the mandatory training, I was less than
thrilled at the idea of spending four hours learning about policies and
procedures regarding sexual harassment.

During the training, however, I found myself taking pages of notes.
It fascinated me that California has many laws in place intended to
protect employees from workplace harassment and discrimination. Part
of the presentation was even dedicated to LGBTQ-specific workplace
discrimination.

As pleasantly surprised as I was to see diversity included in the
presentation, I was disappointed to see that it was also filled with language such as "sexual and gender preference" and "lifestyle choice."
As we learned in chapter 2, language can be a source of subconscious
shame. Using "preference" or "lifestyle" is problematic and sends the
subtle message that being LGBTQ is a decision we make rather than
being inherent in us. Another aspect of the presentation that stood out
for me was the emphasis on "workplace prevention." In fact, the entire
presentation was focused on helping companies *prevent* workplace harassment or discrimination before it begins—which is my intention for this
chapter, as it pertains to shame.

During the presentation, we reviewed multiple cases of large corporations that were found guilty of harassment and discrimination, thanks to laws protecting LGBTQ employees. While I'm grateful for the extensive workplace protection that I have as a gay man living in the state of California, I thought about the LGBTQ youth who face the same, if not worse, kind of discrimination at home, in school, or on the playground.

According to the Trevor Project, a suicide prevention and crisis intervention organization:[1]

- Two-thirds of LGBTQ youth reported that someone had tried to convince them to change their sexual orientation or gender identity.
- Some 71 percent of LGBTQ youth reported experiencing discrimination due to either their sexual orientation or their gender identity.
- Around 58 percent of transgender and non-binary youth reported being discouraged from using the bathroom that corresponds to their gender identity.

I wondered how there could be specific laws protecting people from discrimination and harassment in the workplace—laws that a judge and jury would recognize when and if they were broken—yet LGBTQ youth experience the same kind of discrimination and harassment at home and at school, religiously and institutionally, but without the same legal recourse.

After the presentation, I asked the instructor whether any of the laws designed to protect employees in the workplace could be applied to LGBTQ youth at home, in school, or on the playground so as to protect them from shame and its harmful effects. The instructor said, "Unfortunately, when it comes to parental rights and something like homophobia or transphobia, the law gets a little tricky."

"So while an employee could file a lawsuit against their employer for workplace harassment, there isn't anything protecting LGBTQ children from experiencing at home, in school, or on the playground what a judge or jury would consider to be harassment if it took place in the workplace?" I asked.

"That's where it gets a little tricky, as parental rights and religious freedom are often protected under the First Amendment of the US Constitution," he said.

I'm not suggesting we should police parental beliefs, or even that it's something we could realistically do. Instead, I desire more parents, caregivers, and educators to consider the following questions:

1. How can we create safer homes, schools, and playgrounds for the next generation?
2. How do we prevent shame before it begins?

The Trevor Project's 2019 National Survey on LGBTQ Mental Health also found that 39 percent of LGBTQ youth had seriously considered attempting suicide during the past twelve months, with more than half of all transgender and non-binary youth having seriously considered doing so. Additionally, 76 percent of LGBTQ youth reported feeling that the political climate had adversely impacted their mental health or sense of self.[2]

Although children today are being raised in a more diverse and inclusive world, shame still continues to negatively affect the lives of LGBTQ youth. Dr. Brené Brown, one of the world's leading experts on shame, says, "When we have conversations about shame we either shut down, change the subject, or deny that we have it."[3] As a result, Dr. Brown often encourages people to use a different word to talk about shame, which is, in addition to being a tool to explore subconscious beliefs, another reason why I chose "messages from the playground" as the theme of this book.

Using the metaphor has helped me to address shame within the LGBTQ community, which can influence the choices LGBTQ youth make, as well as how they perceive themselves today. In the following sections, we're going to peel back the layers of shame and explore how they particularly impact the lives of young people.

TRICKLE-DOWN EFFECTS OF RELIGIOUS SHAME

We need to talk about shame just as much as we do about pride.

—*Consciously Queer*

Since living in Los Angeles and working closely with the LGBTQ community for more than fifteen years, I've known far too many people who have overdosed from drugs or alcohol or died by suicide.

Just recently, I was told a young man I once worked with at a gay bar, who from the outside appeared to have it all, killed himself that very week. He was handsome, charming, in good shape, and commanded attention wherever he went. Even in the sharing of his death, everyone I spoke to said, "He was so handsome."

Similarly to others I've known who have died or taken their own life, he embodied what, for most people, especially in the LGBTQ community, would consider as ideal: external beauty and strength. But each of us has an inner world that is more than what appears on the outside.

None of us can say for sure why this young man took his own life, and we cannot know what it's like to walk in another person's shoes, nor do we know what the journey is for someone else's soul. What I do know, though, is learning to love myself is what saved my own life after I came out of the closet and turned to drugs and alcohol as my source of strength.

Being young and part of a culture that prizes beauty from the outside in, I thought about the importance of seeing someone from the inside out. It's one thing to look around and see people through the lens of what they show us from the outside, but another to fully embrace someone wholeheartedly and unconditionally for who they are on the inside.

While correlation is not causation, when I first moved to Los Angeles, I worked for a national LGBTQ organization. One of my primary responsibilities was to help organize new-member recruitment events. The events always took place at gay bars across the United States and were a way of attracting new members.

Once, when I secured a venue for a new market at a non-bar location, I was called to meet with the president of the organization at the time. He told me I'd have to find a new venue. Even though the location was perfect for our event, and they were going to give us a great deal, we couldn't have our event somewhere that wasn't a gay bar. I was told, "The bar is for gays what the church is for straights."

At first glance, the comment sounds problematic. But if we were to examine the history between the LGBTQ community and the church, his comment was pretty accurate. Throughout generations and around the world, bars have served as a safe haven for lesbian, gay, bisexual, transgender, questioning, and queer people. Although gay bars have historically been a place for LGBTQ people to connect, unhealed shame combined with substances is a recipe for self-destruction.

While working at a gay bar, I regularly saw people overdose from drugs or alcohol. Seeing young men carried out by security from taking too much G (a kind of liquid ecstasy popular among gay men) was a common occurrence.

It's not that gay bars themselves are bad. But if a young person holds unresolved shame and doesn't have a strong enough foundation to sustain themselves while subconsciously numbing their pain through substances, or only being seen externally and less for who they are on the inside, the results can be devastating.

LGBTQ generations from the past paved the way for same-sex marriage and transgender rights today. Now, it's up to the current generation of LGBTQ parents, people, and allies to heal our messages from the playground so that we don't carry them into tomorrow.

WHEN EXTERNAL MESSAGES SEEP INSIDE: INTERNALIZED HOMOPHOBIA

> Seventy percent of the people who raised me, who loved me, who I trusted, believed that homosexuality was a sin, that homosexuals were heinous, subhuman, pedophiles. 70 percent! And by the time I identified as being gay, it was too late, I was already homophobic. And you do not get to just flip a switch on that.[4]
>
> —Hannah Gadsby

One of Sigmund Freud's many defense mechanisms studied in psychotherapy is called "introjection."[5] Introjection occurs when we internalize the outside ideas and voices of other people. "Introjection is about taking inside something that's outside. So making it one's own, really. Taking in qualities, feelings, emotions, and so on, that come from outside oneself,"[6] says Ann Phoenix, psychologist and professor of psychosocial studies at the Institute of Education, University College London.

Introjection is considered normal and common between children and caregivers, occurring when children internalize the beliefs of the people around them. Some parents might ask, "Well, why doesn't my child introject eating more vegetables and less candy?" According to Freud, in order for us to experience introjection, or any defense mechanism, it has to be unconscious. We can't be consciously aware of its occurrence. Besides, even if we raise children to like vegetables, the dominant societal messages they receive promote sugar and sweets.

Something not openly talked about or widely addressed in the LGBTQ community, specifically with gay men (because I'm a gay man and so am speaking from my experience), is how internalized homophobia affects us. We cannot talk about homophobia, or queerphobia, without addressing internalized homophobia or internalized queerphobia. No matter our gender or sexuality, each person in the LGBTQ community experiences internalized queerphobia living in a heteronormative world.

In her 2014 viral talk from the National Theatre of Ireland, celebrated LGBTQ activist and drag queen Panti Bliss said, "I do, it is true, believe that almost all of you are probably homophobes. But I'm a homophobe. I mean, it would be incredible if we weren't. I mean, to grow up in a society that is overwhelmingly and stiflingly homophobic and to somehow escape unscathed would be miraculous."[7] Without explicitly doing so, Panti named internalized homophobia.

What *is* internalized homophobia, and why is it important to talk about? In an article on Mashable.com called "Internalized Homophobia: The Next LGBT Movement after Same-Sex Marriage,"[8] the author describes internalized homophobia as being a "fancy clinical term" most familiar among therapists and mental health professionals. He says definitions vary, "but it generally refers to the internalization of a society's homophobic attitudes within lesbian, gay or bisexual people."

Internalized homophobia is when we introject the shameful messages we learn as children about what it means to be LGBTQ, that is, messages from the playground. It's queerphobia from the outside we take inside. Once internalized, it becomes shame an LGBTQ person carries inside about themselves, others, or the LGBTQ community—consciously or subconsciously. It's safe to say that by virtue of being socialized in dominant culture, the young people in your life have internalized a shameful message about being LGBTQ to a certain degree.

If any of us, gay or straight, has guilt or shame, we may subconsciously seek punishment. That could look like many things, but includes unhappiness, unhealthy relationships, substance abuse, and other self-deprecating behavior. Everything we hear, see, and perceive, whether it's at home, in the media, on the playground, or from a non-affirming religion, can seep inside. Left unaddressed, it can negatively affect our life, our choices, and our children.

One year, while I was bartending, we began serving Moscow Mules. Our drink menu featured two kinds: the original, "Masculine Mule," and fruit-flavored, "Fruity Mules." Each time a customer looked at the menu to order a Moscow Mule or an employee rang one up on the computer, they received a subconscious impression of internalized homophobia. Distinguishing between "masculine" and "fruity" drinks is an example of gender policing. It also demonstrates how prevalent and pervasive shame is, even inside the sacred spaces where LGBTQ people socialize.

How can we prevent something from occurring in the next generation if we aren't willing to see it within ourselves or our communities?

Internalized homophobia can be challenging to address because it's a term mostly used inside the confines of a therapist's office. It's not engaged openly enough within the LGBTQ community or in our relationships. The less we acknowledge shame in our lives, the more it continues to thrive. One of the most important contributions LGBTQ people can make for the sake of the next generation is to heal internalized queerphobia.

During an LGBTQ event I worked at recently, an intoxicated older man stood up on a chair, frantically waved his hands at me, and yelled to get my attention. When I told him he didn't need to yell, he shouted, "You're a bitch!" A few minutes later a young woman walked up to me and said, "I'm sorry about my uncle. He's really drunk."

We teach by our demonstration, and in this case, the "guncle" (a popular term used for gay uncles) was demonstrating his own internalized homophobia. Some of it might have been the pain he carries from feeling invisible in a community that glorifies youth, but mostly he was projecting unresolved shame onto me. Although she may not be familiar with internalized homophobia, the young woman could subconsciously sense it in her uncle. I'm sure that wasn't the first time he lashed out at someone or got as drunk as he did.

I once bartended with a young lesbian woman. When she first started, she told me one of the customers thought she was straight. I had only known her a few days, so when I responded, "Oh, I didn't know you were gay." She excitedly replied, "Yay! You thought I was straight, too!" Here we were, two gay people, both working at a gay bar, yet not only was she excited to have been mistaken for being straight, she had no problem expressing it to me nor was even aware of the implications it had.

As more members of the LGBTQ community step into the role of parents, aunts, and uncles, it's vitally important to look within our own life and heal our shame so that we don't teach it to youth. We have to value ourselves before we can ask anyone else to value us. We also have to value our community before we can ask anyone else to value it.

One of my best friends, Alex, who is a third-grade teacher, told me about a recent conversation he had with his eleven-year-old nephew. Alex has been in a relationship with his boyfriend for more than two years and often brings him to family functions. He's been out to his parents and siblings for more than fifteen years and, in fact, has a younger brother who is also gay. Recently, after Alex answered a question from his nephew about dating, his nephew responded confusedly, "What the fuck?! You're gay?"

When Alex told me this, I replied, "Wait a second. Your boyfriend has been going to your family functions for more than a year. You're an LGBTQ advocate and a teacher. You're one of my go-to people to talk about shame and the effects it has on LGBTQ youth, and you haven't introduced your boyfriend to your family as your boyfriend? Your nephew intuitively already knew."

We looked at each other, and I could see from his facial expression what he was thinking: "How is it possible someone who actively does work to help shine a light on homophobia is someone who can still teach it at home? What was behind my silence?"

That's the thing with benign neglect and internalized homophobia, or any kind of shame, it's so ubiquitous, it can hide inside the conversations we choose not to have.

The Importance of an Answer

The questions children ask are indicators of what they're learning. They can also tell us what they're intuiting about themselves, life, and the world in which they live. Not long ago, I heard an openly gay father say that his children don't know he's gay. As a gay uncle with five nieces and nephews, it caught my attention. I'm also writing a book that specifically addresses how being open and honest with children from a young age can prevent queerphobia and bullying. I was curious about why his kids didn't know.

I continued listening to the openly gay father share that he's a single parent and that his almost-five-year-old son has been talking to him about wanting to have kids and get married in the future. His son recently asked, "Why didn't you get married?" He replied, "Well, it hasn't happened for me, but I'd love that in the future." The father said, "I then quickly changed the subject." He explained that he didn't feel the need to introduce his sexuality if his children hadn't explicitly asked.

While I respect a parent's choice on how they raise their child, as someone who works with youth, it's important for me to bring awareness to what parents, educators, and caregivers can sometimes overlook.

Similarly to my friend Alex, I was curious about his conscious choice to not be open and honest. What was behind his decision to "quickly change the subject?" If a child is old enough to talk about marriage and having kids, they're surely able to be introduced to what it means to be gay. Love between two men or two women is just as normal as the dominant heterosexual examples they've already seen on television and in cartoons. When our answers don't align with what children intuitively know, we can unintentionally teach them shame.

To the degree that we are willing to name internalized homophobia, we can refrain from teaching it to children. Addressing shame within ourselves, as well as within our communities, is a required part of a proactive prevention process.

PROACTIVE PREVENTION

A good doctor cures the disease, but a great doctor cures the cause.

—Amit Kalantri

A few days ago, I was talking to my six-year-old niece. She told me how earlier in the day two of her friends came by. I said, "Oh, how fun. Did they come over to play?" She replied, "No, they came over to say sorry for pulling my hair."

Surprised, I asked my niece, "What did you say after they apologized?" She immediately said, "I accept your apology!" I had to laugh at how cute she was. Then I asked where she learned such a mature response. She told me it was something they learned at school, so I asked her to give me an example of how it's taught.

She said, "Well, if one student is mean to another student our teacher will bring us together and ask them to apologize. The apology isn't complete until the other person says, 'I accept your apology.'" Then, in the most matter-of-fact way, and in her cute six-year-old voice, she said, "I don't know why we don't do that at home. Home is just the same as school, so I don't understand why it's not something we do at home."

I had to take pause with what she said because it's true. What I've learned teaching social-emotional learning for the past six years is how important it is for parents to reinforce at home concepts students learn in class.

Most children of marginalized groups, including LGBTQ youth, have received some form of shameful message about their identity—especially if their identity isn't spoken about or affirmed by an adult when they are young. The more we engage in open and honest conversations with children at home, the more we can proactively prevent bullying and shame—including some of their most harmful effects, like addiction, suicide, and depression.

The Centers for Disease Control and Prevention (CDC) published a study in the *Journal of the American Medical Association* (*JAMA*) in 2019 that shows the suicide rate in the United States among fifteen- to twenty-five-year-olds has increased to its highest point since 2000, with a recent increase, especially in males fifteen to nineteen years old.[9] Not long afterward, *US News and World Report* reported on a study, published in *JAMA Pediatrics*, showing that while depression rates for heterosexual teens have dropped since 1999, the rate for LGB teens hasn't dropped. In fact, depression rates for LGB teens have remained the same (the study didn't include results for transgender youth).[10]

According to the study, each year between 1999 and 2017, roughly 33,500 teens were surveyed on their struggles with sustained bouts of depressed moods, such as sadness and hopelessness. Among the teens who identified as straight, about three in ten reported being depressed for two weeks in a row or more in 1999. By 2017, the number dropped five percentage points.

For sexual-minority teens, the numbers were much worse. In 1999, approximately 51 percent of LGB teens reported being depressed. And nearly twenty years later, the figure hasn't changed. Caitlin Ryan, director of the Family Acceptance Project at San Francisco State University says that while images of LGB people have become more positive over the past twenty years, "there is an enormous gap between need and reality when it comes to social services for LGBT youth."

Caitlin talks about the importance of getting families and more social services involved to support youth. She says, "Kids are coming out earlier and parents are much more aware of sexual orientation and gender identification than ever. That's great. But that means we now have to step up and fill a huge and continuously growing need for more and more child development and family support to help these kids."

My goal with the next section is to help prevent LGBTQ bullying, which is both a cause and effect of shame, and also to help increase support for LGBTQ youth. "The answer to the bullying problem," says Dr. Brené Brown, "starts with this question: Do we have the courage to be the adults that our children need us to be?"[11]

In the following sections we will:

- develop a plan we can implement to prevent bullying;
- receive tools on how to prevent bullying's harmful effects;

- bring awareness around what to look out for; and
- continue to take inventory of our "messages from the playground" and how they can contribute to a world in which bullying still exists.

KEY FACTORS RELATED TO LGBTQ BULLYING

> We don't tell them what to believe. We don't tell them what they need to do in terms of what action they need to take, but we help them develop a framework and a language in the sense that their voices matter.
>
> —Liz Vogel

This week, one of the youths I work with told me how badly he was bullied during high school. I was shocked because he's such an outgoing and gregarious young man. When I expressed my disbelief, he said, "Why is that so surprising? I'm a little gay boy." Even though he's twenty-two and comes from a completely different generation from me, it's still the rule, not an exception: LGBTQ youth get bullied. Also, his language, referring to himself as "a little gay boy," makes it seem as though he subconsciously blames himself for getting bullied.

As parents and caregivers, we must continue to reinforce at home that, no matter what, a child is never the cause of getting bullied. Nothing about an individual needs to change in order to prevent bullying. That's like saying a person who dresses a certain way is responsible for being harassed. The bully and the reasons they choose to bully are what need to change. Creating a new narrative and shifting the focus will prevent shame from continuing to be the subconscious self-talk for youth who are bullied.

Each of us is familiar with bullying. We've been either bullied ourselves or indirectly touched by it in our lives. For LGBTQ youth, the numbers are consistently higher. In 2019, roughly 78 percent of transgender youth reported being discriminated against because of their gender identity, and 70 percent of LGBTQ youth experienced discrimination due to their sexual orientation.[12]

Institutional, cultural, familial, and interpersonal discriminatory beliefs are the root cause of violence toward LGBTQ individuals. There are many intersectionalities related to these types of discrimination, but the key factors related to LGBTQ bullying are: sexism, racism, classism, misogyny, toxic masculinity, queerphobia, heteronormativity, and shame. What LGBTQ bullying boils down to is fear. And as we've learned, fear can manifest itself in many ways.

What drives bullying is usually related, but not limited, to: a lack mentality, unhappiness, insecurity, disempowerment, having no feeling of purpose, hurt, anger, blame, peer pressure, group dynamics, rites of passage, a need to fit in, and power dynamics.

If we look deeply enough into LGBTQ bullying, we will often find within the perpetrator: self-judgment, projection, shame, insecurity, or internalized queerphobia. Ultimately, LGBTQ bullying looks like: *Fear + Misguided Beliefs = LGBTQ Bullying.*

One of the principles of nonviolent communication is that we are always operating from our values. In any given moment, our actions reflect our values. One of the most significant ways we can prevent bullying is by helping youth consciously connect to their values. Only when we're aware of what our values are can we know when we aren't connected to them (chapter 10 includes a fun and creative exercise to help youth connect more fully to their values).

Types of Bullying

In order to holistically address bullying, it will help to become more familiar with its varied types:[13]

- Physical—can include hitting, hurting someone, or damaging/stealing their property.
- Sexual—harassment that is sexual in nature, including name-calling, spreading rumors about sexual behavior, and assault or rape.
- Verbal—name-calling or insulting someone about physical characteristics or other attributes including race, sexuality, gender, culture, weight, or religion.
- Cyber (social media)—sharing information or images without permission. It can also include any online version of harassment that overlaps with most other forms of bullying.

- Social—consistently excluding another person, being ignored.
- Prejudicial—verbal, physical, social, and/or cyber harassment based on race, religion, sexual orientation, or gender identity.
- Benign Neglect—subtle yet pervasive, what happens when parents, families, teachers, and caregivers don't affirm or acknowledge the identities of LGBTQ youth.

Note: All forms of bullying are harmful and feed shame. It's especially important to keep a careful watch for nonphysical bullying. Nonphysical bullying lives in the shadows and doesn't leave an outward, physical mark. This is why not only speaking with our children openly is important but also reflecting to them what it's like to be vulnerable can help shine a light on nonphysical harm.

Bullying Scenarios

Bullying scenarios to consider include:

1. peer to peer;
2. adult to youth;
3. youth to adult;
4. organizational, institutional, and cultural; and
5. self.

Note: To help create open dialogues around bullying and nip shame in the bud, ask youth for examples of bullying they've witnessed for each scenario. Are there stories or experiences you can draw on from each scenario? Using examples from your own life can help open the door to honest conversations.

Bullying Roles

When it comes to bullying, it's important to know what roles there are. Most of us are familiar with the bully. More often than not, though, there is a bully, bystander, target, and defender. By understanding more about bullying, we can empower the children in our lives to advocate for themselves and be allies for LGBTQ youth and other marginalized groups.

"I AM Authentic" is the name of a class from Tilly's Life Center that I've been teaching for six years. It's a class specifically to address bullying. To help youth better understand the dynamics of bullying, we use, "Bully Boards." There is a board for each of the key characters involved in a bullying scenario, including the bully, bystander, target, and defender.

During the closing discussion of every class, I always ask youth what role they hope to play in real life should bullying ever occur. Some say they want to be the defender, some choose to be the bystander, some even say they'd like to be the bully. After six years of teaching the class, no one has ever wanted to be the target. Not once has anyone ever raised their hand to be the target. When youth from all backgrounds see that no one wants to be the target, not even in a pretend scenario, a new level of awareness around LGBTQ bullying occurs. What I've learned from teaching this class is that authentic and honest conversations help prevent bullying in all of its forms.

What If Your Child Is the Bully?

While doing research for this book, I asked parents I knew what they wanted to see addressed more in schools. One of the mothers I spoke with said, "I'd like to learn what to do if my child is the bully."

Most parents want to think of their child as the defender or bystander in a bullying scenario. But sometimes, our child can be the bully. When we create space for authentic communication, we can proactively address that possibility.

To help, here is an easy five-step process for all ages:

Step 1—Acknowledge behavior, language, and conversations.

Step 2—Be aware of groups, friends, and social dynamics.

Step 3—Be willing to uncover, address, and challenge negative messages.

Step 4—Address and take action by calling out, speaking up, and naming what's said.

Step 5—Apologize and accept (I borrowed this step from my niece).

Where possible, it's important for children to learn when they've made a mistake. It's also important to help children learn how to forgive themselves, as well as others. Forgiveness is never something they do for another person. It's for their own benefit and helps to dissolve subconscious shame. When approaching step 5, do so mindfully and not forcefully. Forcing anything isn't necessarily effective. There are various degrees of bullying, and each one requires an appropriate approach. Being willing to engage with children in subjects and scenarios that are oftentimes swept under the rug is what matters most.

Not long after writing this chapter, I had an article published about what to do if your child is the bully. I had no idea the article would bring back memories from people's childhoods. I had many people reach out to me from across the country sharing detailed stories, of either getting bullied or being the bully, from when they were children. We all do things when we're young that we aren't proud of when we revisit our past. The purpose of my article was for parents and caregivers to have open and honest conversations with children—not to make assumptions because we think our kids are the most wonderful, but because peer pressure is a real thing.

In the twelve steps of Alcoholics Anonymous, step 9 includes making amends. Sometimes we aren't able to personally make amends with the people we've wronged from our past. But I believe we still can. If anything you've read so far has brought up a memory from your own childhood, I would invite you to write a letter of apology to the person or situation. After you write the letter, you can say a prayer and then, in a safe place, burn or bury it. I would also invite you to write a letter of forgiveness to your younger self. In the nonphysical realm, your apology is impactful in more ways than you can ever know.

Ultimately, having systems in place at home, in schools, and on playgrounds will help us to not only empower youth but also prevent LGBTQ bullying. It also prevents the negative effects of shame from continuing to cause harm in the lives of young people, today and tomorrow.

THE ANTIDOTE TO SHAME

Trauma is the gun and shame is the bullet.

—Ilene Smith

As we conclude this chapter, I want to share with you a personal story that continues to inspire me to speak out against LGBTQ bullying and shame. Left untreated, unhealed shame becomes trauma—which is what we'll learn more about in chapter 7.

One day, while I was bartending a few years ago, a nervous young man sat at my bar. I could sense his energy and so I walked over to greet him. He also seemed young, so I asked for his ID. Something told me to make small talk to help put him at ease. His ID was from Colombia, so I asked if he lived in Los Angeles or was just visiting. He said he was visiting his mother for the holidays but lived in Colombia.

He was so nervous, he could barely make eye contact. I asked him how he liked living in Colombia. He said he really liked it, but that it was challenging being himself. He said that this was his first time at a gay bar. He had googled *gay bar*, and that's how he wound up sitting in front of me. He told me he just came to terms with his sexuality and finally acknowledged he was gay. He was twenty-five years old. As he looked to his right and to his left, almost as if he was checking to see if anyone was watching him, I found myself looking into a mirror. He was me. He was me when I was twenty-five years old. I felt the urge to take him into my arms, hug him, and tell him everything was going to be okay.

While working at a gay bar, I met many people at various stages of their coming-out process. This particular occasion was the first time I had felt and seen myself in someone so clearly before. It was a huge reminder of the connectedness of our human condition. It also reminded me although the LGBTQ community has made great strides, there is still more for us to do. The young man I met that day said it wasn't safe for him to be out. There weren't even gay bars or places to hang out where he lives.

It made me grateful for what I have and that I live here in the United States. I think being gay or lesbian and living here—especially in larger cities like New York or Los Angeles—we tend to take for granted our freedom and forget the young people growing up in places where they continue to be bullied for being themselves.

I recently read that one of the fundamental keys to success is humility. I think it goes beyond success, and that it's one of the fundamental keys to life. It was in my humility that I saw myself in the young man and shared compassionately my experiences. I told him he reminded me of myself. He looked up at me, smiled, and asked, "Really?" I said, "Yes, and it's an honor to meet you." I bought him a Bud Light, gave him a glass of water and my email address. He emailed me a few days after we met to say thank you for supporting people like him. I replied:

> It was really great to meet you and I'm glad you came in. I was really struck by how much you reminded me of myself. I can completely relate to what you're going through right now and so I just want to let you know you aren't alone. You seem like a happy, successful, and healthy young man, but I remember what I was going through on the inside when I was your age. Coming out is a process, so make sure you remember to love yourself. That was one of the things I didn't know to do while I was coming out and it eventually caught up with me and my choices.
>
> The best thing you can do for yourself and for the entire LGBTQ community is to love yourself on the inside and not be afraid to show who you are. *Cuídate mucho y nos hablamos pronto!*

The old adage says that when we give a person a fish, we feed them for a day. If we teach them how to fish, we feed them for a lifetime. Demonstrating to youth how to love themselves from the inside out is the antidote to shame and LGBTQ bullying. Giving young people the space to discover who they are, while encouraging them to share authentically their lives with us, helps prevent shame before we have to treat its harmful effects.

In the following chapter, we're going to explore trauma and discover what shame actually is. My hope is to help shift your perception of shame and its relationship to LGBTQ youth and trauma.

7

TRAUMA, RESILIENCE, AND HUMAN DIGNITY

Raising a New Generation

> Young children look to caring adults to help them un-
> derstand the expectations of their society and to develop
> a secure sense of self. Children are more likely to become
> resilient and successful when they are valued and feel that
> they belong.
>
> —Healthy Gender Development and
> Young Children, National Center on Parent,
> Family, and Community Engagement

Among the biggest takeaways I learned from bartending at one of the largest and most well-known gay bars in the world is how much unresolved intergenerational trauma there is in the LGBTQ community. I was privileged to hear the stories of hundreds, maybe even thousands, of LGBTQ people and community allies from across generations and around the world. I became a collector of stories and considered myself a "fly on the wall" because of everything I observed. Even the stories of trauma and shame were endowed with themes of resilience.

A story I don't think I'll ever forget is from one of my regulars, Donna, and is an example of the unresolved trauma so many members of the LGBTQ community carry today.

Donna was an ICU nurse at one of the largest hospitals in Los Angeles for ten years. She had always dreamed of being a nurse and so moved to LA from Michigan to attend nursing school in 1980. After she graduated from nursing school, she moved to West Hollywood. She had a lot of gay friends, and being a young twenty-something professional, she wanted to live closer to them.

107

Like many of the regulars I served, by the time I met Donna, she was an alcoholic. As wonderful as they were, most of the people I saw on a daily basis had a drinking problem. Donna used to visit me after her shift at the hospital and drink to the point where she could forget her past. It wasn't until I started to ask my regulars questions about their lives that I began to see themes of unresolved trauma.

One night after her shift and a few drinks, Donna shared with me what it was like being a nurse in the 1980s and 1990s in West Hollywood during the AIDS crisis. She told me about the friends she lost and how quickly everyone around her began to die. She specifically told me about one night early on in her career when she was a "fresh new nurse— bright-eyed and ready to save the world." She went out to dinner before her nursing shift to one of her favorite restaurants in West Hollywood. One of her favorite waiters, a young, handsome, gay man in his twenties, waited on her. After her meal, they said their goodbyes, and she said she'd see him again soon, not realizing how soon it would actually be.

An hour or so into her shift, a doctor urgently called her to a room to treat a dying patient. After she rushed inside, she looked down and saw the young waiter from the restaurant earlier that day. While telling me the story, her body began to tremble and she started to cry. Through her tears she said, "That's how fast everyone died back then. Here I was helping the guy who had just helped me. One minute he was fine and the next I was holding his body as he died in my arms from AIDS."

In his book *The Body Keeps the Score,* which I discuss more in the next chapter, Bessel van der Kolk, MD, one of the foremost experts on trauma, says, "People who suffer from flashbacks often organize their lives around trying to protect against them. They may . . . numb themselves with drugs, or try to cultivate an illusory sense of control in highly dangerous situations. Constantly fighting unseen dangers is exhausting and leaves them fatigued, depressed, and weary. . . . As a result, shame becomes the dominant emotion and hiding the truth the central preoccupation. They rarely are in touch with the fact that these sensations have their origins in traumatic experiences."[1]

We pass down trauma intergenerationally. Unless we acknowledge, name, and heal the trauma many members of the LGBTQ community still carry, we won't be able to completely prevent it from being passed on to future generations.

In the 2017 Netflix documentary *One of Us*, about the lives and struggles of three ex-Hassidic Jewish people, one of the film's commentators, Chani Getter, addresses intergenerational trauma. She says, "The Hassidic community that exists today is an answer to after World War II. And so it's an entire community built on survivors with trauma and they bring that in."[2]

While watching, I paused the documentary to record what Chani Getter said. I sent the recording to a friend and asked him what it reminded him of. He replied, "The LGBTQ community." When it comes to trauma, we don't just experience individual trauma; we also experience trauma from our communities.

The LGBTQ community today is an answer to closets, shame, religious persecution, familial rejection, heteronormativity, and the AIDS crisis. It's an entire community built on trauma. It's also a community built on hope, perseverance, and the resilient backs of survivors. Not addressing our individual and collective trauma, though, does a disservice to the next generation. The intention of this chapter is to explore LGBTQ trauma so that we can raise a new generation of LGBTQ youth without passing on trauma's harmful effects.

PASS ON OUR WISDOM, NOT OUR TRAUMA

> Some of the strongest forces that drive us are subconscious, and have roots from generations long before us—and it behooves us to recognize this today.
>
> —Adrian Pei

We cannot fully address homophobia, transphobia, bullying, shame, and their effects without exploring trauma. When we think of trauma, most of us think of a rape, murder, death, catastrophic event, or natural disaster. And while these are unequivocally traumas, a trauma is also experienced as a daily microaggression, such as homophobia, transphobia, bullying, and time spent in the closet. Any child who has experienced the closet has known shame—and shame itself is trauma.

For years, while working at a gay bar and being a part of a culture where drugs and alcohol were intrinsically connected, I looked at high rates of drug and alcohol abuse in the LGBTQ community through the lens of shame. Having seven years of sobriety myself, I used to attribute my close and personal relationship with drugs and alcohol to shame. It wasn't until a presentation I saw given by Jeremy Treat, LMFT, director of research and evaluation, and his team at Penny Lane, one of LA County's largest child welfare agencies, that I discovered how minority stress, daily microaggressions, and the implications for LGBTQ youth living in a heteronormative world are, in fact, traumatic.

Jeremy's presentation completely changed my advocacy and propelled me down a path of learning more about trauma. I contacted him after the conference to see if I could review his research, and what I found was astonishing. Jeremy's research showed what I already intuitively knew. It's what *Raising LGBTQ Allies* is trying to prevent; I just didn't realize it was considered trauma.

After discovering the impact of trauma on LGBTQ youth, I enrolled in the Narrative Focused Trauma Care training at the Allender Center of the Seattle School of Theology and Psychology. The Allender Center's theory is based on the principle that we can take others only as far as we've gone ourselves. Thus, to be more effective in my advocacy, for the past two years I've been exploring my story to be able to take others further along in their own.

In order to understand how living in a heteronormative world, daily microaggressions, minority stress, and the closet can be traumatic for LGBTQ youth, we have to take a few steps back. Each of us, as children, develops physically, mentally, emotionally, spiritually, and personally based on our unique backgrounds and experiences, what experts consider "identity formation." The children in your life, right now, are establishing their own identity formation based on their individual experiences and will develop accordingly. For minorities and marginalized groups (in this case, LGBTQ youth), childhood development comes with what are considered to be "barriers to development"—things in the world that can complicate a child's healthy identify formation.

According to Jeremy's research,[3] the top four common barriers to development for LGBTQ youth are:

1. Minority Stress. Which includes stigmas associated with being LGBTQ, outright prejudice and discrimination, and daily

microaggressions, for example, blatant name-calling, physical bullying, or benign neglect.

2. Homonegativity. As we learned in chapter 1, the misguided belief that sexual orientation and gender identity (SOGIE) outside a heteronormative standard is wrong—consciously or subsconsciously.

3. Anomie. A sense of normlessness, lack of social control, and feeling alienated. This is connected to why using words like "different" versus "difference" when describing an LGBTQ person can be harmful. The *Merriam-Webster's Dictionary* definition of *anomie* is "Personal unrest, alienation, and uncertainty that comes from a lack of purpose,"[4] which is what I specifically hope to remedy at the end of this chapter.

4. Internalized homophobia. Something we learned about in chapter 6 and is so important for us to be aware of, especially among LGBTQ youth. According to research, by age twelve, most children (including LGBTQ children) have already internalized the message that being LGBTQ is shameful and being straight and cisgender is normal.[5] This doesn't, however, account for the subconscious mind, which is where most of our early childhood beliefs are born, that is, messages from the playground.

While little t trauma, including bullying, heteronormativity, and queerphobia, may seem less threatening or significant than big T trauma, the symptoms LGBTQ youth experience are often the same as those of someone with post-traumatic stress disorder, including hypervigilance, blunted awareness, poor concentration, depressed mood, worry or panic, illness, and physical pain.[6]

In her book *Trauma and Grace*, Serene Jones writes, "Traumatic events are not necessarily limited to one-time occurrences of cataclysmic proportions; they can also be repeated events of the low-intensity variety, like the constant threat of violence in some forms of domestic abuse or hostile workplace environments. In such instances, the assault on the psyche is no less disabling than a frontal attack; but because it never reaches the explosive level of violence we associate with traumatic harm, its corrosive effects are more likely to go unnoticed—and uninterrupted—for years."[7]

Addiction rates are higher for LGBTQ people than the overall population. Compared to their straight peers, LGB youth are 90 percent more likely to use substances.[8] The Adverse Childhood Experiences (ACE) study shows how exposure to emotional, physical, or sexual abuse and household dysfunction during childhood, compared to those who had experienced none, led to a four- to twelvefold increase of the risk of alcoholism, drug abuse, depression, and suicide attempts.[9]

I remember one day while bartending, a young man ordered a drink from me. I only heard "Red Bull." To confirm what he had said I asked, "Just Red Bull?" He looked at me, laughed, and said, "No, no, no. Red Bull and *vodka*—you know, gay water."

His comment made me think about how normalized drug and alcohol use are among people who are LGBTQ. I wondered how many of us have subconsciously accepted the belief that being LGBTQ is the cause of increased rates of drug and alcohol use. The purpose of this chapter is to explore trauma and show how its effects are the main culprit for drug and alcohol abuse. It's also to give parents, teachers, caregivers, and allies tools to prevent trauma from being a shared experience for new generations of LGBTQ youth.

LGBTQ youth are also at increased risk of suicide ideation and attempts. Recently, Sam Brinton, Head of Advocacy & Government Affairs for the Trevor Project, released a statement in response to the Federal Communications Commission (FCC) report on the National Suicide Hotline Improvement Act of 2018. He said, "Today's FCC report on the National Suicide Hotline Improvement Act of 2018 recognizes young LGBTQ Americans as an acutely high-risk population for suicide attempts. The report also recognizes a need for specialized services for at-risk populations, specifically LGBTQ youth."[10]

What's more, FCC Chairman Ajit Pai said, "There is a suicide epidemic in this country, and it is disproportionately affecting at-risk populations, including our Veterans and LGBTQ youth."[11]

Additionally, 1.5 to 2 times the general population of youth I've worked with in the child welfare system identify as lesbian, gay, bisexual, transgender, or questioning.[12] According to a study by the Administration for Children and Families, 39 percent of them were forced from their homes due to their sexual orientation or gender identity. Despite large numbers in need, many service professionals receive no training on how to support LGBTQ youth.[13]

While there is a disproportionately low number of service professionals trained to work with LGBTQ youth, the Department of Research and Evaluation at Penny Lane emphasizes three important considerations for any professional to make when working with LGBTQ youth:[14]

- Awareness of personal bias. Nearly half of gay men and lesbian women surveyed in treatment experienced a homophobic therapist. One of my good friends, a transgender woman, shared with me recently that she's on her third therapist. The two prior ones were transphobic, and she had to painfully terminate the relationships.
- Internalized queerphobia, or shame, that is, messages from the playground, create a negative self-image and lack of self-worth.
- Familial, cultural, or communal rejection is no different from grief from losing a loved one.

That is why this book carries an important message for parents, families, caregivers, and teachers to consider when raising new generations of allies and LGBTQ youth. Rejection of any kind, especially when it comes to youth, is an embodied experience.

LGBTQ YOUTH AND THE TRAUMA OF REJECTION

> The brain makes no distinction between a broken bone and an aching heart. That's why social exclusion needs a health warning.
>
> —Elitsa Dermendzhiyska

In her 2019 article "Rejection Kills,"[15] author Elitsa Dermendzhiyska references a 2003 landmark experiment by psychologist Naomi Eisenberger. The experiment helped researchers conclude that social rejection is as damaging to the body as physical harm.

While earning her doctoral degree at UCLA, Eisenberger was curious about popular expressions like "My heart was broken" or "He hurt my feelings." She noticed how even though they're used to describe rejection, they also imply physical pain. She organized an experiment that researchers replicate even today to demonstrate the harmful effects of social rejection.

According to Eisenberger, when it comes to feeling rejected, "The significance of social pain goes back to evolution. Throughout history, we depended on other people for survival: they nurtured us, helped to gather food and provide protection against predators and enemy tribes. Social relationships literally kept us alive."

When LGBTQ youth are rejected by families, friends, churches, or communities, there isn't just emotional pain or trauma from grief; there are harmful physical and neurological effects as well. Regarding rejection, the article further states, "The harm goes beyond emotions. A growing number of researchers now recognise that threats to our social identity, such as being negatively evaluated by others, can tamper with crucial neurobiological systems."

Most young people will have an experience with some form of rejection growing up. My niece just turned thirteen and is beginning to have arguments with her friends at school. She's at the age when young people are beginning to form cliques. Now, add the possibility that a young person faces possible rejection from their friends, family, school, or church because of their gender identity or sexual orientation. It's no wonder that some youth take refuge in the closet. But the closet is also a hotbed of shame, and as we've discovered, shame itself is trauma. No child deserves to develop with shame or trauma, especially when each is preventable.

In "Rejection Kills," Elitsa Dermendzhiyska further states, "Rejection doesn't have to come from family, or even people you know, to do harm. Nor does it have to be particularly overt. In insidious forms, it lurks woven into the very fabric of society. The rejection might be implicit but, if anything, that makes it even more pernicious because it goes unquestioned: we often accept social inequality the way we inhale polluted air, or we justify it as a matter of merit."

I'll never forget, when I was in junior high and still in the closet, I got into a fight with my best friend on our way to school. Because of our argument, he walked ahead of me to school. When I eventually arrived, no one spoke to me. It was as though he had made an announcement to the entire school. I found out later he had started a rumor that I was gay and that I tried to hit on him. For a solid week I came home and sat in my room waiting for my friends to call. They never did, and I eventually transferred to a different school because the stress from being rejected was beginning to affect my grades. Rejection from our tribe is traumatic and affects the neural pathways of our brains the same way pain does.

With an increased awareness of the trauma associated with LGBTQ rejection, we can strengthen our willingness to affirm, acknowledge, and include LGBTQ youth in conversations and classroom examples. Our impact on young people can be quite different from our intent. We may not intend to cause harm, but the conversations we *don't* have about the communities we *don't* include can unintentionally imply rejection.

A study by San Francisco State University shows increased rates of substance abuse, mental health challenges, and risky sexual behavior are attributed to family rejection.[16] The entire study shows the direct link between parents and caregivers who reject lesbian, gay, and bisexual youth and the negative health problems the youth face as a result. During a recent conference call organized by Gender Spectrum, they talked about the ways to help make people care about the lives of LGBTQ youth. They encouraged advocates and allies to talk about the real experiences of youth—"lived experiences versus policies"—for example, how some transgender youth haven't peed at school for an entire year because of their anxiety around which bathroom to use.

I recently went to lunch with a friend, a thirty-two-year-old gay man. He told me about the recent news he received about one of his best friends, also a thirty-two-year-old gay man, who had died from suicide the week before. He told me it was the young man's third suicide attempt. He was raised in a religious household and so hid in the closet growing up. He dated girls and wound up getting one of them pregnant while he was in high school. The young girl had an abortion because he came out of the closet after finding out she was pregnant. The shame about being gay and an abortion was too much to bear, so his first suicide attempt was when he was sixteen. Unhealed shame is trauma and, while I can't say what ultimately caused this young man to take his life, the shame in his story is far too prevalent among gay men.

My friend told me that when they called his mom to give her the news, she said, "You're calling to tell me my son killed himself, aren't you? I've been waiting for this call." He also told me LA County recently announced that they were going to begin tracking suicides among LGBTQ individuals in an effort to protect the high-risk community.[17] In 2019, I personally knew four gay men in their twenties and thirties who died from suicide. And so far in 2020, another young gay man I know recently took his own life. I'm also one of three openly gay chapter members from my college fraternity's pledge class. Two of them have died—one of chronic alcoholism and the other from suicide. Both men were in their late thirties and died within the past five years.

From what I've seen in my own life and from the vantage point that I've had, one of the biggest threats facing the LGBTQ community today is the effects from unresolved childhood trauma. We carry our past with us wherever we go, and unless more parents, caregivers, allies, and teachers are affirming and inclusive of LGBTQ identities, we run the risk of perpetuating a preventable cycle of trauma. My hope by sharing lived experiences is that we'll begin to understand how much not being seen affects a young person growing up.

Adrienne Rich states, "When someone with the authority of a teacher describes the world and you are not in it, there is a moment of psychic disequilibrium, as if you looked into a mirror and saw nothing."[18] If we don't make space for LGBTQ youth at home or in the classroom and only look through a heteronormative lens, where can LGBTQ youth see themselves? Relying on pop culture to teach our children about people who are LGBTQ isn't responsible. That's like feeding kids fast food for breakfast, lunch, and dinner and expecting them to get their daily nutritional requirements.

While attending a lecture not long ago, the instructor used a typically heteronormative example in class. He said, "Imagine if you're at a party and there's a really attractive girl you're interested in . . . ." I thought about all the young people in the room who aren't straight men and wondered how they felt hearing his example. On a certain level, there's a feeling of not being included.

I'm sure my teacher is a lovely father and a caring husband. Like most of us, though, his belief system is reflective of the dominant patriarchal worldview. The reasons we reject individuals and groups vary, but oftentimes they can be from an unintentional lack of awareness. Part of becoming a more aware parent or caregiver is that we can pass on our wisdom and challenge limiting stereotypes about LGBTQ youth.

STEREOTYPES AND CONFIRMATION BIAS

> Show a people as one thing, as only one thing, over and over again and that is what they become.
>
> —Chimamanda Ngozi Adichie

I don't know about you, but I love watching TED Talks. In fact, in this book, I reference four of them, including my own (shameless plug). In one of my favorite talks, "The Danger of a Single Story," Nigerian novelist Chimamanda Adichie talks about stereotypes and the consequences of using a single story to define a group or person. She draws on her own experience as a woman from Nigeria going to college in the United States. Although her talk was given in 2009, the examples she uses are relevant today.

She specifically references a trip she took to Guadalajara, Mexico, when she was in college. There was a lot of negative news about the border, and she recalled constantly reading one-narrative stories about Mexican people. Being from Nigeria, she didn't know much more than what she read and heard about Mexico while living in the United States. So when she was visiting in Guadalajara, she looked around one day and noticed people around her walking, shopping, dining at restaurants; suddenly she felt a sense of shame. She said she had bought into the single story of what she read in the papers about the troubles along the US Mexico border and didn't consider anything more.

Her talk reminded me of a time when I was living in Monterrey, Mexico, and some friends came to visit me from the United States. I took them to one of the city's popular shopping malls to explore and look around. As we pulled up to the mall, one of my friends asked, "There are shopping malls in Mexico?" In her talk, Chimamanda says, "The single story creates stereotypes and the problem with stereotypes is not they are untrue, but they are incomplete. They make one story become the only story."

I draw the same parallels with the single story of the LGBTQ community. For my entire time growing up, the messages I received—consciously, subconsciously, overtly, or covertly—told me LGBTQ people had increased rates of addiction, suicide, and mental illness and that these experiences were a result of being gay, lesbian, bisexual, or transgender. Drawing on what Chimamanda says about the dangers of the single story, we begin to see entire groups of people in a singular way.

She says, "The consequence of the single story is this: it robs people of dignity. It makes our recognition of our equal humanity difficult. It emphasizes how we are different rather than how we are similar." While it's important to acknowledge the shared experiences a particular group has, when we reduce them to one narrative, we tend to see, *and seek*, only that. If we look at the entire LGBTQ story, and not the single story, we'll see the lives of LGBTQ youth being lived at home, in church, in the classroom, and on playgrounds. We'll also be more willing to see how increased rates of suicide, addiction, and mental illness are not a result of being LGBTQ; they are a result of heteronormativity, the closet, bullying, rejection, and trauma.

At the conclusion of a panel I spoke on recently, a young boy asked me, "Why do stereotypes exist, and why do we have to have them?" I answered, "That's a really great question, and you're so smart to even ask. Stereotypes exist if we don't question why we believe something we do. They also continue to exist if we don't speak up to challenge them otherwise."

I told him how grateful I was for his question and for the entire class. I was there to share my story and speak with them about how they can support their LGBTQ friends and family members. I let them know it's through their questions and the information they learn that they'll be able to help challenge stereotypes and be allies for the LGBTQ community.

In addition to learning how stereotypes inform our lives, it's important to understand *confirmation bias*. When we believe something based on an experience or what we've learned, we tend to gather information to confirm this belief. Take, for example, a parent who has unexplored queerphobia, conscious or subconscious, from either religious beliefs or what they heard growing up. According to confirmation bias, they will seek out information to prove themselves right. The parent will collect data to support their misguided beliefs about people who are LGBTQ while disregarding anything that doesn't support the narrative.[19]

For example, remember the story I shared about when I came out to my dad? His immediate reaction to my sexuality was a result of his confirmation bias. Not only was it confirmation bias, but his suddenly seeing a lawn chair in my backyard as a tool to solicit sex was relying on a single-story narrative about gay men: walking sex acts. Although similar, confirmation bias and messages from the playground are not to be confused. Messages from the playground are the beliefs we have on the inside, and confirmation bias is like a private investigator we hire to gather evidence on the outside to support our beliefs. The function of confirmation bias is to collect only the evidence we believe is true.

When it comes to confirmation bias, it's a two-way street. Being aware of my own confirmation bias was very important to consider while doing research for this book. As much as Google represents the collective conscious, it can also serve as a private investigator to prove our case right. If I didn't use discernment while gathering research to support my message, I would only gather evidence to support my bias as an LGBTQ person and advocate.

The good news is that once we're aware of our confirmation bias and messages from the playground, we become better equipped to challenge stereotypes on behalf of LGBTQ youth.

RESILIENCE AND HUMAN DIGNITY

Resilience is the ability to adapt with change.

—Simon Sinek

While working on this chapter, I hopped on a train to San Francisco from Los Angeles. The purposes of my trip were varied, one of which was to intentionally walk the streets and connect to the resilience of the city's LGBTQ history. The last time I had visited San Francisco was ten years before when I was at a completely different place in my life. On the outside, I seemed fine. But on the inside, I had lost my way. I was using drugs and alcohol to escape my unhappiness and the pain from feeling disconnected from my purpose.

It was a rather beautifully redemptive experience being back in the city and reflecting on my life between visits. Sometimes life takes us places we never anticipate going—physically, spiritually, and emotionally. And, sometimes, life calls us back to revisit and reclaim.

As I walked around the city, I imagined all the lives lost during the AIDS epidemic. I wondered how many of them also walked across the Golden Gate Bridge or wandered down Fulton Street after spending an afternoon at the beach. I thought about the resilient people who fought for the lives of the loved ones they lost—demonstrations of human dignity. During a lecture I attended before my trip to San Francisco, the woman speaking said human dignity is the most important quality to behold. She said, "It's through human dignity we gain access to our calling."

One of my favorite subjects to teach young people about is purpose and calling. Helping a young person discover their purpose is one of the most empowering tools we can give them. For LGBTQ youth, learning how to love themselves is part of their purpose and the ultimate act of resilience in the face of trauma and rejection.

Growing up, we don't often teach children about purpose and calling. Rather, we encourage them to get a job or pursue a career, and as a result, fewer of us are familiar with calling or what it means to offer it a blessing.

To bless our calling is to know our scars and learn the truth of who we are. It's to intentionally, and purposefully, claim and align with love. Especially when our calling touches areas where there's been deep harm, engaging from a place of love, not fear, is the only way to justly serve our calling. A good indication of a calling is that it's always about love. It's always about leaving the world better off than how we found it. And claiming our calling through blessing is what helps us discover our purpose.

A calling isn't defined by what we do; it's part of who we are. A calling is an extension of our soul—the purpose for which we are here.

So often the youth I teach get confused and think that what we do for a living, or how we earn an income, defines who we are. It doesn't. If we don't make a living from our calling, it doesn't mean we aren't living purposefully.

A purpose is similar to a calling. A purpose, though, serves as a function of our calling. It's easy to live purposefully when we've said yes to our calling.

To help youth understand the concept of calling, we have to help them read their lives. For LGBTQ youth who have experienced the effects of trauma, we have to listen to their stories, face areas of their lives where there's been harm, and learn where they're from. Most importantly, we have to encourage them to begin asking themselves:[20]

- What do I love?
- What are my gifts and talents?
- What do I stand for and against?

These aren't easy questions for young people to answer. In the pursuit of answering them, LGBTQ youth can heal their trauma, embrace their calling, and connect to their purpose. Even if they don't consciously have an answer to one or more of these questions, if they look inside their lives, they'll have a glimpse of what their calling is.

What I've learned in working with youth from all backgrounds is that the more challenges a young person has faced, the more resilient they can become. By no means am I implying that the trauma LGBTQ youth experience is good. The familial and cultural abuse I've heard about would break your heart. What I am saying is that the youth I work with who have faced the most adversity are often the wisest and most empathetic. While working at Juvenile Hall and at LA's LGBT Center's Homeless Youth Shelter, I learned more about the power of the human spirit than I did anywhere else.

Despite trauma, the LGBTQ youth I've worked with are still making a positive contribution to the planet. Mike, the young man I mentored, is a perfect example of someone who demonstrates resilience. After being part of the system and living in a group home while in high school, he graduated and started working at Disneyland. He makes everyone around him smile and feel good about themselves. It's no wonder he was selected to be a part of the special opening team for Disney's new theme park, Star Wars Land.

The biggest act of resilience is when we rise above harm and forgive those who hurt us the most, not out of guilt, but because we've transformed our pain into personal power. When I attended Mike's high school graduation, I was shocked to learn he had invited his entire family. Even though he had been emancipated from his family due to physical and emotional abuse, he continued to share his life with them. His entire case-management team and I were motivated, inspired, and humbled by his constant acts of resilience. Resilience is part of his purpose.

Each of us is here to help make a positive contribution to the planet, to somehow leave the world better off than how we found it. As we conclude this chapter, I'd like to leave you with a few tenets you can use to help LGBTQ youth turn trauma into purpose:

1. Purpose is something we can never lose, nor can it be taken away. It's something we must continually choose.
2. Calling is a constant companion that can carry us through the unknown.
3. Resilience is purpose and calling in action.

For more than six years, I've participated in support groups for LGBTQ youth and their family members. I speak on panels with LGBTQ people who share their coming-out stories. The common thread among all the stories I've heard is that one person made the difference. One person helped a young person decide to be themselves and not give up. Author and youth advocate Josh Shipp says, "Every kid is one caring adult away from being a success story." The thing is, we never know who that one kid will be. It might be our own child. It might be an LGBTQ youth we positively impact by challenging stereotypes and our misguided beliefs.

As I'm finishing this chapter, I can hear laughter from kids playing on the playground next door to my home. Children's laughter is the sound of resilience and human dignity. Jeremy Treat's final recommendation from his presentation "LGBTQ Youth and Trauma" is to use humor. He credits humor as an essential part of creating change. While trauma is a serious subject, and naming its effects is no easy feat, my ultimate hope is for LGBTQ youth to have fun while learning to be themselves. A world full of young people living purposefully through their calling is a world full of laughter and a gift that keeps on giving.

Ultimately, each of us is responsible for treating all children with dignity if we want to help raise a resilient new generation without trauma. In the next chapter, we'll learn more about what we can proactively do to take a more LGBTQ-inclusive parenting approach.

III

CHANGE

8

BUILDING A NEW PLAYGROUND

Six Simple and Effective Steps

> Not being seen, not being known, and having nowhere to
> turn to feel safe is devastating at any age, but it is particu-
> larly destructive for young children, who are still trying to
> find their place in the world.
>
> —Bessel van der Kolk, MD, *The Body Keeps the Score*

After working with young people, I've learned a lot and noticed
even more. Something I've noticed, and that I find particularly
fascinating, is that no matter where I teach or what age the youth are,
the same social dynamics exist in groups and are comparable to those
from when I was a child. I've also learned that, although technology has
changed and youth today have access to far more than what I had as a
child, they still use the same derogatory words to put down, denigrate,
and make fun of each other, so I wanted to do an experiment.

One day I called my nephew, Jacob (who was ten years old at the
time), on his cell phone. While I listened to the phone ringing, I re-
membered how it wasn't until high school that I even had my first pager.
The realization made me laugh because not only did it confirm my age,
but it's also a perfect example of something some youth have access to
today that I didn't have when I was ten years old. I said, "Hey Jacob, I
have a really cool project I think you could help me out with. You're
a really good leader and I could use your leadership skills. You want to
help me?" He replied, "Sure! What is it?" I told him, "I want you to
call all of your cousins, ask each of your friends from school and baseball,
even talk to your sister and her friends, and put together a list of words
that kids use to make fun of other kids." His immediate response was,
"Huh?" I continued, "I'm trying to put together a list of words that kids

127

use to make fun of other kids, so I need you to help me to try and find out what those words are."

Jacob is one of the brightest and kindest kids I know; he was also bullied pretty badly during the fifth grade. The harassment was so bad that his parents had to get involved, and he almost wound up transferring schools midyear. I thought, because of his experience being bullied, he'd be able to understand what I was talking about and want to help me with my project.

After my second attempt at explaining to him what kind of list I was looking for, he replied, "What words?" I was surprised he still didn't understand what I was talking about given his personal experience, but if he didn't bring it up, I wasn't going to remind him. I said, "You know, Jacob, the words that maybe a bully would use to make fun of someone he or she was picking on at school." He then replied, "I haven't heard any words." That's when I felt it: *shame*. The shame he still carried from his experience was preventing him from talking to me about it on the phone.

I could feel his discomfort and could sense he was beginning to shut down. I didn't want to push it anymore, so I thanked him for his help and told him I didn't want to pressure him into doing something he wasn't interested in doing. We chatted about the baseball practice he was driving to with his mom and current events, and then we said our goodbyes. My sister-in-law called me back about an hour later and told me she couldn't believe he said he hadn't heard any words. After Jacob and I had hung up, she asked him why he didn't want to tell me what words he's heard, and she said he told her, "I didn't want to tell Uncle Chris those words."

That's when I realized the importance of creating a safe space with a young person to address anything that has to do with bullying, shame, or trauma.

Calling Jacob on the phone while he was on his way to baseball practice with his mom wasn't creating a safe space. There wasn't a container to contain the shame I unknowingly triggered while talking to him about bullying. So I thought of approaching it in another way. I called my sister and let her know what I was up to and asked her to sit down with each of her kids and talk to them about the words they've heard kids use to make fun of other kids. In creating a safe space first to contain any shame, the goal was the same, but the approach was different.

The next day, my sister carefully and intentionally sat down with each of her children and a few of their friends and cousins, and asked them to take ten minutes and write down any words they've heard kids use at school to make fun of other kids. After she put all of the words together on one list, she emailed them to me. I immediately noticed three things:

- First, the same derogatory words are still being used. Glaring back at me on my sister's list from 2017 were words I'd heard on the playground nearly thirty years ago.
- Second, "that's gay" or "gay" is still being used in an offensive way. It's also a phrase or word most young children equate with being bad, wrong, or "less than." *There's still shame associated with it on the playground.*
- Third, out of twenty-two words from ten different kids, ages seven to twelve, there were two specific words I intuitively felt were directed at one of my nieces, who, to my sister's knowledge, had never been bullied.

After I reviewed the list, I called my sister to ask her whether the two words were specifically addressed to my niece. She said, "Yes, I had no idea she was being called those words. I was completely shocked and it made me really sad she never told me. I just didn't think she was ever bullied, so I never knew to ask her about anything negative she's ever been called." I told her the good news is that, now that she's aware of the negative words my niece had been called, she can intentionally create new positive words and messages to use to affirm her daughter, helping counter the negative ones.

The earlier we can identify any negative words or messages a child hears about themselves, the sooner we can begin to imprint new messages of empowerment and confidence. By doing this, we are taking a proactive approach at preventing specific negative messages from taking root inside of their belief system and formulating a negative self-image based on that particular word or message.

I explain to parents that it's kind of like visiting the doctor—if you were to go to the hospital for a hurt elbow, and the doctor took a look at your knee and said, "I don't see anything wrong with your knee, it's perfectly fine." Having a doctor treat your knee will do nothing for your hurt elbow. My sister's not knowing the negative messages her daughter had received was like paying attention to her elbow, not knowing it was her knee that was hurt. Having open conversations with children and proactively asking specific questions can help prevent low self-esteem and lack of self-confidence. Especially as it pertains to LGBTQ youth, being able to identify early on which negative words and messages they associate with, or see or hear about, being gay, lesbian, bisexual, or transgender can help prevent a negative self-image and the internalization of shame, that is, internalized queerphobia.

For example, the common phrases "you're gay," "don't be gay," or "that's gay" can be particularly harmful for young children and contribute to the negative association they begin to subconsciously formulate about what it means to be LGBTQ. No one ever gives high fives after a touchdown and says, "That was so gay!" It's usually used to indicate something bad or wrong, or to denigrate and put someone down, which leaves a lasting impression on the conscious *and subconscious* perceptions youth have about people who are LGBTQ, whether it's themselves, friends, or people they know.

Not all children will go to their parents, caregivers, or a teacher if they're being bullied. According to PACER's National Bullying Prevention Center, 43 percent of bullied students report notifying an adult at school about the incident. However, "students were less likely to report having experienced homophobic bullying."[1] I believe this specifically speaks to the negative association, shame, or trauma youth pick up from the playground about what it means to be lesbian, gay, bisexual, or transgender. The degree to which an LGBTQ child is out and feels safe, or doesn't feel shame for their sexual orientation or gender identity, is the degree to which they'll report homophobic bullying. And the degree to which we are attuned to a child is the degree to which we can prevent the negative effects of bullying, shame, or trauma from causing further harm as they get older.

ATTUNEMENT

We need attunement to read our children's lives.

—Dr. Dan Allender

One of the most important things we can offer a young person is attunement. "Parents who are insufficiently attuned produce children who grow up with a sense of inner emptiness," says Dr. Susan Heitler in an article in *Psychology Today*.[2] To attune to a child is to say, "I see you and I am a witness to your life." It requires engagement, both verbal and nonverbal. Something else important to offer a young person is the space for them to become who they are.

I was recently listening to the *Moth Radio Hour* on NPR, and during one of the stories, a father said to his daughter, "It's not the child's responsibility to teach the parent who they are, it's the parent's responsibility to learn who the child is."[3] I knew I was gay from a very young age. I was really good at keeping my sexuality hidden, though, so I can't fault my mom for saying she never knew. But if I were to be completely honest, I'd have to recognize the fact that as wonderful of a mother as I had, she was not attuned to me or what was going on in my life. My mom loved me, and I knew she loved me, but everyone knows everything on a subconscious level, and I truly believe my mom intuitively knew that I was gay. She was, for religious reasons, in denial and not willing to see me fully. Therefore, she couldn't entirely understand what my needs were growing up.

In the groundbreaking book *The Body Keeps the Score*, Bessel van der Kolk, MD, shares a study by Karlen Lyons-Ruth, a Harvard attachment researcher, that concludes that children who are not truly seen and known by their mothers are at high risk to grow into adolescents who are "unable to know and to see" (in this context she's referring to dissociation). Her research shows that what cannot be communicated to the mother (i.e., needs, wants, feelings, etc.) cannot be communicated to the self. She says, "If you cannot tolerate what you know or feel what you feel, the only option is denial and dissociation." This dissociation, per Lyons-Ruth, "is manifested in feelings of being lost, overwhelmed, abandoned, and disconnected from the world and in seeing oneself as unloved, empty, helpless, trapped, and weighed down."[4]

I started getting bullied a lot in junior high. From seventh to eighth grade, I had lost most of my friends. During one particularly hot afternoon day while walking home by myself after school, before I had even left the playground, I suddenly felt someone walk up behind me and whisper "faggot" in my ear. I literally froze. I was petrified. The first thing I thought was, "Oh my God, people know." The secret I had worked tirelessly to hide was suddenly acknowledged. If he knew, then others must know as well. I remember feeling so much shame I didn't even turn around. I just kept walking, pretending I didn't hear what he said. Similarly to my niece, I had been called names my mother had no idea I was being called. I can't say for sure, but I wonder, had there been opportunities for me to talk about names I had been called, or words I heard on the playground, would my mom have been better able to anticipate my needs or recognize that her intuition about my being gay might be right?

One of the fundamental needs all humans share is safety, and for LGBTQ youth, not feeling safe can be life threatening. Lack of safety within the early caregiving relationship, says Dr. van der Kolk, leads to "an impaired sense of inner reality . . . and self-damaging behavior."[5]

CONTAINMENT

> In psychotherapy, containment is the atmosphere created
> by the therapist to convey a sense of safety, thereby allow-
> ing the patient to move through their emotions.
>
> —Dr. Suzanne Lacombe

Attuning to what a child is going through and anticipating their needs equips us with a container where we can take in their suffering. When we can take in a child's suffering and hold it as sacred, we offer them containment.

Dr. Brené Brown shares from her research on shame that kids start shutting parts of themselves down around middle school. She actually refers to fourth and fifth grade as the "creativity slump" because that's the age kids begin to compare themselves to each other. Her studies show that shame-prone children are more likely to die from suicide, drop out of school, engage in high-risk sexual behavior, and experience increased drug use.[6] The Trevor Project shows that suicide is the second leading cause of death for people ten to twenty-four years old. Lesbian, gay, and bisexual youth are four times more likely to attempt suicide than their straight peers. And nearly half of transgender youth have seriously thought about taking their lives.[7]

Matthew Shurka, founder of the Born Perfect Campaign, an organization working to end conversion therapy, shared that during a recent visit to Virginia, an elected official in support of keeping it legal in the state openly expressed at a public meeting that "homosexuality is the cause of suicide." I think most intelligible adults would recognize how problematic and false the proclamation is; however, the purpose of this book is to uncover the negative conscious *and subconscious* beliefs that still exist about being gay, lesbian, bisexual, and transgender. There are still beliefs held in the collective consciousness that being LGBTQ is the cause of suicide, addiction, risky sexual behavior, and HIV and AIDS. Being LGBTQ isn't the cause of any of these things; *lack of childhood acceptance, recognition, affirmation, celebration, attunement, and containment are.*[8]

I often speak on panels with parents of LGBTQ youth, and even the most affirming and accepting parents share their fears and concerns of having children who are gay, lesbian, bisexual, and transgender. All children will face challenges. It's our job as parents, caregivers, teachers, uncles, and aunts to attune to our children, offer containment, affirm their identity, help them know their own worth and their own strengths, and to support them in whatever challenges life brings them.

DISMANTLING OLD PLAYGROUNDS

Despite the false sense of security given by the advances in queer liberation, there are still many forces threatening queer rights and people today.

—A. Pallas Gutierrez

While at an educational event a few months ago, I spoke on a panel with an elementary school teacher who has two decades of experience as well as a daughter who is a lesbian. She shared a personal revelation about heteronormativity in the classroom: even though she is a supportive and affirming mother of an LGBTQ child, it had never occurred to her that the questions she asked her students and the examples she used in the classroom always put forth a heteronormative perspective. It wasn't until she recently ran into one of her former students, now in high school and openly gay, that she realized how important it is to not make assumptions when teaching children or raising a child.

Not everyone is straight or cisgender. Yet we live in a heteronormative world, and many young people spend their days in classrooms and homes that are extensions of the world outside them. Through everything from pop culture to K–12 materials, the main messages children receive inside and outside the classroom often put forth a heteronormative worldview.

According to a 2017 article from the American Marketing Association, the average consumer in the United States is exposed to ten thousand brand messages a day.[9] In addition, research from Michigan State University Extension's Stress Less With Mindfulness program, finds that the average person has eighty thousand thoughts per day.[10] Because we live in a heteronormative world, from the moment a child is born, families can unintentionally pass along homophobic beliefs and encourage heteronormativity simply by the toys, books, and movies their children are exposed to at home.

It's made me wonder how many heteronormative messages, images, and impressions an average youth receives on a daily basis in the United States, from both the media and their environment. Compounded with the number of thoughts the average person has per day and the intersectionality of familial, religious, cultural, and societal beliefs (and just by doing basic math), we have an overwhelmingly straight and cisgender equation, thereby helping give us a dominant straight and cisgender lens through which to interpret the world.

Just the other week, I was at the grocery store with my youngest nephew. We were waiting in the checkout line, and a woman at the register complimented his brown eyes and long eyelashes. She told him, "You're gonna be trouble for the ladies. I'm sure all the girls have a crush on you." It may appear to be a harmless and sweet comment, but if you look beneath the surface, the message is rooted in heteronormativity.

As my nephew and I left the store, I thought about how, when I was eight years old and knew I was gay, comments like hers were part of the reason I hid in the closet. How did she know my nephew wasn't gay? Furthermore, not all girls will have a crush on him.

In math, if you want a different outcome, you have to plug in different numbers or change the equation. If we want to build new playgrounds and help create an open and affirming world for all children, we have a responsibility to not make assumptions about children's identities—and that includes their sexual orientations and gender identities. To effectively create more LGBTQ-affirming homes, classrooms, and playgrounds and dismantle the old, I want to highlight a few of the most important takeaways we've explored in this book so far:

- No matter who we are or where we come from, we subconsciously learn or are exposed to certain societal messages. They mold our beliefs, and our belief systems become the lens through which we interpret the world. Building an awareness of our implicit biases is key to interrupting heteronormative thinking.
- Beneath heteronormativity lies homophobia and transphobia. Homophobia and transphobia are multilayered, and each can include conscious or subconscious beliefs that someone else or a group of people is "bad," "wrong," or "less than."
- Biological sex, sexual orientation, gender identity, and gender expression cannot be equated. This is important to understand when working with youth.
- Not communicating something still communicates something. When teachers do not have LGBTQ-inclusive curricular materials or lesson plans, or parents don't talk to their children about an out and openly LGBTQ family member or don't make a concerted effort to use LGBTQ examples in conversations, they are still sending a message.
- Heteronormativity perpetuates the closet, and the closet is a hotbed for shame.
- Shame itself is trauma.

During her keynote address at the 2017 SXSW EDU Conference, Dr. Brené Brown spoke to an audience full of teachers about shame and the negative impact it has in the classroom. She shared that learning is inherently vulnerable, and if students can't be vulnerable, it's impossible for them to learn. *For LGBTQ youth in the closet, it isn't possible to be vulnerable without first feeling safe.*

As we're continuing to explore, it's not enough to support same-sex marriage and be a passive ally for the LGBTQ community. We have to become willing to prevent heteronormativity, homophobia, and transphobia from taking root at home, in the classroom, and on the playground by raising LGBTQ allies.

BUILDING A NEW PLAYGROUND IN SIX STEPS

> Every outcome has its cause, and every predicament has its solution.
>
> —Anthony Doerr

In 2018, I attended a reunion with eight guys I went to college with, all of whom are married and have kids. During dinner one night, the conversation centered around fatherhood and what they all enjoyed most about being dads. While waiting for our food to arrive, one of the fathers asked each person in the group to say one thing they were really good at as a dad. After each person answered, I could sense the attention and anticipation shift toward me. To help me feel included, and because they all know how involved I am with my nieces and nephews, one of the guys asked, "Chris, what is something you're really good at as an uncle?" I immediately said, "Listening. I'm a really good listener. I can hear what someone says even if they don't say it." They all replied, "Yeah, we can totally see that!"

As a good listener and because of my personal experience growing up hypervigilant in a homophobic home, I'm able to hear and interpret what even the best-intentioned parents might miss otherwise. Just recently, I was part of an LGBTQ educational forum for teachers, administrators, parents, and mental health practitioners. I sat alongside parents of LGBTQ youth who, although they love and support their children and in fact were there on their behalf, made some subtlety homophobic and problematic comments. Hearing what they weren't explicitly saying,

I was attuned to their deeper, subconscious, and unresolved homophobia, which they haven't become aware of yet and were unintentionally and unknowingly continuing to pass along.

Something that keeps me motivated to continually work on myself and my life is that, in order to say my room is really clean, I have to be willing to look underneath the bed. In addition to dismantling old playgrounds, we have to proactively uncover the deeper layers of homophobia and transphobia that can continue to cause harm and be a source of shame for even the most accepting families.

What I've learned over the years is that if we don't consciously build love, fear-based forces will come right in. To help, I put together six proactive steps for parents, caregivers, and teachers to consider when raising or working with youth to help heal homophobia and transphobia, prevent bullying, and create allies. Following these steps will help build new playgrounds for *all children*.

Six Proactive Steps

1. Consider that at least one child in your class or family is lesbian, gay, bisexual, transgender, or queer. Even if you don't have an LGBTQ child, they will jump rope or play tag with someone who is LGBTQ on the playground. Being aware of this helps to interrupt heteronormative thinking and heal homophobia and transphobia before they begin, and it also helps create allies early on.

2. Proactive confrontation. In his parenting book *Becoming Attached*, Robert Karen, PhD, states, "The problem we have as parents, then, is not usually a lack of love or good intentions, but more often an unwillingness to face who we are."[11] I think the most powerful step any parent, caregiver, or teacher can take is to proactively confront their own *messages from the playground,* or subconscious beliefs, they have within themselves. We can't change something we can't see, so in order to confront any bias or negative belief, we have to be willing to acknowledge that it exists. As with any behavioral modification, lasting change comes from the willingness to recognize, acknowledge, and accept what we want to change.

3. Be inclusive and incorporate LGBTQ examples in discussions and everyday conversations. For parents and caregivers, it means using same-sex examples when you talk to your children like "Does your friend Billy have a boyfriend or girlfriend?" For teachers in the classroom, use same-sex stories whether you teach math, science, history, or art. By incorporating more LGBTQ-related examples in conversations and classrooms, we're helping to create a world where being gay, lesbian, bisexual, or transgender is normal and natural.

4. Show support by having LGBTQ-related books, signage, stickers, or resource materials. This sends a powerful message to children who are gay, lesbian, bisexual, or transgender. Even seeing a book or sticker sends a subtle message that this space is safe. Once, I was enrolled in a training program at the Seattle School of Theology and Psychology. I was hesitant about whether I should attend and even mentioned to the admissions director that I had reservations about being an openly gay person at a religion-based institution. When I walked into the main office during my first week and began looking around, I noticed handouts on one of the desks about the "Genderbread Person," a figure similar to the one we saw in chapter 4 that's used as a teaching tool to talk about gender identity and sexual orientation.[12] I breathed a sigh of relief. Seeing something LGBTQ-affirming sent a huge message to me that I was in a safe place and that my sexual orientation would be validated. Having LGBTQ-related children's books whether you have LGBTQ children or not is also a really great idea. Encouraging my nieces and nephews to read is its own gift, but getting them LGBTQ-related children's books has been one of my favorite gifts to give. In chapter 10, I share which books I love giving that you can easily add to your annual holiday and birthday present shopping list.

5. Create an open, safe, and affirming space (containment). Before beginning a new program, no matter how long it will be, I always have students create their own "class agreements." I let them choose the agreements, but I do my best to have some variation of non-judgment on the list. I let them know we practice "non-judgment" in the room. As I shared in the example

with my nephew Jacob, creating a safe space is vitally important to ensure youth feel comfortable and confident that whatever they share is safe and will be held as sacred. Creating an open, safe, and affirming space starts with the parent, caregiver, and teacher, and it allows children who are LGBTQ to be who they are and express themselves without fear of being judged.

6. Be vulnerable, ask questions, and have authentic conversations (attunement). Recently, a friend of mine, a Presbyterian minister, asked me, "Chris, what are some tips you can give me about what the church shouldn't say to people who are LGBTQ?" We were talking about his interest in helping to create a more open and LGBTQ-affirming congregation. I told him, "How about I tell you what *to say* instead of what not to say? Be vulnerable and ask me questions about my life, my relationships, my family, who I'm dating (or not dating), and my interests." Sometimes when we're uncomfortable talking about something, we ignore it or don't say anything at all. Just like a form of bullying, our silence speaks volumes. Being vulnerable, asking questions, and having authentic conversations helps a youth who is LGBTQ know that who they are matters. Even if you don't know what to say, saying that you don't know but you are curious and want to learn more lets them know they are seen and you are a witness to their life.

By using these steps and not making assumptions, we can help keep children out of the closet. Outside the closet is the only place appropriate for a child to learn, feel safe, and thrive.

Once while teaching, I shared the quote, "To save one human being is to save the entire world."[13] After sharing it, I asked the class what they thought the quote meant. One girl raised her hand and said enthusiastically, "Every person matters!"

If a young girl in seventh grade can recognize what it means to be able to save one person, then I think as parents, caregivers, family members, and teachers, we're called on to take action at home, in the classroom, and in our communities so that we can as well.

Dr. Bessel van der Kolk further states in *The Body Keeps the Score* that as children, "If our parents or grandparents keep telling us we're the cutest, most delicious thing in the world, we don't question their judgement—we must be exactly that. And deep down, no matter what else we learn about ourselves, we will carry that sense with us: that we are basically adorable. As a result, if we later hook up with somebody who treats us badly, we will be outraged. But if we are abused or ignored in childhood, or grow up in a family where sexuality is treated with disgust, our inner map contains a different message. Our sense of our self is marked by contempt and humiliation."[14]

It's perfectly okay to not fully understand being lesbian, gay, bisexual, or transgender—yet. Gender and sexuality may be something new for you to consider talking about with youth. Remember, the journey we've been on together is a process of unlearning. All we need is our willingness, and where there was once fear, open hearts, open minds, and open conversations can heal.

To assist you in building new playgrounds, chapter 10 is dedicated entirely to experiential exercises you can use on yourself and with the children in your life, including sample questions and suggestions for parents, a powerful visualization, as well as empowerment statements for adults and youth alike. Also included are LGBTQ-inclusive tips and suggestions for parents and caregivers to consider making when engaging the young people in their lives.

Before we move on to the next chapter, I'm going to invite you to envision the new playgrounds you're building by virtue of reading this book. The following is a special meditation you can repeat to yourself and share with your loved ones.

BUILDING A NEW PLAYGROUND MEDITATION

Go ahead and get into a comfortable position. Slowly breathe in to the count of five and exhale to the count of six. Do this three times. Breathe in 1, 2, 3, 4, 5 and breathe out 1, 2, 3, 4, 5, 6. Repeat twice more. Continue to breathe in and out slowly and deeply. Consciously tell yourself, "I am relaxed, my scalp is relaxed, my forehead is relaxed, my face and jaw are relaxed. I relax my shoulders, my chest, my arms, my abdomen, my hands, and my palms. My upper body is completely relaxed and I feel grounded where I sit. I relax my upper thighs, my hips, my legs, and my feet. My feet are connected to the ground and I am safe.

I bring to my mind's eye somewhere I love to be. Maybe I've been there before; maybe it's a place I've always wanted to go. I feel safe here. I feel relaxed and at ease. I understand that not all of my beliefs are my own. Some of my thoughts and some of my beliefs I learned and that's completely okay. I now realize my thoughts and beliefs are ever-changing. Each thought I think and each belief I have can change. I can choose what I want to think and what I want to believe. It's safe for me to change my thoughts and safe for me to change my beliefs. I am open and accepting of new thoughts and new beliefs, and I welcome change. I believe all children are the future and that each and every human life matters. I believe the world is connected and all children deserve to be loved and are lovable. If I can help inspire, uplift, and empower a young person to be exactly who they are, I can help create a more peaceful planet.

Building new playgrounds begins with me, and I have the strength, capacity, support, and motivation to help inspire change. Where there was once fear, I now stand for love. Where there was once hatred, I now actively embrace true acceptance. The privilege of a lifetime is for me to fully embrace, love, and accept myself exactly as I am. If I know that for myself, I'm willing to believe it's also true for every child on the planet. I embrace myself and therefore embrace each and every child I know. I'm willing to open my heart, and it's safe for me to embrace my new thoughts and my new beliefs. I'm excited to see, speak, and listen through my heart. I share peace, love, and acceptance wherever I go.

I believe in love, I believe in the human spirit, and I believe in change. I will do what I can to help create new and safe playgrounds for each and every child, regardless of background, race, culture, religion, gender, or sexuality. I am helping to build new playgrounds with each and every thought I think. It is my joy to build new playgrounds. Building new playgrounds begins with me and what I believe and I am safe. I look around and I see new playgrounds. I see all children laughing and smiling. I see what's possible when I embrace and accept all children. A peaceful planet begins with peaceful playgrounds. My new mantra and my new belief is: a peaceful planet begins with peaceful playgrounds. And so it is.

9

NEW MESSAGES, NEW PLAYGROUND, NEW WORLD

A Mother's Faith

Be authentic with your kids and they will follow your example.

—Monica Berg

When I was younger and coming to terms with my sexuality, I used to pray to God to help me not be gay. I thought I could "pray the gay away." When I turned forty, I took a three-week vacation to celebrate. While on my trip, something began to happen inside my heart. I've since healed my relationship with God and have spent the better part of a decade reestablishing a relationship with my version of a higher power—a higher power of my own understanding who created me exactly as I am. Prayer has always been a big part of my life, and the daily prayer I found myself saying during my trip was, "Dear God, continue to work on my heart." I'm not sure why that was the prayer I chose to say, but it was the one I intuitively said for twenty-one days. Throughout the days, at the beach, while walking, taking tours, visiting historical sites, or even eating, I would mentally say, "Dear God, continue to work on my heart."

After I returned home, I was on the phone with my mom. She wanted to know how my trip was, and I told her something inside of me shifted. After a decade of being single, I told her I had a desire to share my life with someone.

She quietly replied, "I've been waiting years for you to say that." Chills went down my spine and tears welled up in my eyes. Hearing the genuine love, celebration, and joy in my mom's voice made me recognize how far our relationship had come and how much healing we'd both done. Her response was a stark difference from what she first told me when I came out fifteen years earlier. When I first came out to my mom, she said, "You know what my religion says: I can hate the sin, but love the sinner."

It was during winter, and we were sitting in her car. We had gone to dinner while I was in town visiting. I had planned on coming out to her but didn't want to do it in the middle of the restaurant for fear of how she might respond. Instead, I asked if we could take a walk to have a heart-to-heart talk. When we arrived at her car, I was visibly nervous—rubbing my hands against my thighs and breathing heavily. I couldn't look her in the eye, so instead stared at the ground in front of me. Concerned with how I was acting, she asked if everything was okay. I told her I needed to tell her something and she fell silent. Then, suddenly she asked, "Chris, did you get a girl pregnant?" As if coming out wasn't challenging enough, her question made me realize how disconnected she was from my life. The pain of not sharing my complete self with the person I loved most suddenly hurt more.

After I came out, my mom went into the closet. I remember shortly after my coming out, my mom turned fifty. My brother, sister, and I decided to plan a surprise for her birthday. I was a little nervous about contacting her friends after recently telling her I was gay. I thought surely they'd know. Not once did anyone mention anything when I called to invite them to her party. When the day came and everyone eventually arrived, it suddenly occurred to me that not everyone knew. My coming out wasn't exactly a family celebration, and so over the next five years, it was something we didn't talk about. I lived my life openly gay socially, but whenever I was with my family, our familiar foe, benign neglect, tagged along.

My mom and I have both come a long way since that cold winter day I sat in the passenger seat of her car. She remains my biggest supporter and has already told everyone she knows about my newfound desire for a relationship. She's even been dropping hints at becoming a grandmother again, which, to me, are precious gifts of her love and a celebration of my life. Her coming-out journey wasn't easy. She lost friends, she's had to change churches numerous times because of anti-LGBTQ theology, and she's also had to face her own misguided beliefs about people who are LGBTQ.

When it comes to familial healing around LGBTQ matters, each family is unique. There are beliefs carried in my family that may be different from the ones you heard growing up. There are also collective societal beliefs we learn from playing on the same playgrounds. In the first section of this book, we explored some of the misguided beliefs about LGBTQ people and where these beliefs come from. In this chapter, we're going to revisit other misguided beliefs to clear the way for entirely new playgrounds. We're also going to further explore spirituality and religion. I'm going to share the specific steps my mom and I have taken in our own lives to offer hope, love, and, ultimately, healing to parents of faith.

Shining a light in dark places can heal limited generational ideology and break systemic cultural beliefs. And sometimes, we need to bring the dark to the light.

OTHER MISGUIDED BELIEFS:
BRINGING DARKNESS TO THE LIGHT

You can't solve a problem that you won't name or that you won't even recognize as real.

—Tim Wise

Books are like messengers. They come into our lives when we are ready to receive their gift. Recently, I read *Night*, by Nobel Laureate Elie Wiesel. I've been familiar with Wiesel and his work; however, I hadn't read any of his books until now. Although the content of *Night* isn't for the faint of heart (it's Wiesel's personal story of being in Nazi concentration camps as an adolescent in the 1940s), it's powerfully written, and his story is unforgettable. His writing touched my soul. While the story deeply affected me, there was one part of the book I found troubling. In describing one of his German camp leader's fondness for children, Wiesel wrote, "In fact, this affection was not entirely altruistic; there existed here a veritable traffic of children among homosexuals, I learned later."[1]

Although it was published in 1958 and is Wiesel's personal account of surviving the horrors of the Holocaust, the book saw a slow rise to worldwide acclaim. In fact, Oprah Winfrey selected it for her book club in 2006, nearly fifty years after it was originally published. Afterward, it stayed on the *New York Times* bestseller list for eighteen months, selling more than two million copies from the Book Club edition. While an important book, Wiesel's observation about "homosexuals" imprints itself on the consciousness of those who read it, including students who are required to read it in high schools nationwide. It's an example of the messages from the playground about LGBTQ people and speaks to the misguided association between being gay and sexual deviancy. He didn't refer to men who abused children as pedophiles—he referred to them as "homosexuals."

After I finished the book, I wondered how LGBTQ youth who are required to read it in school feel when they come across that part—youth who are out, in the closet, or questioning their sexual identity. This isn't to say that Wiesel's important book shouldn't be read. I'm bringing it to your awareness to help parents and teachers create a dialogue around a long-held belief that continues to feed stigmas today.

I told my mom about how much I enjoyed *Night* and Wiesel's writing. I also mentioned to her how I'm writing a book about the subconscious beliefs some families have that perpetuate queerphobia. One of the most damaging is equating being gay with sexual deviancy or pedophilia. She proceeded to tell me that when she was a teenager, her high school boyfriend was sexually assaulted by a Catholic priest at their school. When her boyfriend came to her window in the middle of the night to tell her what had happened, her reaction at the time wasn't grief, but shame. She didn't see her boyfriend as a victim of sexual abuse or the priest as a perpetrator. She convoluted being gay with what had occurred—her boyfriend's assault was intertwined with a sexual orientation.

I've had many conversations with parents who associate a male perpetrator of childhood sexual abuse with being gay. Last week, while at an LGBTQ parents' support group, one of the parents said that when her high school–age son recently came out, she told him to be careful of pedophiles. I asked if she had talked to her son about being careful of pedophiles the week before she knew he was gay and she said, "No." It wasn't until she began to see him as gay that she started to think of pedophiles abusing her son.

Sadly, we live in a world where sexual abuse occurs. It's important for us as parents, teachers, and caregivers to keep careful watch over our children's lives. Also important is to name the subconscious association between being gay, sex, and sexual deviancy that some families still have, an association that can prevent parents from having open and honest conversations with their children at a young age.

In a 2017 study, "Sexual Victimization Perpetrated by Women: Federal Data Reveal Surprising Prevalence," researchers explore the statistics surrounding sexual abuse perpetrated by women. The report discusses the prevalence of female sexual perpetration and shows how it wasn't until the 1990s that systematic studies were even undertaken. One study from the U.S. Census Bureau's National Epidemiologic Survey on Alcohol and Related Conditions (NESARC) shows, out of 43,000 adults sampled, that there was little difference in the sex of self-reported sexual perpetrators. "Of those who affirmed that they had 'ever force[d] someone to have sex . . . against their will,' the study said, 43.6% were female and 56.4% were male."[2]

By no means does this minimize the prevalence of sexual abuse perpetrated by men, especially during the necessary rise of the Me Too movement. Yet it sheds light on how we stereotype sexual abuse. Researchers from the study also reference a 2013 survey of 1,058 male and female youth, ages fourteen to twenty-one, who self-reported perpetrating sexual victimization. The results showed: "While 98% of perpetrators who committed their first offense at age 15 or younger were male, by 18–19 self-reports of perpetration differed little by sex: females comprised 48% of self-reported perpetrators of attempted or completed rape."[3]

After I graduated from college, I lived off the coast of California on Catalina Island for a summer. I wasn't out of the closet and still dated women to hide my sexuality. It was an easy way to distract people from suspecting I might be gay. One of the girls I became friends with had a crush on me. At first, I liked the attention because I thought it was good for my "straight image." I wasn't interested in a sexual relationship with her, but the more we hung out, the more sexually aggressive she became.

One night, while asleep in my apartment, I awoke to someone crawling through my bedroom window. It startled me at first, then I realized it was her. I could tell she had been drinking, so I asked what she was doing. She said she wanted to have sex. She jumped on my bed and forcibly tried to take off my clothes. Her aggressiveness caught me off guard. I worried how she'd respond if I told her no. I didn't want anyone to suspect I was gay and thought about the rumors she might start if I said no. I was petrified and wanted to crawl out of my skin. After she tried to take advantage of me, I got up and demanded she leave. Despite my fear and her anger, I was willing to risk the rumors. When she left, I immediately felt shame wash over me.

During a narrative-based trauma training, one of the straight male participants of our group shared his story. He told us he had been sexually abused by seven different people during his childhood. He also told us that six of the seven perpetrators were women. He said that for a long time he never told anyone. He said, "The shame I felt for being abused by a woman wasn't something I could understand, let alone expect others to understand." I wondered how many of us assumed his abusers were only men. I also thought about how most of us didn't question whether his sexual orientation (heterosexuality) was a result of sexual abuse—which is often the assumption about gay men.

Being gay or transgender isn't a result of something. The belief that it's from a sexual abuse experience is misguided. Making this distinction and shifting societal perceptions on what it means to be LGBTQ can encourage more young people to speak up about abuse. For a lot of men who have been abused by another man, they fear reporting the abuse because they don't want to be considered gay. Taking the shame away from both abuse and being LGBTQ can help survivors of childhood sexual abuse.

My mom's response to her high school boyfriend's sexual assault, which to this day is something she regrets, was a manifestation of the subconscious belief that being gay is a result of sexual abuse. I have many gay friends who at one time questioned whether sexual abuse had something to do with their sexuality. In fact, I wish I could say otherwise, but it's something I, too, once questioned along my coming-out journey. It wasn't until I consciously began doing the inner work that I was able to uncover and challenge the misguided beliefs I carried about my sexuality.

Once, I dated a guy who told me he was abused by a family friend when he was a child. He said he always thought the incident is what made him gay. When he shared this with me, I looked him in the eyes and said, "What happened to you wasn't your fault nor was it something you caused. Have you ever considered you were gay before you were abused and that someone took advantage of you? They might have sensed your shame of being gay and knew you wouldn't tell anyone." It was like a huge weight lifted from his shoulders, and he began to sob.

I began thinking about other children who know they're LGBTQ but don't know how to talk about it. How they have feelings of being different or that something is wrong with them. Children who feel guilty or as though something is wrong with them often isolate themselves and withdraw. During an episode of *The Oprah Winfrey Show* I watched years ago, Oprah interviewed four convicted child sex offenders. She wanted to understand why pedophiles do what they do, and she discovered that they intentionally and methodically seek out vulnerable children—children who are away from the group, detached, quiet, and otherwise withdrawn.

By talking about something shameful, we're bringing darkness to the light. Having uncomfortable conversations doesn't put children at risk. Instead, it does the opposite. It keeps children from risk. Dr. Brené Brown says, "If you put shame in a Petri dish, it only needs three things to grow exponentially: secrecy, silence, and judgment. If you put shame in a Petri dish and douse it with empathy it can't survive. Shame can't survive being spoken."[4]

While I've been writing this book, the Jeffrey Epstein story has been in the news. Epstein, a financier, was arrested and charged with sex trafficking of minors and conspiracy to commit sex trafficking of minors in July 2019.[5] In 2008, he had been charged with and pleaded guilty to procuring a minor for prostitution and felony solicitation of prostitution.[6] After a controversial "sweetheart deal," he only served thirteen months in jail before being placed on work release. Shortly after his arrest in 2019, he died by suicide in his jail cell. What's been interesting to me about the case is how the media has covered the story. Epstein has been deemed a pedophile; however, his abuse of young girls isn't connected to his sexuality as a straight man. Heterosexuality isn't conflated with the abuse. However, when there's a story about men who have abused young boys, there's an automatic association with the violator's sexuality. His sexuality is seen alongside the abuse.

For example, when speaking to numerous parents before I began working on this chapter, a mother I spoke to asked me to specifically discuss "child abuse and homosexuality." Although she said she assumes it's a myth, she continued, "People relate the two. It's a big topic from Michael Jackson to Catholic priests, etc."

This is a very sensitive subject and one that is not easy to address. Changing the narrative for future generations of LGBTQ youth means navigating difficult conversations about long-held misguided beliefs. To do so is courageous. It also requires the capacity to hold the discomfort for the sake of healing. When conducting research of any kind, it's important to pay attention to themes. Four out of the five conversations I have about misguided beliefs about LGBTQ people include some sort of sexual deviancy—which makes the conversation all the more necessary.

The individual healing work we do influences others in more ways than we can ever know. It may take time and will require courage, but if I can share anything from my own family's journey, it's that *beliefs can change, and open hearts heal.* No matter what the world does to try and make us think otherwise, where there was once fear, love's promise can overcome.

How we raise children today determines the playgrounds future generations will play on. The second half of this chapter touches on the importance of individual healing work. As parents, teachers, and caregivers, personal healing directly impacts the change we desire to see in the world.

A NEW WAY OF THINKING

Children can read your face sometimes more than they can hear your words.

—Rachael Clinton

We just marked the fiftieth anniversary of the Stonewall Riots, which are considered a catalyst for the LGBTQ movement in the United States and around the world. While fifty years is a long time, it's also not a very long time. In fact, it's fewer years than a lot of parents and grandparents I know have lived. Maybe even some of you.

An article *Time* published three days before the fiftieth anniversary, "Young Americans Are Increasingly 'Uncomfortable' with LGBTQ Community, GLAAD Study Shows," highlights how legal equality is not the same as social acceptance. Rich Ferraro, GLAAD's chief communications officer, told *Time*, "Acceptance cannot be legislated." GLAAD, an LGBTQ media advocacy organization, has taken a survey for the past five years called Accelerating Acceptance Index. The survey reports the average American's beliefs toward LGBTQ people and tracks how they shift.[7]

The *Time* article reported that GLAAD's fifth annual survey results showed a sharp drop in acceptance among Americans, specifically among millennials and Gen-Z. The survey included questions and scenarios for tracking the comfort level Americans have with the LGBTQ community, including scenarios of children learning about LGBTQ history in school, having an LGBTQ family member, having an LGBTQ doctor, and having a child in a class with an LGBTQ teacher. Each scenario saw a rise in "uncomfortable" responses.

The sudden drop in acceptance redefines whom GLAAD considers "allies" versus "detached supporters." Sarah Kate Ellis, president and CEO of GLAAD, said lack of education on the LGBTQ spectrum has been a contributing factor to the younger generations becoming increasingly more uncomfortable. She concluded, "Closing the gap to full acceptance of LGBTQ people will not come from legislation on judicial decisions alone, but from creating a culture where LGBTQ people are embraced and respected." The most significant place for this to begin is within our own belief systems at home, in classrooms, and on playgrounds. We can't move forward with *what* to accept without first exploring *why* we have an aversion to accepting something in the first place.

The political climate in the United States and across the globe is swinging toward more conservatism. I heard an interview on NPR a few weeks ago about how the younger generations in Japan are becoming more conservative than their parents. There are many speculations about the rise in conservatism among millennials and Gen-Zs. In an article, "Generation Z and the Rise of Conservatism," author Laura Reiff refers to it as "counterculture dynamic in action"—a sort of cultural pendulum swinging back.[8]

Reiff says, "Sure, if you're ten years old, you don't really know what's going on. But you can intuit a tenseness and a fear. If you're ten, you can still pick up on the notion of adult fear and that leaves a fairly penetrating, indelible mark." As it pertains to gender and sexual minorities, the "mark" is "messages from the playground" about people who are LGBTQ. Empowering youth of the next generation begins by injecting a new way of thinking into our consciousness of today.

NEW CONSCIOUSNESS = NEW PLAYGROUNDS

In every community, there is work to be done. In every nation, there are wounds to heal. In every heart, there is the power to do it.

—Marianne Williamson

Throughout this book, we've been using tools to recognize and uncover the deeper subconscious beliefs we may have about people who are LG-BTQ. In the next chapter, you're going to learn even more tools to help integrate what you've learned in this final section, "Change." It's a way to clean up our room, or rather, our consciousness. We've also been able to name some of the most pervasive and shame-based misguided beliefs about people who are LGBTQ. So what do we do with the information? How can we encourage our friends, families, and communities to become better allies?

For more than fifteen years, I've been fighting to change people's minds about the LGBTQ community. I've had countless arguments with family members and strangers and with people I love and people I don't know. I've cried and I've yelled and I've hit my head against the wall. That is to say, I've learned that the deeper we go within ourselves, the bigger the potential to heal communities, cultures, and families. When we enter pain and heal the wounds from our past, we're better prepared to guide others through uncharted territory.

One of the biggest realizations I've had writing this book is that I couldn't have arrived any sooner. I didn't have the consciousness to write, or even share, any of these lessons. It wasn't until I acknowledged, and committed, to healing my own messages from the playground that I could invite others to uncover and heal theirs.

It Takes a Village

We can be queerphobic, or have misguided beliefs about people who are LGBTQ, and still love a family member who is gay, lesbian, bisexual, transgender, or queer. Becoming an ally or celebrating an LG-BTQ loved one can be a journey with nuanced paths. Our hearts and minds have the capacity to experience a variety of emotions, including love *and* bias. We can't see what we aren't willing to face, though.

I've met many parents with LGBTQ children who resist acknowledging their own LGBTQ bias. They think that if they do, it means they're a bad parent. That's not the purpose of my message or what I hope to accomplish with this book. As I mentioned in chapter 1, it's important for us to hold in our hearts two truths: we've made tremendous progress, and there's still work to do. Acknowledging our own queerphobia is the very answer to healing it.

Just like coming out is a process for people who are LGBTQ and is continual throughout their lifetime, so is the journey for parents. As I shared in chapter 5, after I came out, my family tolerated my identity. I didn't come out of the closet to my family's immediately celebrating my sexuality. It happened in phases. There was tolerance, acceptance, embracing, appreciation, and now, celebration. Although each person in my family arrived at a specific phase on their own, it was only from an increased awareness that they were willing to change their beliefs.

Recently, while in a spin class, the instructor told us there'd be few times during class where we'd feel like we were going to die. It's indoor hot room spinning and one of the hardest forms of exercise I've done. She told us that although we'll feel like we're going to die, we probably won't. She also told us it's during the most difficult times in class when we're developing the most strength. Each of the challenging parts in our ride will help us become stronger and the process will prepare us for the next.

What she said made me think about life—how most of our day-to-day challenges don't necessarily kill us, but make us stronger. In spinning, if I don't experience a challenge and work through it, I don't get a good workout. I don't sweat as much, and my body doesn't reap the rewards of good exercise. When I embrace the challenging times and look at the process as a means of transformation, they become the most important part of the entire ride. Similarly, the process through which we learn how to celebrate LGBTQ youth is where the gifts of transformation lie.

After I spoke at a recent LGBTQ educational event, a parent in the audience raised their hand and asked, "What does LGBTQ equality look like for you?" I told her, "LGBTQ equality is when we not only have the same rights, but we're seen as deserving and worthy of the same rights. It's when we can celebrate the lives of LGBTQ youth." I also told her it's not something we can do on our own. It takes a village to raise a child. It also takes a village to raise allies and create a world in which all children are equal. A village of parents who say, "Queerphobia, racism, xenophobia, anti-Semitism? Not with my kid and not on my watch."

The last section of this chapter is for any parent who has struggled to support their LGBTQ loved one because of religious beliefs. The purpose is not to condemn religion or people of faith. It's to inspire conversations and help those with a religious background to consider another way—embracing religion or spirituality *and* celebrating LGBTQ youth. What I know from my own life and from the work I do with young people is that religious guilt and shame can cause tremendous harm. The number-one recommendation I make for anyone who has questions concerning non-affirming LGBTQ religious doctrine, or who carries religious trauma, is to work on themselves and consider the five steps that follow.

FIVE STEPS TO CELEBRATING LGBTQ YOUTH

> What cannot be spoken to the mother cannot be told to the self.
>
> —John Bowlby

When I asked my mom, a woman of faith with a gay son, what the most important step was that she took along her journey, she told me there were a few. She also told me it was a process she committed to and that it didn't happen overnight. She had to get to know God in a new way and relearn how she engaged with religion and her spiritual beliefs.

Whether religious or not, we can improve our relationships with LGBTQ youth. As an ally, parent, teacher, caregiver, or guncle, by committing to the following five steps, we can help heal queerphobia. We can also better support the lives of all children. The journey of any personal development or spiritual path must first begin within.

1. **Love yourself.** I once had a high school student ask me in class, "How do we love ourselves?" I told her, "It begins with letting go of who we think we should be and embracing who we are." When I was her age, I had never heard the concept of self-love. But just like physical exercise, unless we actively do the work, we won't see the results. By consciously committing to loving ourselves, we begin the first step to improving the world. When we love ourselves and work on correcting our own lives, we become more accepting of others. The moment I became willing to look at the parts of myself I didn't want people to see and accept that even those areas were worthy and deserving of love, my life began to improve. I no longer projected my fear and judgment onto the outside world. We can only learn to love ourselves if we are willing to learn who we are. Self-love is not only a gift for ourselves; it's also a gift for future generations.

2. **Cultivate a *new* spiritual connection.** Life is beautiful, and it's also very big. There is so much beyond our understanding and control. A spiritual connection of our own understanding is something we can lean on to navigate life's most difficult moments. It requires nothing from us, but it gives us everything.

3. **Be willing to change your thinking and challenge your beliefs.** Most of our beliefs aren't our own. There are collective societal messages we absorb as children from the outside world—consciously or subconsciously (i.e., messages from the playground). Challenging our beliefs gives us the keys to unlock a life that's true for us. It releases us from generational suffering and helps us create a new world full of hope and healing.

4. **Take full responsibility for your life and choices.** This is the step I find most confronting. Taking full responsibility for our lives helps us reclaim our power. If I'm stuck in resentment from something I believe, I'll take the time to write down my current version of the story. There's usually blame in this version, so I'll set it aside and review what I wrote the next day. Then, I'll ask myself, if I retold this story as if it were happening to support me and my growth, what would I say? I give myself permission to rewrite my story from a new perspective.

5. **Forgive yourself and others.** A young girl I once taught in Juvenile Hall asked me if it was okay if she forgave herself for having a miscarriage. It was as if she became lighter just by asking the question. It reminded me that one of the biggest obstacles to building new playgrounds can be self-forgiveness. I told her forgiveness is courageous and an act of self-love. As parents, teachers, and caregivers, self-forgiveness is especially important. Each of us is doing the best we can with the knowledge and information we have *in this moment*. By incorporating self-forgiveness in our lives, we let ourselves off the perfection hook. We also release ourselves from outcomes beyond our understanding and control.

Being a parent, caregiver, or teacher requires sharing. The more at peace we are with ourselves and our lives, the more we can share our wisdom and not our suffering. Maybe you've used one or more of these steps before, or maybe they're new. Regardless, when we bring awareness to the change we are willing to make, we become conscious creators. Each of these steps has been instrumental to my mom's and my healing. They also continue to be an essential part of our relationship today.

When we commit to these five steps, we become better listeners, our energy has more impact when we're around others, and we're only interested in speaking and hearing the truth. Most importantly of all, we make better role models for the youngsters in our families, and we can see them more clearly.

A MOTHER'S FAITH

The stone that the builder refused shall be the head cornerstone.

—Bob Marley

Earlier this week, I emailed my mom to ask her a few questions about her journey. I wanted to learn about the process she went through to reestablish a relationship with God and religion. I also asked her what advice she would give to another parent with a religious background whose child just came out. Even though I came out to her fifteen years ago, I hadn't ever asked about her process. As I typed my questions, I realized how layered it actually was. I knew she was going to have to dig deep and revisit a painful part of our journey.

A few days later, on my way to my car after speaking to a religious group about *Raising LGBTQ Allies*, I received her reply. Once inside the car, I began to read her email. It was honest and heartfelt and made me cry. It was the first time I really saw the distance my mom traveled to reestablish her relationship with God and reclaim faith on her own terms. I saw courage, strength, redemption, and mostly, I felt loved.

Rather than tell you what she said and offer the advice she gave, I've included her response. Her words aren't just for me, they're for anyone who has been hurt by anti-LGBTQ theology.

★ ★ ★

Hi Honey,

First of all, I came to the realization that God does not make mistakes. As a woman of deep faith, I had to take a really long and honest look at my hardcore stance on my religious beliefs and homosexuality. I had to also reconcile my beliefs on having a gay son.

It was truly a huge, life-changing understanding that took place in my heart and then my mind. I knew I would lose many of my Christian friends. But most importantly, I knew God doesn't make mistakes. How could I possibly play God? How could I hate or reject a gift from God, such as my beautiful son? God is Love. He says you will know my people by their love for one another, without judgement.

A lot of my friends in the church rejected, not only my stance, but me for taking a stance. I came to the realization that as deep as my love was for you, God created you, and must love you even more. I also knew, within my heart of hearts, how very hard your coming out was, especially to me. I knew this is how God created you. Period. When you told me at 24 when you were in town visiting from Mexico, I cried. I had to look within my heart, soul, and mind. The shift wasn't instant. I was frightened at first and scared of the unknown. By reexamining my religion, I no longer judged you but loved you even more for all the years I was blinded by the truth.

The guilt was overwhelming. Then came understanding, acceptance, and eventual appreciation of what I've learned along the way. If I could share my experience with another person of faith and offer them any advice, I would say:

1. It might be challenging at first. I'm not going to say I wasn't questioned, rejected, and hurt by some of my closest friends. I questioned my own beliefs. I went to counseling, which gave me a better understanding of myself.
2. God doesn't punish us by giving us children we think are a mistake. I had even thought God was punishing me at first, through my children for my past. I came to realize that's stinking thinking and just bad theology.
3. God's Love is unconditional and all-encompassing.
4. Research the interpretations of scripture. Through revisiting scriptural text on same-sex relationships and being gay, I actually learned more about theology and it brought me closer to God. I realized how easy it is to misinterpret scripture and so learn to be a critical thinker, even when it comes to religion. And especially when it comes to using God as a means of persecuting another human being.
5. Look at your child and listen to them with an open heart and mind.
6. And lastly, but most importantly, look into your own belief system and dig deep. Shame is a heavy burden no mother would want their child to bear.

★ ★ ★

Despite my mom's and my continued personal work, homophobia can sometimes still rear its ugly head, which is one of the driving forces behind *Raising LGBTQ Allies*. The purpose of this book is to help families see the nuanced forms of queerphobia and to lovingly address them should they unexpectedly arise.

As we conclude this chapter, I invite you to consider a principle I base my life on today: the greater the challenge, the greater the blessing. Often, it's during the most challenging times in our lives that we learn how to be the strongest. This doesn't discount the pain we experience during a difficult challenge. Challenges can be overwhelming, especially when it comes to some families' coming-out journeys. What this does do is give us an expanded view from which to see a challenge and embrace the fullness of life. When we look at our lives linearly from now until the end, we see challenges as inconvenient or bad. If we imagined standing at the end of our lives and looking backward, we'd be more open to receive the gift each challenge can give.

When I look back on my own life, it's been the most painful experiences that have blessed me the most. The coming-out journey I've traveled with my mom continues to bring us closer. It's also helped give me empathy and feel a deeper sense of connection to the human experience. What's more, to witness my mom's beliefs shift from "I can hate the sin but love the sinner" to her desire for grandchildren has helped me to not only believe in the power of redemption but to know it in my soul.

We don't have to believe in gravity for its effects to work. If we walk off a bridge, we will fall. Religious or not, challenging long-held misguided beliefs and reestablishing a relationship with a higher power of our own understanding will help build new playgrounds. Every parent is meant to bless their child. Building new playgrounds, together and connected versus divided and separate, creates new worlds.

10

NEW TOYS

Instructional and Interactive Exercises

Kids are making up their mind, we've got to change ours.
It's a lot easier to make up your mind than it is to change
it.

—Bob Proctor

A *little boy was watching his mother prepare a fish for dinner. His mother*
cut the head and tail off the fish and then placed it into a baking pan. The
little boy asked his mother why she cut the head and tail off the fish. His mother
thought for a while and then said, "I've always done it that way—that's how
babicka (Czech for grandma) did it."

Not satisfied with the answer, the little boy went to visit his grandma to
find out why she cut the head and tail off the fish before baking it.

Grandma thought for a while and replied, "I don't know. My mother
always did it that way."

So the little boy and the grandma went to visit Great-grandma to ask if
she knew the answer.

Great-grandma thought for a while and said, "Because my baking pan was
too small to fit in the whole fish."[1] "The Fish Baking Story," courtesy of
NRI RISE Plus.

This story is from a training program called NRI RISE Plus (Non-
Racially-Identified Rewriting Inner Scripts), by Kip Castner and the
Maryland Department of Health & Mental Hygiene. The group primar-
ily works with gay men around coming-out challenges. They changed
the child's gender from the original story to reflect the population they
served and also to disrupt gender stereotypes. It's a perfect demonstration
of what we've been learning about in *Raising LGBT Allies*. Often, when
it comes to familial beliefs, we don't know where they come from. Only

until we begin to consciously learn about our beliefs do we understand why we have them.

Our entire life is a journey of self-discovery. There's a point at which we become consciously aware of walking along the personal or spiritual development path. For me, it was in 2011. I began reading tons of personal and spiritual development books, and most of them encouraged me to ask questions about my parents' or caregivers' pasts. When we start to ask questions about our family's history, it gives us a glimpse into their worldview. We also learn more about ourselves through our family's traditions.

There isn't a person on the planet who hasn't taken issue with something their parents did when they were a child. It's part of human experience. Another aspect of human experience is to get to a place where we live life on our own terms. Part of living life on our own terms is reconciling our past and recognizing that each of us is doing the best we can with the knowledge and information we have.

When we inquire into the lives of our parents, or the past of people who've influenced our lives growing up, we gain a better understanding of why we were raised a certain way. It also helps us choose which traditions to pass on to the next generation. Just recently, I had a conversation with a friend about one of the classes I taught over the summer at a Los Angeles County residential program. Two of my students were parents—a sixteen-year-old boy with a two-year-old child and a sixteen-year-old girl with a three-year-old. My friend couldn't believe how young the parents were, just kids themselves, really. We began to talk about the importance of having honest and age-appropriate conversations with youth.

I shared with her how a lot of youth I work with aren't informed or educated about relationships, including sex, sexuality, and gender. I also shared that most LGBTQ youth learn about sex through gay porn because of the lack of education. By the time a child is twelve, they will have already seen or have been shown pornography. She expressed shock, but when I explained to her that most youth in general aren't having educated conversations with parents, caregivers, or teachers, the internet is the only place for LGBTQ youth to go.

In a funny and powerful talk at the Maker's 2019 women's conference, actress and activist Jameela Jamil addressed the importance of having open and authentic conversations about sex. Jamil says, "I believe that learning sex from porn is like learning how to drive from watching, *The Fast and the Furious*. A f★★★ing terrible idea." When parents, teachers, and caregivers can have open and age-appropriate conversations with children about sex, sexuality, and gender, and include same-sex relationships and other LGBTQ experiences, we prevent inaccurate information from being introduced to a young person. We also stop pushing queer people's sexuality into the shadows, which feeds stigmas, shame, and trauma.

This isn't about forcing any child out of the closet before they're ready; this is about creating a world where closets don't exist. And one of the ways we do that is by creating a safe place for children to learn about who they are, without shame and trauma.

A mom I know recently told me that when she brought up gender and sexuality with her fourteen-year-old son, he said, "Mom, you're weird." She asked me what she should do. I told her it's a normal response for a lot of teenagers, but it doesn't mean we stop talking about it. The more we're able to have healthy conversations with our children, the more we affirm their identity, whatever it may be. We also help normalize all genders and sexualities, especially gender and sexual minorities.

A few questions you can use to help include the experiences of all youth are:

1. What am I doing to prepare my children (or nieces, nephews, students, etc.) for the new world in which they'll live?
2. What proactive action am I taking to inject an expanded awareness into my children's lives?
3. How am I intentionally, mindfully, and actively raising allies?
4. How am I accounting for the gender and sexual diversity of all youth?
5. Is there a way I can take proactive steps to help youth access age-appropriate information?
6. If I don't know how to have conversations about gender and sexuality, is there a person or an organization I feel comfortable learning from?

A parent I know reached out to me a few weeks ago asking for help. Two of their adolescent kids just came out as LGBTQ, one gay and the other bisexual. They wanted to know what they could do to continue the conversation with their children and to "affirm what they feel and know in their hearts." I let them know that the most important things for any parent or caregiver to do to support a child who comes out are to affirm them, let them know they can talk to you, and to believe them. I also reminded them that their kids are the same today as they were last week. I always recommend that parents be prepared, affirming, and aware, but not hyperaware. It can sometimes send a conflicting message if we start to see/treat our LGBTQ children differently once they come out.

In the following sections, I'm going to share sample questions, suggestions, and exercises for parents, teachers, and caregivers to help empower all youth. I've also included tips on LGBTQ-inclusive actions you can easily and effectively take. Ultimately, I want this chapter to be a practical resource you can use for ongoing support—beginning with a life-changing concept called the Rule of Expectations.

RULE OF EXPECTATIONS

What makes us sick are those things we cannot see through, society's constraints that we have absorbed through our parents' eyes.

—Alice Miller

One week while teaching a class on forgiveness, I asked a group of boys what they wanted to let go of. One of the boys replied, "self-loathing." He was a young, handsome, and seemingly confident eighteen-year-old whose pain in his reply was palpable. Another boy said he wanted to let go of the issues he had with his body and feeling fat. There wasn't an ounce of fat on his body, but it wasn't what I saw, it was how he felt inside.

During my time teaching social-emotional learning at Juvenile Hall, I came to realize two things: the first was clear from the beginning—kids don't just wind up in juvie. They come from experiences, families, places, or events that contribute to choices that reflect a low self-concept or lack of self-worth.

After teaching SEL to youth of all ages throughout Los Angeles County for the past six years, I've come to believe the most valuable tool we can teach a young person is to love themselves. Some of the most excruciating experiences in my life came as a result of low self-esteem and lack of self-worth. The biggest gift I ever gave myself was to consciously begin loving myself, from the inside out. Applying principles in this book, and specifically this chapter, to my own life is what helped turn it around and inspire me to want to help others.

Another question we asked the boys that day was what they wanted to create. They all wrote the same answer: a better life. The second thing I've learned during my time teaching is that no matter who we are or where we come from, we all inherently want and value the same thing: a life that reflects the good we feel about ourselves.

I ended class by letting the youth know that how they feel about themselves right now may not change overnight, but with time and some willingness, it can change. The power of redemption is as real as it is available for us all.

According to the Rule of Expectations, the actions we take and decisions we make can be influenced by expectations in relationships. We tend to play out in our lives what others expect of us. As someone who has worked with youth from all backgrounds, including LGBTQ homeless and incarcerated youth, I've come to learn that my perceptions influence behavior. One of the most powerful ways to positively impact a young person's learning is to affirm who they are while speaking to the potential of who we know they can be. This goes beyond individuals, and touches not just our lives but the wider communities of which we're a part. We impact those around us based on what we believe and expect through our language, our tone of voice, our faces, our thoughts, our energy, and our awareness.

I once worked with a man who had served time in prison for killing someone. When word got out that he had been convicted of homicide, people began to treat him differently. My coworkers avoided interacting with him, and not a day went by when I didn't hear a negative comment about him. I began to notice his behavior change—he became more aggressive and defensive while at work. It was almost as if the gossip and judgment contributed to how he acted.

One time, I had an altercation with him, and so we were both called to the manager's office to discuss what had occurred. I remember being in the office and listening to him tell his side of the story. He barely made eye contact with me or my manager and during his explanation of what had happened, he commented, "Chris is scared of me." I looked directly at him and said in a calm and empathetic way, "Andrew, I am not scared of you at all." He looked up at me, as if surprised, and said, "Really? You aren't?" I smiled and said, "No."

The next day while walking into work, I heard someone yell out my name. It was Andrew, standing across the street waving at me. Never before had Andrew ever greeted me, let alone yelled my name from across the street. It was clear from his facial expression that he saw me in a different light. I wasn't different—I had not changed. He was simply responding to the impact of feeling affirmed and being seen, which is something we have the ability to do for LGBTQ youth when we acknowledge gender and sexuality minorities in our classrooms, families, churches, conversations, and communities.

We are responsible for our actions; however, when we explore our beliefs and create new expectations, we have the ability to change other people's behavior. When it comes to things like age, race, sexuality, gender, or socioeconomic status, according to the Rule of Expectations, my beliefs have an effect on you and how you show up in the world.

What we believe about a person matters. The messages from the playground we have about youth who are LGBTQ impact how they feel about themselves. As parents, teachers, and caregivers, we can proactively strengthen a young person's self-esteem by affirming their identity. When we don't acknowledge LGBTQ youth or talk about gender and sexuality with children at a young age, we miss an opportunity to help them connect to their authentic selves.

In the following section, you'll find fun and creative exercises to use on yourself and with the children in your lives. Regardless of whether you think you have or know LGBTQ youth, these exercises will help raise allies and create a world in which all children can hold hands together on the playground.

BACK TO SCHOOL: NEW TOYS FOR THE NEW YEAR

If you have supportive family and friends combined with
a strong will; there is no limit to what you can achieve.

—S. J. Hailey

The following are what I call "backpack" exercises, questions, and suggestions. Each one is a simple, yet effective, tool we can share with
youth and take with us wherever we go:

1) Tattoo and Values Exercise

I've had quite a few conversations about values lately. I even attended a workshop, Fundamentals of Nonviolent Communication, and
one of the things I learned is that our values are at the root of all human
behavior.

Some of our values change over time, but each of us possesses a set
of core values that influence the choices we make. When we're consciously connected to them, we feel good about our choices. I know in
my own life, whenever I experience discomfort, guilt, or some sort of
inner conflict, it's usually because I'm out of touch with my core values.

A fun way to creatively connect to your values and introduce this
concept to young people is to google "core values." You'll find countless words to choose from. The difficult part is to identify which resonate
with you most. The fun part is to pick seven to ten words you'd be
willing to have tattooed on your body. Not because of what you want
someone else to see, but because these are qualities you'd be willing to
permanently possess. From there, it's easier to narrow down your core
values.

Once you have your set, see where in your life you're holding true
to what you value most and where you can improve. For instance, if you
value peace, love, and kindness, how are you teaching those qualities to
the children in your life? For youth, this exercise is powerful in a mul-
titude of ways: it introduces them to values, helps establish a conscious
connection to them, and offers a sort of North Star they can use with
decision-making. A young person who not only values respect but is
consciously connected to it isn't going to bully. An adult who not only

values authenticity but is consciously connected to it is going to have open and honest conversations.

2) New Word Exercise

This exercise was inspired by Caroline Myss (see "The Power of Words" section in chapter 2). It's pretty simple and is an especially powerful concept for young people. All you need to do is get a jar and create the label "Fear and Judgment." Then, ask a young person to answer the following questions on a piece of paper: "What do you judge, fear, and dislike?" and "What groups or people are judged at your school, and what words are they called?" What they write is private and not to be shared. The point is for them to be honest and feel safe enough to include the things in the world they fear, dislike, or judge about other people. Once they write down a few words, fold up the papers, and throw them into the jar. For the next twenty-four hours, the jar is going to hold their fear, dislike, and judgment. Then, before you dispose of the papers, ask:

1. What would happen in your life if those were no longer people, places, or things you feared, judged, or disliked?
2. What would the world look like?
3. What will your day look like without this fear, dislike, or judgment?
4. How does it feel in your body to give up fear, dislike, and judgment?
5. How does the day feel?
6. Is the feeling connected to any of your core values?
7. What would it be like to forgive fear and judgment?

For adults, consider asking these additional questions: "Without this fear, dislike, and judgment, what world am I helping to create? What can I avoid teaching? What am I passing along?" Then, make a list of the beliefs and values you'd like to pass down instead.

Another aspect of this exercise is to have youth write down what negative things they've heard on the playground about people who are

LGBTQ. After they've written a word or sentence, have them cross it out and write *fear*. Then toss the paper into the jar. This opens up a dialogue around fear and how most of the hurtful comments they hear about people who are LGBTQ come from fear.

3) Gender and Sexuality Belief Dump

One of my favorite exercises to do is called "The Belief Dump." Write a word at the top of a piece of paper. For example, "gay" or "transgender." Then, set a timer for two minutes and without stopping, write all the things you think, believe, and have heard about *gay* or *transgender*. Circle anything negative and see if there are areas in your life that reflect the negative belief.

You can also use this exercise with youth to identify where they've been influenced by gender policing. It can be done in a conversation or as a written exercise. Simply ask the following questions:

1. What are boy activities? What are girl activities?
2. What can boys wear? What can girls wear?
3. What are boy colors? What are girl colors?

The beauty of the Belief Dump exercise is it creates a healthy discussion around gender roles. We unknowingly contribute to gender policing by the roles our family members have at home. Important questions to ask yourself are "What activities do my children see me do at home?" and "What roles do the men in my family have and what roles to the women have?" This isn't to condemn a parent's role; it's to help families become more aware of gender policing. I recently had a conversation with a female friend. She said, "I had to go over to my sister's house to help clean her bathrooms before her guests arrived. She's been working overtime and her bathrooms looked terrible." I asked her, "Why can't your brother-in-law clean?" She paused for a second and said, "Well, he works." I replied, "And so does your sister, right?" We began to speak about gender roles and how easy it is to keep them alive, even in the most subtle ways.

4) See and Speak to the Light Within

This exercise is simple and goes along with the Rule of Expectations. It's a sort of namaste we can carry off the yoga mat and into our children's lives. All you need to do is consciously speak to and see the light within youth. Whenever I teach, part of my lesson planning includes mentally telling my class, "The light within me recognizes the light within you." It's a practice we can use with children of all backgrounds and especially for youth who are LGBTQ. Seeing and speaking to the light within helps affirm their identity from the inside out. It also helps youth subconsciously feel safe.

5) Messages from the Playground Guide:
Seven Simple and Effective Steps

In 2017, after I gave my TEDx Talk, I created a Messages from the Playground guide for parents to use with the children in their lives. To help you with this next exercise, you can visit my website, www.aroadtriptolove.com, to download and print a free guide, or you can simply draw the outline of a page-sized person on an 8½ by 11 sheet of paper.

In order to find a solution, we have to first identify the problem. Uncovering hurtful messages children have heard about themselves will help to identify a problem before it becomes something we need to treat. Once you've drawn an outline or downloaded a guide, use these seven simple steps to uncover a misguided message from the playground:

1. *Create a safe space to uncover messages.* An example is my sister sitting down with her kids and talking to them about words they've been called and messages they've heard rather than my phoning my nephew unexpectedly while he was on his way to baseball practice.
2. *Ask what messages have been heard or received—have youth write specific words in the outline.* It's important to ask the person completing the guide whether they want to write the words they've heard inside or outside the outline. Where the word is placed can indicate how strongly they've internalized its message. If a word is written inside the outline, they might identify with it more strongly than if they wrote it outside.

3. *Talk about each message—notice where it was written, inside or outside the outline, and any corresponding feeling in the body.* Shame and trauma are carried in the body, and helping a child to develop full-body awareness can help heal shame and trauma on a cellular level. We can all relate to having heard a word that makes us cringe. Our body might react by a feeling in the pit of our stomach or having shortness of breath. Bringing full-body awareness to words and messages can help prevent youth from re-experiencing shame or trauma as they get older.

4. *Consider and talk about how a negative message impacts life and self-esteem.* If someone walked up to me today and called me a big pink elephant, it wouldn't bother me because I have zero identification with being a big pink elephant. Nothing about me, consciously or subconsciously, identifies with being a big pink elephant. The reason we're triggered when someone calls us something is that part of us believes it's true. Not only is it important to learn what messages a child hears, but also knowing whether or not they believe them can prevent low self-esteem.

5. *Create a plan to identify how a message shows up once it's in conscious awareness.* Once something is in our conscious awareness, we cannot become unaware. Awareness precedes change, and this step helps empower parents, teachers, and young people. Not only does awareness precede change, but also it's the very answer to change. My sister knowing the words her daughter had been called made her more aware of certain behaviors. She was attuned to her daughter's needs and knew what to look out for when it came to specific areas of her life.

6. *Forgive, and release the old message.* This step isn't easy, so I recommend asking, "Are you *willing* to replace the old message with something more empowering?" I also make sure to let young people know that forgiveness isn't saying bad behavior is okay. Forgiveness is for themselves. It's to set themselves free to be who they *truly* are.

7. *Develop affirming words, messages, and actions to replace old messages.* It's not enough to say something isn't true. If we want to proactively grow a new garden, not only do we have to pick out the old weeds but we also have to plant new seeds.

Another empowering concept we can share with a young person is the notion their thoughts are creative. Introducing young people to the power of their mind is important for all youth, especially marginalized youth. If there's anything I've learned from working with at-risk youth is self-aware, happy, confident, and supported young people rarely bully and are more inclined to speak up for themselves. Here are some of my favorite empowerment statements and new beliefs to share with youth:

6) Affirming Statements and New Beliefs

- You are loved because of who you are.
- I'm proud of you.
- I'm here for you.
- I see you, I hear you, and who you are matters.
- I love you just the way you are.
- You are lovable because you exist.
- I love you.
- You are worthy of becoming anything you want.
- I support you.
- It's okay for you to express yourself.
- You are special and so are your friends.
- It's okay for boys to like boys.
- It's okay for girls to like girls.
- It's okay for boys to play with _____.
- It's okay for girls to play with _____.
- There are no boy toys or girl toys; there are only kid toys.

7) Empowerment Statements for Youth

- I am loved.
- I am worthy.
- I am confident.
- I am kind.
- I am compassionate.
- I am safe.
- I am supported.
- It's okay for me to express myself.

- Who I am matters.
- I am lovable because I exist.
- My opinion matters.
- It's okay for me to feel the way I do.
- It's okay for me to like what I like.
- I trust myself.
- Being me is all I need to be.
- I love myself for who I am.
- I love myself.
- I attract supportive and loving people into my life.
- I am strong.
- I deserve to live the life of my dreams.
- I am deserving.
- I am worthy.
- I can do anything I put my heart and mind to.
- It's safe to follow my heart.
- I listen to my heart.

An affirmation, or empowerment statement, is something positive and, in the present tense, what we want to create more of in our lives. Using these statements with LGBTQ youth doesn't just affirm their identity, it also helps with their emotional development. In his book *What Happy People Know*, Dr. Dan Baker wrote about a study done with children. He showed how the quality of language can either help or hurt a young person. Dr. Baker says, "The quality of words made a profound impact upon emotional development. The kids who were exposed to the most constructive language excelled at bonding, good behavior, and self-esteem. The other kids didn't. . . . The biggest difference in their lives was simply the language they were reared with."[2] Words and language matter for all youth. For LGBTQ youth raised in a heteronormative world, it's especially valuable to hear affirming language that celebrates their identity.

8) Questions for Parents, Teachers, and Mentors to Ask Youth

1. Have you ever wanted to play with a certain toy, but didn't feel like it was okay because of what people would think?

2. Have you ever wanted to wear something, but didn't feel like it was okay because of what people would say or think?
3. What do you think about the way boys/girls are supposed to act?
4. Do you think it's possible for someone to be born in a body that doesn't match who they are on the inside?
5. Have you ever seen bullying at your school? What were some words used? Why were kids picked on?
6. Have you ever been called something by someone that made you feel sad, angry, or upset?
7. Have you ever felt like you didn't belong?

9) Out with the Old, in with the New—a Few Tips and Suggestions

1. Replace, "Hey guys" with "Hey friends" or a gender-neutral phrase. Air Canada recently announced that it was going to drop "ladies and gentlemen" from its announcements and greetings in an effort to be more inclusive for people who identify as gender X.[3] Using "friends" instead of saying "guys" is something I try to say when speaking with youth. Even with family and friends, I try to refer to everyone in a gender-neutral way. It's a small way we can begin to help youth see beyond the dominant masculine worldview and be more inclusive. Every day that there's a class outside, I can hear the preschool teachers directly next-door to my house using "friends" to refer to their scholars. Just like anything—the more we practice, the easier it becomes.
2. "Itsa . . . ." Blank page versus gender reveal parties. I once had a work meeting with a pregnant woman. She was due to give birth any day and when she began to speak about her baby, she complained that it was a boy. As she sat there rubbing her belly, she remarked on how much she wished it were a girl. I thought about the child inside and how horrible it must be to feel its parent's disappointment. Our thoughts and feelings are just as important as the food we eat. I understand getting excited over the gender of a child, especially if a parent has always wanted

a little girl or boy. However, complaining about the child's gender and preferring it to be different is harmful. Rather than throwing gender reveal parties, begin with a blank page. Embrace the new world and welcome whatever gender your child tells you they are. Beginning with a blank page and celebrating the gender your child tells you they are helps prevent gender oppression and gender policing. We also create space for children to be themselves fully.

3. Have conversations. A parent recently asked me for ways to bring up gender and sexuality with children by age group. She also asked me how to start the conversation around being LGBTQ. The first thing I told her to consider was that being LGBTQ is normal and natural. One of the main takeaways I hope you get from this book is that the only real thing for children to have to understand is that there are many ways of being human. If you're someone who needs a little more support or has fear of what to say, a great tool for any parent or caregiver to use is books.

10) LGBTQ-Affirming Books

Because I live out of state, gifting books has been a fun and creative way to keep the conversation around gender and sexuality alive. Helping my family unwrap a more inclusive world is a gift idea for not only parents but also for teachers, guncles, and allies. Below is a list of a few of my favorite LGBTQ-affirming children's books, as well as some recommendations from "Healthy Gender Development and Young Children: A Guide for Early Childhood Programs and Professionals."[4]

BOOKS FOR AGES TWO AND UP

1. *And Tango Makes Three*, by Justin Richardson and Peter Parnell—the heartwarming true story of two penguins who create a family that reflects the new world in which we live (2–5 years old).[5]

2. *Of Course They Do! Boys and Girls Can Do Anything*, by Marie-Sabine Roger and Anne Sol—a book that debunks commonly held gender myths in a cheerful, no-nonsense fashion (2–5 years old).[6]

BOOKS FOR AGES THREE AND UP

1. *The Story of Ferdinand*, by Munro Leaf—all the other bulls run, jump, and butt their heads together in fights. Ferdinand, on the other hand, would rather sit and smell the flowers (3–5 years old).[7]
2. *Who Has What? All About Girls' Bodies and Boys' Bodies*, by Robie H. Harris—this is a helpful book for parents or families when their children start to ask questions about their bodies (3–7 years old).[8]

BOOKS FOR AGES FOUR AND UP

1. *I Am Jazz*, by Jessica Herthel and Jazz Jennings—the story of a transgender child based on the real-life experience of Jazz Jennings, who has become a spokesperson for trans kids everywhere (4–8 years old).[9]
2. *Jacob's New Dress*, by Sarah and Ian Hoffman—this heartwarming story speaks to the unique challenges faced by boys who don't identify with traditional gender roles (4–8 years old).[10]
3. *Not Every Princess*, by Jeffrey and Lisa Bone—a book that helps readers gently question the rigid construction of gender roles, while challenging societal expectations in an inspirational way (4–8 years old).[11]
4. *Red: A Crayon's Story*, by Michael Hall—a story about being true to your inner self and following your own path despite obstacles that may come your way (4–8 years old).[12]
5. *Love Makes a Family*, by Sophie Beer—this fun, inclusive board book celebrates the one thing that makes every family a family . . . and that's LOVE (preschool and up).[13]

11) LGBTQ Organizations:

There are many wonderful LGBTQ organizations doing good work in the world to advocate for LGBTQ youth. As far as resources, a few national groups I recommend for parents, teachers, and allies are:

1. The Trevor Project—the leading national organization providing crisis intervention and suicide prevention services to LGBTQ young people under twenty-five. Youth can text "START" to 678678 or call the TrevorLifeline at 1-866-488-7386 24/7 (www.thetrevorproject.org).
2. Gender Spectrum—Gender Spectrum's mission is to create a gender-inclusive world for all children and youth (www.genderspectrum.org).
3. Family Acceptance Project—a research, intervention, education, and policy initiative that works to prevent health and mental health risks for LGBTQ children and youth in the context of their families, cultures, and faith communities (https://familyproject.sfsu.edu).
4. GLSEN—a national organization working to ensure that LGBTQ students are able to learn and grow in a school environment free from bullying and harassment (www.glsen.org).
5. PFLAG—the first and largest organization for LGBTQ people, their parents and families, and allies. They have chapters throughout the United States and are an excellent place for families to turn to for support. Especially for parents with kids who are LGBTQ, they have support groups where you can connect with other parents who have walked this same journey. You can find local chapters on their website (www.pflag.org).

Each of these organizations provides free online information on how to advocate and be an ally for LGBTQ youth. No matter where you find yourself along the phases of acceptance, these organizations can help.

INSTILLING EMPATHY

Teaching our children empathy is the number one thing
we can do as parents to make our kids' future a better
place.

—Dr. Steve Silvestro

While in college, I was involved with an organization called the Ability
Experience. Its mission was to raise money and awareness for people
with disabilities. One of my favorite activities we conducted to raise
awareness for people with disabilities was to host "empathy dinners." As
each guest arrived, they were assigned a physical disability. Some were
given a blindfold, while others had to tie their dominant had behind
their back. Before dinner, we shared a personal story of someone we
knew with a disability. We also paired each guest with an advocate who
would sit alongside them to provide support while they ate dinner.

Each time I was a part of an empathy dinner, I saw transformation.
It's one thing to hear someone tell you what it's like to be blind, but to
eat a three-course meal while blindfolded is an entirely different experience. Opening up someone's heart and instilling empathy is an unforgettable experience. After I graduated from college, two of my friends
involved with the Ability Experience had children born with disabilities.
I've often thought how the work they did with people with disabilities
while in college equipped them with not only experience but also the
empathy to be better parents.

I recently read an article published in *Yale News* and funded by the
National Institutes of Health that shows how early-career doctors had
less bias toward lesbian women and gay men depending on their direct
experience with LGBTQ people during medical school. The article also
reported that sexual minorities are less satisfied with their healthcare than
heterosexuals. Not all medical professionals or healthcare providers have
experience working with LGBTQ people. Just as people in classrooms,
families, or the workplace can, they can show bias. The article noted,
"Early exposure to people with different sexual orientations and more
vigilance against bias in medical schools could help improve doctor-
patient relationships."[14] One of the best ways to combat queerphobia is
by getting to know *people*.

My last suggestion is to contact one or more of the organizations I mentioned from above. PFLAG and GLSEN are run by chapter-based volunteers. Chances are, you have a chapter in your community. Invite them to provide a panel or speaker for your company, classroom, or church. For more than five years, I've spoken on PFLAG LA's Speakers Bureau, and it's where I've witnessed the most change. Gender Spectrum hosts online groups and trainings for both youth and adults, which I highly recommend for all things gender. In addition to crisis intervention and suicide prevention, the Trevor Project is an online support network for LGBTQ youth and allies. And the Family Acceptance Project does groundbreaking work to support LGBTQ youth and their families through everything from research to resources.

It's not enough to say we're an LGBTQ advocate or consider ourselves an ally because we have friends who are LGBTQ. In order to create change and prevent queerphobia and bullying, we have to take action. Applying what we've learned helps complete the process. One of the most effective forms of advocacy is empathy.

According to Carl Rogers, a well-known psychologist credited for the humanistic therapeutic approach, empathy is one of three requirements a person needs for growth. Rogers believed each person needs to experience congruence (being able to feel open, connected, and genuine in one's own life), respect (feeling accepted for who a person is), and empathy.[15] Cultivating a sense of empathy can be done in many ways. Whether it's through one or more of the "backpack" exercises in this chapter or from hearing LGBTQ people's stories, empathy grows our capacity to care for LGBTQ youth.

Empathy, Rogers thought, isn't needed only to help a person grow. It's a necessary quality of an effective therapist. The ability to insert ourselves into another person's experience to understand what they're going through can make us better parents, caregivers, teachers, and allies. Empathy creates a world in which all children are safe to learn, thrive, and grow.

Before each and every class I teach, I visualize the class going well. I see each student confident and articulate. Before I arrive, I send love to the place I'm teaching at, and I visualize blasting it with light. It doesn't mean every class is perfect or without challenges. By holding space for the potential of each class, I help call it forth. Even if I don't see it that day, what counts is I know it's possible.

Each of us has the ability to bring so much goodness to a young person's life. It starts by what we believe is true for them. Before we conclude this chapter, I want to leave you with a Rule of Expectations visualization to help instill empathy. It will also help you visualize communities, classrooms, and churches for what they are capable of being: affirming, loving, and supportive of LGBTQ youth. It also brings us to the final chapter, where I tie everything we've learned during our time together and I share with you my personal story.

RULE OF EXPECTATIONS VISUALIZATION

Go ahead and get into a comfortable position. Close your eyes and take a deep breath in through your nose to the count of 1, 2, 3, 4, 5. Now gently exhale through your nose. Repeat this two more times.

See in your mind's eye a classroom full of students. Maybe it's one of the classrooms you were in as a young person. As you look around, you see all the students talking to one another and smiling. You notice the room feels light and free. Everyone is in a good mood. The sunlight is bright and shines through a big window. You look up at the front of the room and see a teacher with their back to the class. You notice they're writing on the board. The bell rings and they begin to write: *Who you are matters.*

When they turn around you see their face and realize it's you. You're the teacher and the classroom is your life. Each person you interact with every day is someone sitting in your classroom—smiling, happy, and free. You realize that how you feel impacts everyone around you, especially young people. You begin to notice how your heart feels in the middle of your chest. It feels full of loving energy. You remember how good it feels to be able to share something positive with someone and so you begin to smile at each person in the classroom.

You see youth of all backgrounds standing in a big circle in the middle of the classroom holding hands. You see their faces and notice the warmth of their smiles. You see them achieving their dreams, you see them laughing, you see them capable, you see them free, you see them enjoying life, you see them making a positive contribution to the planet. You hold each student's smiling face in your heart and you look them in their eyes and say:

Who you are matters. Your life matters. You have potential and are capable of achieving anything your heart desires. You deserve to be happy, healthy, and free. May you be blessed and may you know peace.

Because you know this for each student in your classroom, you know this for all youth around the world. You hold a vision in your mind's eye of a planet full of playgrounds where all children are laughing and free. You now carry this vision with you everywhere you go. And so it is.

11

UNCLE CHRIS

The Journey of a Soul

Once there was a man who was afraid of his shadow. Then
he met it. Now he glows in the dark.

—Ben Loory

My friend, Sushant, has traveled to parts of the world where it's
unsafe to be LGBTQ. And he's heard stories of inspiration and
unyielding courage. He once told me about a Thai LGBTQ activist who
has since changed how he sees the responsibility each of us has in telling our story. He said, "We heal not only by sharing our stories, but by
people listening to our stories."

As we conclude our journey together, I'd like to share with you
my story. When I first set out to write this book, I thought I was writing
something for "other people." After my nephew's question that changed
my perception of familial homophobia, I thought the work was with my
family. At the time, I didn't realize as a gay uncle, I too had a role to
play in my nephew's understanding of gender and sexuality. As we've
explored, we can't heal what we don't reveal, though. If we aren't aware
of our blind spots, we'll continue to pass on the parts of ourselves we
are unwilling to see.

When it comes to family expectations, it can be challenging to live
authentically. It's one thing to live away from home and be who we
are, but something else entirely to be ourselves around people whose
opinions carry the most weight. After taking the journey with *Raising LGBTQ Allies*, I realized how easy it was for me to code-switch
and hide comfortably behind heteronormativity whenever I visited my
family. I haven't been in a long-term relationship while my nieces and

nephews have been alive, so I've never brought a boyfriend home with me to visit. Until my nephew's question, I didn't realize the importance of taking a proactive approach as an LGBTQ family member—not only with my words, but in my actions, my energy, and how I live my life.

Part of my family's healing has been from the conscious inner work we've done to explore our subconscious homophobia and name the harmful effects of heteronormativity. Through this process, I've also learned I can only take others as far as I've gone myself—which means revisiting my past in order to change the future.

I once heard that when we speak to someone at the level of the mind, we reach them at the mind level. When we speak to someone at the level of the heart, we reach them at the heart level. And when we use stories, we create transformation. Here is my story.

ANSWERING THE CALL

The witness has forced himself to testify. For the youth of today, for the children who will be born tomorrow. He does not want his past to become their future.

—Elie Wiesel

I knew I was gay when I was six years old. At the time, I didn't know what being gay meant. However, I knew there was something about me that wasn't the same as most of the other boys with whom I grew up. I had a lot of friends who were girls, but unlike the other boys, I never had crushes on any of them. Growing up in a religious household, the messages I received about boys who liked boys were that it was wrong and sinful, and I could go to hell if I was, in fact, gay.

I never recall anyone sitting me down and telling me, "Chris, if you are gay, you are going to hell." It was something I picked up from my surroundings. I also picked up what wasn't being talked about, the benign neglect—which informed *my* messages from the playground.

I used to jokingly tell people I could have won an Oscar for the role I played as a straight person. Because of my hypervigilance as a gay child growing up in a heteronormative world, I had a heightened sense of awareness for how straight men were supposed to dress, walk, and talk.

I trained myself to act like the guys I knew. For my entire adolescence I gender-policed myself to ensure my truth remained hidden. I felt like the more I could blend in, the better my chances were at being accepted, staying safe, and avoiding hell.

I had girlfriends in junior high and high school, and when I got to college, I joined a fraternity. When you're in college, it's easy to hide who you are. There's a club or activity for everything, so I was able to disguise my sexuality behind busyness and the clubs I joined. After graduation, it became increasingly more difficult to hide who I was. My friends started getting married and everyone seemed to ask me why I didn't have a girlfriend or wasn't married. Being asked heteronormative questions was like hearing nails on a chalkboard. It was also a constant source of anxiety.

When I was twenty-four, I took a job in Monterrey, Mexico. The idea of moving to a foreign country where no one knew me or would ask me about a girlfriend was like an answer to prayer. I used to pray for God to take the gay away, so Mexico was an opportunity for me to start over. The questions followed me with the move, though. So I signed up to run a marathon to not have to go out on the weekends. It was too exhausting to pretend to hit on women, trying to be someone I wasn't. Running a marathon was a reason to avoid being set up and have to answer questions about why I didn't have a girlfriend. "Sorry guys, can't go out tonight. I have to train in the morning," became my saving grace.

I didn't realize it at the time, but I hadn't signed up to run a marathon. I had signed up for something that kept me running from myself.

Before I moved, my aunt used to tell me, "You're going to move to Mexico and fall and love with a beautiful Mexican woman and never come back." Well, part of what she told me was true. I did fall in love, but it wasn't with a beautiful Mexican woman.

I came out while living in Mexico. I remember going to an internet cafe on the corner where I lived. I used to research being gay to see if there was something I could easily do to not be. I never found anything helpful, so I set up a fake email account to anonymously email my old pastor. Before I moved to Mexico, I went to a pretty open and liberal church. I emailed my pastor about a "friend" I knew who was attracted to men and so I wanted to get his perspective. I knew what messages I heard growing up, but I thought (and hoped) that maybe he'd give me a different answer.

Instead, he sent me an article from a Christian magazine about a man who had "homosexual desires." This man was married with a beautiful wife and had two young children. He was successful in keeping his "homosexual desires" at bay for more than six years, and each night, he and his wife would get on their knees and pray, thanking God for delivering him from his "sin."

After reading the article, I felt a sense of despair. I thought about the man's wife and how women in general need to feel loved. They need to feel attractive and desired, and I wondered if he was ever really able to do that for her. Sure, they had two kids and a seemingly successful marriage, by my old pastor's standards, but how did she feel in their marriage?

Then I had an image of a scenario in my mind: I envisioned the two parents at a soccer meeting after school. In the article, it said one of their kids was on a soccer team. I thought, what if one day, a new father who had just moved to town brought his kid to a meeting. As he walked in the room, what if the father with "homosexual desires," who every night was on his knees with his wife in prayer, glanced at the new father. For a split second, he checked him out. And in that split second, his wife noticed. I thought about how it would make her feel. A marriage has to be built on trust and in that moment, her trust in him would be fractured.

I realized I wouldn't ever be able to marry a woman for the very reason that it could cause another person to feel uncertain about their own life. When I thought of the man's wife, I couldn't imagine she ever truly felt secure in her relationship.

For Love

While living in Mexico, I worked for a North American company. One afternoon, they sent me to the airport to pick up some visitors from our Texas office. The plan was that I would bring them back to our offices and give them a tour. Once I picked up the all-male visitors, they began to ask me about the women in Mexico and wanted to know how many girlfriends I had—an example of how heteronormativity informs even the most basic interactions.

Their questions made me nauseous. Little did they know, I was at the lowest point in my life. I breathed a sigh of relief when they asked me to drop them off at their hotel instead of going into the office. I realized I couldn't keep up the facade any longer, but I didn't know what to do or who I could turn to for help.

After I dropped them off, I drove to a Subway down the street for a sandwich to take with me back to work. As I walked in, a man walked out. We passed one another, almost brushing shoulders. He looked at me as if he knew me. To justify feeling completely seen, I told myself, "Oh, I must look like his cousin's friend." I had butterflies in my stomach and my palms began to sweat. It was like time slowed down, and I could hear the sound of my heartbeat. I had been attracted to guys before, but this was the first time I had a physiological reaction. I wondered what was happening, but at the same time, already knew.

I walked to the register and noticed the guy who gave me butterflies and made my heart beat was in his car watching me, pretending to read a magazine. I thought, "It's the middle of the day on a Tuesday. How can this be happening?" The sexually deviant messages from the playground my dad had about gay men had been passed down to me. I didn't think gay men met at sandwich shops in the middle of the day on a Tuesday.

As I walked outside, something inside of me shifted. I felt a sense of fearless freedom. I thought, "I don't know anyone in Mexico, I barely speak Spanish, what do I have to lose?" It was like my heart took over and pulled me toward his car. Although I was nervous, it felt as natural as it does to breath. I walked up, and he rolled down his window. With a shaky voice and a terrible accent, I said in Spanish, "Hola, nada más quería decir, hola." Which means, "Hi, I just wanted to say hi." It's a good thing my heart was in the lead and not my head. Otherwise, my worst possible pick-up line would've been the reason I blushed and not because I had a crush.

In perfect English and a hint of an accent he said, "Oh, you aren't from here. My name is Rodrigo." It was one of those moments where even though I didn't know what I was doing, everything felt right.

He asked for my number, but I didn't feel comfortable giving him my phone number yet. I took his and promised I'd call.

After we said our goodbyes, I drove back to the office. When I sat down at my desk, I couldn't think of work or eat my Subway sandwich. All I could do was think about Rodrigo and the feeling I had in my chest. I wanted to stand on a mountaintop and announce to the world how I felt. I immediately started to write a poem. Me, who had never written poetry in my life; I was sitting at my cubicle in the middle of the day on a Tuesday, writing a poem. Never before had I felt as free.

It took me a few days, but I eventually called. For the first time, I acted from a place of love, not fear. Love helped me break the facade I had lived for more than twenty years.

Recently, I shared my coming-out story at a local junior high school. Afterward, a young girl stood up and came out to her entire class for the first time. Through her tears, I saw her courage. I was reminded about the power we have when we share authentically from our hearts and how no one can take authentic power away.

Sometimes, we'll go to pretty great lengths to avoid looking at our lives and keep something about ourselves hidden. We might stay in a marriage we don't feel safe in, we might move to another country to come out of the closet, we might code-switch and hide behind societal norms, or we might run a marathon in hopes of running from ourselves.

And sometimes, we'll do something as a symbolic gesture to show ourselves that how we did it before was simply because we didn't know any better. By doing it again, in a different way, we're telling ourselves it's now okay.

This final chapter is for any young person who has ever felt that they had to hide something or couldn't fully be themselves. I wrote it as a symbolic gesture for anyone else who has ever knelt in prayer asking God to help them to not be gay. I wrote it for the little girl who came out to her class and for any other young person struggling to accept themselves. I wrote it for parents to encourage them to read their children's lives. I wrote it for families to inspire proactive conversations. I wrote it for the LGBTQ community as a call for us to heal the parts of ourselves we still find shameful. And most importantly, I wrote it for my six-year-old self.

A RETURN TO THE VILLAGE

I ask for the movement to continue, for the movement
to grow, because last week I got a call from Altoona,
Pennsylvania, and my election gave somebody else, one
more person, hope. And after all, that's what this is all
about. It's not about personal gain, not about ego, not
about power—it's about giving those young people out
there in the Altoona, Pennsylvanias, hope. You gotta give
them hope.

—Harvey Milk[1]

In 2008, my LGBTQ advocacy work relocated me to Los Angeles. After coming out of the closet, I had this deep drive to make a difference
in the LGBTQ community's vision of equality. They say hindsight is
twenty-twenty, and what I've since discovered is my fight to change
everyone's mind about the LGBTQ community was an internal fight—
one that ultimately led me to where I am today. Although I was out
of the closet and working for a national LGBTQ organization, I hadn't
faced my messages from the playground.

In one of my favorite shows, *Sex and the City*, there's an episode
where one of the characters, Samantha, gets an HIV test. A new guy
she's dating insists that before they have sex, she have an HIV test. When
she tells this to her girlfriends, one of them jokingly says that as long as
she isn't escorted to the "little room" to get her results, she'll be fine.
Fast-forward to the scene where she goes to get her test results, and she
faints while being escorted to a little room. In this case, the character
from *Sex and the City* was HIV negative. The nurse wanted to give her
advice on practicing safe sex.

I recalled that episode as I was escorted to a little room about ten
years ago after returning to get my test results from a visit to the clinic.
I had gone in for a standard STD screening. The nurse who helped me
was a nice little old man who asked way too many questions. Normally
when you go for a screening, they ask you a few questions and draw
your blood. This guy was really going for it. He kept asking if I wanted
an HIV test, which I kept declining. Getting an STD test was one thing,

but an HIV test seemed so official. Besides, HIV was something I heard about other people having, not anyone I thought I knew personally.

A week or so later I got a call from a very friendly nurse who asked me to come by the clinic to go over my results. She said everything was fine; it was standard protocol to speak with me in person. After arriving the next day, she walked me to a little room at the end of the hallway—a scene I was all too familiar with thanks to one of my favorite shows. The man in the room introduced himself and let me know I tested negative for all STDs. I was relieved, but nervous as to why I was there. Was I going to get the same safe-sex lecture they gave Samantha? He let me know that the nice little old man who asked way too many questions had accidentally screened me for an HIV test. By law, he couldn't give me the results unless he had my approval. So we sat in the room for what seemed a lifetime. I knew what he was going to tell me, that I was HIV positive, but I felt that as long as I didn't hear the diagnosis out loud, I was safe. As long as those words weren't spoken, I was in the space that existed before I got there.

Finally, as a means of letting me know the gravity of the situation, he told me people with fewer than 200 t-cells had full-blown AIDS, and a normal range was between 500 and 1,200. He said it was necessary we have a serious conversation. I felt like Samantha and was going to faint. I was lightheaded and could feel my heart beating through my chest. I eventually accepted and he confirmed I was HIV positive. He said I was hovering around 250 t-cells and I'd need to begin treatment immediately.

How was this possible? I was barely thirty years old. I had a bachelor's degree. I came from a loving family. I traveled, spoke two languages, and volunteered. I did things like cycle across the United States and run marathons in Mexico. I didn't think it was possible for someone like me to get HIV.

What I didn't know, and what I do now, is even though I was doing my part to fight for LGBTQ equality, I carried unhealed shame and trauma, which influenced my behavior. I didn't have a clue that my beliefs—conscious and subconscious—affected my sense of self-worth. I also didn't realize a long-held narrative for parents of gay men had become my self-fulfilling prophecy.

I remember looking out the window at the beautiful night sky. I began looking around and noticing people walking below in the court-yard. I thought about their lives and wondered why they were visiting the hospital. I also thought about my life and how different it was now from when I had first arrived.

I had no idea after I left that night that I would embark on a jour-ney of getting to know myself, one that ultimately saved my life. Up until then, I thought I did know myself. What I didn't know, though, was that I had been avoiding myself. Sure, I knew what my favorite food was, that I enjoyed things like traveling, music, and going to the beach. But if I were completely honest, I didn't *know* myself. I was like my own acquaintance instead of my own best friend.

Recently, I was talking to a friend, and she told me my spirituality saved my life. It wasn't something I had ever considered before. When I heard it for the first time, I felt it in my body. Tears welled up in my eyes. I could feel the hair on my neck rise. In that moment, I realized why I had the same reaction when I heard someone describe spirituality as the direct experience of our own essence. It was the experience of my own essence that saved my life.

In her book *Daring Greatly*, Brené Brown writes, "Because true belonging only happens when we present our authentic, imperfect selves to the world, our sense of belonging can never be greater than our level of self-acceptance."[2]

This applies to everyone, but being gay and having HIV, I thought about the LGBTQ community's level of self-acceptance and from where is it cultivated and, more importantly, nourished. It's one thing to be out of the closet, but another to fully accept and embrace ourselves whole-heartedly and unconditionally for who we are. Each person's level of self-acceptance in the LGBTQ community is directly correlated to the vision we hold for LGBTQ youth.

What I've learned from exploring belief systems with people of all ages and backgrounds is that most of us have struggled with worthiness. For LGBTQ youth, not feeling worthy can be especially prevalent.

I once watched an interview where a woman described a sacred tradition on the island of Crete with a group of Greek Orthodox nuns. She said the nuns would walk to a sacred tree to ask for the deepest de-sire of their hearts. Although we're not in Greece and this book isn't a sacred tree, the deepest desire of my heart is for it to help create a world in which all children are affirmed and celebrated.

Part of changing the narrative for future generations of LGBTQ youth is to take full responsibility for our lives, our choices, and our beliefs. When we uncover misguided beliefs and challenge them before we unknowingly teach them to children, we change destinies.

THE HERO'S JOURNEY

What I do know is that there is "response" in responsibility.

—Elie Wiesel

A young man my friend Sushant met in India lives with his parents and two sisters in a room the size of my bathroom in Los Angeles. The young man is openly gay and HIV positive, which in India, Sushant said, "Is risky. Especially when it comes to his family's safety." But the young man's father told Sushant, "It's important for my son to live openly no matter the consequences for our family. Our love and God would take care of everything."

"Something inside of me changed after hearing the young man's story and his father's response," Sushant told me. I had mentioned to him that I wasn't sure if I should share my HIV status in a book for parents, even though a lot of my work encourages open and honest conversations to heal shame. After hearing the young man's story, I didn't feel as though I could fully participate in the conversation if I wasn't sharing the thing that's been the most shameful part of my own life.

I've always loved American mythologist, writer, and lecturer Joseph Campbell's analogy of the *hero's journey* in describing our lives. If you aren't familiar with it, it's a concept Campbell developed based on his life's work. He spent decades studying the stories told throughout history from every continent in the world—everything from stories in the Bible to the Vikings, from the Aborigines in Australia to the Native Americans of North America. What he found is we all tell the same story. The characters and setting may vary, but the soul of the story remains.

Ultimately, the bond each person on the planet shares is that we are all on our own hero's journey. Part of the journey is discovering who we are and what our soul came here to do, and to be able to show our faces fully.

What's Your Favorite Disney Movie?

I often ask people to tell me what their favorite movie is. Especially with youth, a fun way to introduce the hero's journey is to ask them what their favorite Disney movie is. More often than not, the movies we know and love follow the structure posited by Joseph Campbell's, the hero's journey. In fact, the reason most popular Hollywood movies are far-reaching is because we see ourselves inside of the story. From *Legally Blonde* to *Mulan*, from *Black Panther* to *Moana*, the stories resonate with us on a soul level.

Whenever I'm invited to share my coming out story, there's always someone in the room who raises their hand and asks me if I keep in touch with Rodrigo. We may not have all come out in Mexico, but each of us relates to the courage it takes to open our hearts and fall in love for the first time.

A hero's journey always begins with a call to adventure. We don't have to answer the call, but after we do, our life is never the same. Often, when I ask someone to guess the end of a hero's journey, they tell me it's when the hero/heroine accomplishes what they set out to achieve. And when I ask them what that is, they usually tell me it's winning the battle or finding the treasure.

The real end of a hero's journey—and my favorite part—is when we take what we learn from the journey back to the village and share. Sharing the gifts we receive from our lessons of transformation is the true end of the hero's journey. This book is my hero's journey. It's a culmination of everything I've learned along my path. And the only way to successfully complete my journey is to take what I've learned back to the village and share.

A Little More about My Reason for Sharing My HIV Diagnosis

I believe our lives speak to us through others. I had gone in for a quarterly doctor's appointment two years ago after my old doctor transferred to another clinic. I was meeting my new doctor for the first time and so I was a little nervous.

During our visit, we discussed medications, and my new doctor said, "With anyone who is diagnosed with something, I think it's important for them to educate themselves on the disease, treatment options, etc." Her remark made me think of my mom and how any time she comes down with or is diagnosed with something, she researches it until she becomes an expert and then educates herself and others about what the condition is. I told the doctor what she said reminded me of my mom and what my mom does, but it's something I had never done with HIV. She asked me if I'd told my mom and I said, "No."

She looked me right in the eyes and said, "Oh honey, why not?" I told her because I didn't want her to worry or to perpetuate the stereotype her generation has of gay men. Without knowing much more about me than my chart, she replied, "Don't you think you'll be a better healer if that's something you're able to heal more yourself?" It was like she punched me in the stomach with truth.

After we spoke for a little while longer, I asked her what, after thirty-five years of doing this work, she still sees today that she saw in the 1980s during the AIDS crisis? What is the common thread? She said, "After all these years, I still see the same story repeated. I still see young twenty-one-year-old guys who move to LA with a dream and wind up in a relationship with someone who either doesn't know they're positive and exposes them to HIV or who knows and doesn't disclose. The shame the community still carries is what keeps HIV alive." The more we keep the dark parts of ourselves, our communities, and our beliefs hidden, the more we perpetuate their existence.

Despite the battles I've fought, including shame, trauma, HIV, and homophobia, each challenge has led me to my purpose and ultimately, to my truth. The level of our personal development is determined by how much we can transform challenges and share the lessons of transformation with others. Through forgiveness, self-love, spirituality, and taking full responsibility for my life, I've been able to become the uncle and LGBTQ advocate I've aspired to be. Had I not looked inside my own life and done the inner-healing work, my nephew's question wouldn't have inspired me to share my transformation.

That's an aspect of the hero's journey—to look within our own life and face our demons. The deeper we go, the more we connect to the truest part of who we are and discover what we're here to do.

CALLING AND THE SOUL:
WHAT LGBTQ YOUTH ARE HERE TO DO

The soul's guidance always leads us toward growth. It is the life force energy seeking to evolve and expand within us.

—Michelle Bolling

Just like colors or times of the day, life exists on a spectrum. The world in which we live is no longer black and white—the future is fluid. In a beautiful sermon, "The Holiness of Twilight," Rabbi Reuben Zellman said, "Jewish tradition has a unique relationship with twilight: that ethereal moment in every day when dark and light meet. The rising of the sun and its going down are moments that we cannot label with certainty."[3] There isn't only day, nor only night. We have dusk, dawn, afternoon, evening, and twilight. We don't only feel happy or sad, we can feel a variety of emotions in between. In order for us to know an emotion, though, we must also experience its opposite. In order for us to know love, we must also experience fear.

During a training years ago, a woman told me how on a certain level I chose to be gay. I remember getting upset and telling her being gay isn't a choice. I didn't realize it at the time, but what she was trying to tell me was that on a *soul level* I chose to be gay. Each of us is a soul with a call to share its gifts. Part of our purpose is to discover what they are and share them with the planet.

Most of the parents I know who have LGBTQ children all share the same sentiment: their LGBTQ child has taught them how to love more deeply. That's not to say their journey was without challenge. No hero's journey comes without challenge. It's not the "relaxation journey." The journey of the soul is to create transformation in the lives of those who can receive its gifts. On a soul level, LGBTQ youth are calling parents, families, teachers, and playgrounds to love more deeply. By virtue of being themselves, LGBTQ youth can also teach us hope, authenticity, courage, strength, and resilience.

We aren't only our bodies. Our soul is the core of who we are. I was speaking to a parent about transgender youth one afternoon, and I said, "What better way to learn about the soul than to experience someone whose body doesn't match who they are on the inside." The planet is changing and so is our consciousness. LGBTQ youth can help us arrive at a new way of looking at the world if we are open to receive their gifts. My transgender friends have helped me connect to the soul in a way I haven't experienced with my cisgender friends. It's easy to see someone from the outside and think of them as only a body. It requires a lot more to know someone from the inside. The soul can teach us in ways the body cannot.

THE POWER OF A SOUL

> The opposite of love is fear, but what is all-encompassing can have no opposite.
>
> —A Course in Miracles

Over the years, I've known many young people who have died by suicide. After each death, I found myself contemplating life. A friend's daughter recently died by suicide, and when her mother reached out to me for support, I began to speak to her about her daughter's soul. Although there is tragedy in loss, especially when it comes to suicide, death isn't the finality to the soul. Even in suicide, there are gifts from a person's life they continue to share. Each of us has known someone who has died, and while their death was the end of their body, their essence remains.

I told my friend, "In time and space as it exists, we can't truly know what your daughter's purpose was. That's between her and God. What we can do is recognize she is a soul who came here to share with us her gifts. On a soul level, she chose to leave when she did and honoring her life, as well as her choice, will help with the healing."

From the stories I've shared with you in this chapter, whether about my friend's daughter or the young man from India, each person's soul has touched your life. That's the power of our soul. The soul goes beyond boundaries of the body and limits of fear. The soul is to the body what love is to fear. One is all encompassing and transcendent. The other limits, separates, and withholds.

Everything I've been a part of has helped inform the content of this book. If I view my life from the limits of a body, I see the messages from the playground some parents still have for their gay sons: high rates of drug and alcohol abuse, self-deprecating behavior, sexual deviancy, shame, trauma, and HIV. When I expand my consciousness and view my life as a soul who chose to be gay, each of my choices has served my path and purpose. Had I not experienced pain, I wouldn't know forgiveness. Without confusion, I wouldn't know certainty. Had I not known shame, I wouldn't know worthiness. Everything, from coming out to my HIV diagnosis, has become a gift in my life. Gifts I can now share.

We don't need to experience challenges to arrive at our purpose. When we can find purpose in our challenges, though, we create transformation. The real end to my hero's journey is to help transform how we see LGBTQ youth and the stories we hold for their lives. I couldn't have brought this back to the village to share without my soul having answered its call.

EVERYTHING IS BETTER WHEN IT'S SHARED

> Don't worry that children never listen to you; worry that
> they are always watching you.
>
> —Robert Fulghum

You know how, when you see a really good movie, you tell everyone about it? Or when you're at dinner with friends and your meal is so delicious that you let everyone at the table know? Because everything good we experience in life is better when it's shared. From the beginning, the idea for *Raising LGBTQ Allies* has been like discovering something that can improve the lives of young people, including the ones in my own family. Ever since, I've dreamed of being able to share my message by writing a book for parents. Part of having a parenting book is speaking to parents, including some who may not agree with me. Thus, for the past few years I've been using the tips and tools found here to strengthen my voice and empower the lives of LGBTQ youth around the world.

What I've found is that the most powerful way we can teach a child is to embody the very thing we hope to see for their lives. Rather than have a desire for them to be fulfilled, we can demonstrate fulfillment. Instead of *only* talking to our friends about how we wish there was less fear and hate in the world, we can teach love by affirming all youth. Showing our kids how to be versus telling them what they should do is a far more effective way of breaking fear-based generational family structures—including homophobia, transphobia, racism, xenophobia, and anti-Semitism. Teaching children to do something we ourselves don't embody won't be enough to change the system. Kids learn from the energy behind our words and our actions, or the lack thereof. Ultimately, doing the work in our own lives, to be what we desire to see in the world, is the best way we can pay it forward for the next generation.

By healing misguided beliefs about people who are LGBTQ, by having open and authentic conversations with children at a young age, by being more mindful, inclusive, and considerate of all youth, and by stepping into the role of active allies, we prevent queerphobia and bullying before they begin. Sharing what you've learned from our journey together can also help change the story future generations will tell. Through the conversations this book inspires at home, in classrooms, and on playgrounds, each of us has answered the call to help create a more peaceful planet for LGBTQ youth.

As with any journey, it will have its ups and its downs. Speaking from my own experience working with LGBTQ youth, we're not going to get it right 100 percent of the time, and that's okay. Coming out is as much of a process for someone who is LGBTQ as it is for family members and allies. If there was anything I'd want to share with you before we conclude our time together it is to stay present, be honest, and always keep an open dialogue going with your kids. And as my good friend Nia says, "Don't focus on keeping up; stay focused on keeping open."

I'm grateful we've been able to take this journey. It's my belief that we've traveled together for a reason, a season, and, hopefully, a lifetime. May you carry the soul of this message with you in your heart, and may it bless all of the lives you touch. Including your own.

NOTES

CHAPTER 1

1. "Same-Sex Marriage Around the World," Pew Research Center, October 28, 2019, accessed January 28, 2020, https://www.pewforum.org/fact-sheet/gay-marriage-around-the-world/.

2. "Heteronormative (adjective)," *Merriam-Webster Dictionary*, last updated December 26, 2019. https://www.merriam-webster.com/dictionary/heteronormative.

3. Vivek Datta, "When Homosexuality Came Out (of the DSM)," *Mad in America*, December 1, 2014, accessed June 25, 2019, https://www.madinamerica.com/2014/12/homosexuality-came-dsm/.

4. "Egodystonic Sexual Orientation," *PatientsLikeMe*, last updated January 16, 2020, accessed September 2, 2019, https://www.patientslikeme.com/conditions/egodystonic-sexual-orientation.

5. Jack Drescher, "Science & Theology in Human Sexuality," Presentation on History, Science and Politics of Homosexuality, September 19, 2016, accessed May 13, 2019, https://slideplayer.com/slide/11745908/.

6. Neel Burton, "When Homosexuality Stopped Being a Mental Disorder," *Psychology Today*, September 18, 2015, accessed June 25, 2019, https://www.psychologytoday.com/us/blog/hide-and-seek/201509/when-homosexuality-stopped-being-mental-disorder.

7. Nancy Schimelpfening, "'Not Otherwise Specified' (NOS) in the Diagnosis of Mental Disorders," *Verywell Mind*, last updated September 23, 2019, accessed July 14, 2019, https://www.verywellmind.com/not-otherwise-specified-nos-1066918.

8. Burton, "When Homosexuality Stopped Being a Mental Disorder."

9. Terry Gross, "'Fresh Air' Remembers 'Boyz n the Hood' Director John Singleton," NPR, May 3, 2019, accessed May 5, 2019, https://www.npr.

org/2019/05/03/719986809/fresh-air-remembers-boyz-n-the-hood-director-john-singleton.

10. Christy Mallory, Taylor N. T. Brown, and Kerith J. Conron, "Conversion Therapy and LGBT Youth," Williams Institute, January 2018, accessed June 5, 2019, https://williamsinstitute.law.ucla.edu/wp-content/uploads/Conversion-Therapy-LGBT-Youth-Jan-2018.pdf.

11. Christy Mallory, Taylor N. T. Brown, and Kerith J. Conron, "Conversion Therapy and LGBT Youth Update," Williams Institute, June 2019, accessed June 5, 2019, https://williamsinstitute.law.ucla.edu/wp-content/uploads/Conversion-Therapy-LGBT-Youth-Update-June-2019.pdf.

12. "APA Reiterates Strong Opposition to Conversion Therapy," American Psychiatric Association, November 15, 2018, accessed June 20, 2019, https://www.psychiatry.org/newsroom/news-releases/apa-reiterates-strong-opposition-to-conversion-therapy.

13. H. Daniel and R. Bukus, "Lesbian, Gay, Bisexual, and Transgender Health Disparities: Executive Summary of a Policy Position Paper from the American College of Physicians," National Center for Biotechnology Information, July 21, 2015, accessed August 5, 2019, https://doi.org/10.7326/M14-2482.

14. Joelle Goldstein, "Conversion Therapy Founder Comes Out Publicly as Gay after 20 Years of Leading Homophobic Program," *People*, September 4, 2019, accessed September 6, 2019, https://people.com/human-interest/conversion-therapy-founder-comes-out-as-gay/.

15. Jeffrey Mays, "New York City Is Ending a Ban on Gay Conversion Therapy. Here's Why," *New York Times*, September 12, 2019, accessed September 18, 2019, https://www.nytimes.com/2019/09/12/nyregion/conversion-therapy-ban-nyc.html.

16. Devdutt Pattanaik and Jerry Johnson, *I Am Divine. So Are You: How Buddhism, Jainism, Sikhism and Hinduism Affirm the Dignity of Queer Identities and Sexualities* (New York: HarperCollins, 2017), 3.

17. Frank Newport, "In U.S., Estimate of LGBT Population Rises to 4.5%," Gallup, May 22, 2018, accessed September 15, 2019, https://news.gallup.com/poll/234863/estimate-lgbt-population-rises.aspx.

18. Stephen T. Russell and Jessica N. Fish, "Mental Health in Lesbian, Gay, Bisexual, and Transgender (LGBT) Youth," National Center for Biotechnology Information, January 14, 2016, accessed September 12, 2019, https://doi.org/10.1146/annurev-clinpsy-021815-093153.

19. Zoe Schlanger, "A Teen Health Survey Crucial to US Public Policy Is Finally Asking Kids about Their Sexual Orientation," *Quartz*, June 25, 2017,

accessed July 20, 2019, https://qz.com/1014142/a-teen-health-survey-crucial-to-us-public-policy-is-finally-asking-kids-about-their-sexual-orientation/.

20. "America's Top Fears 2018," *Chapman University Blog*, October 16, 2018, accessed September 15, 2019, https://blogs.chapman.edu/wilkinson/2018/10/16/americas-top-fears-2018/.

CHAPTER 2

1. Bailey Maryfield, "Implicit Racial Bias," Justice Research and Statistics Association, December 2018, accessed August 8, 2019, https://www.jrsa.org/pubs/factsheets/jrsa-factsheet-implicit-racial-bias.pdf.

2. Caroline Myss, "Choices That Can Change Your Life—Caroline Myss—TEDxFindhornSalon," YouTube video, 25:55, April 3, 2017, accessed June 20, 2019, https://www.youtube.com/watch?v=-KysuBl2m_w&feature=emb_title.

3. "SB 1019: Amending Section 15-716, Arizona Revised Statutes; Relating to School Curriculum," State of Arizona Senate, 2019, accessed February 5, 2019. https://www.azleg.gov/legtext/54leg/1r/laws/0086.htm.

4. "Chapter 2: The Separation and the Atonement—Fear and Conflict," A Course in Miracles International, accessed August 7, 2019, https://acimi.com/a-course-in-miracles/text/chapter-2/fear-and-conflict.

5. Moira Donegan, "The Jeffrey Esptein-Victoria's Secret Connection," *Atlantic*, August 6, 2019, accessed August 20, 2019, https://www.theatlantic.com/ideas/archive/2019/08/victorias-secret-epstein/595507/.

6. Brit Morse, "The 7 Most Embarrassing Branding Mistakes of 2018," *Inc.*, November 28, 2018, accessed September 2, 2019, https://www.inc.com/brit-morse/2018-biggest-marketing-branding-fails.html.

7. Mollie Reilly, "The Criminal Justice System Disproportionately Targets LGBT People, Study Finds," *HuffPost*, February 25, 2016, accessed July 7, 2019, https://www.huffpost.com/entry/lgbt-criminal-justice-system_n_56ce3108e4b03260bf756d5c.

8. "Unjust: How the Broken Criminal Justice System Fails LGBT People," Movement Advancement Project, February 2016, accessed July 28, 2019, http://lgbtmap.org/lgbt-criminal-justice.

9. Bianca D. M. Wilson et al., "Sexual and Gender Minority Youth in Foster Care: Assessing Disproportionality and Disparities in Los Angeles," Williams Institute, August 2014, accessed August 7, 2019, http://williamsinstitute.law.ucla.edu/wp-content/uploads/LAFYS_report_final-aug-2014.pdf.

10. Wilson et al., "Sexual and Gender Minority Youth in Foster Care."

CHAPTER 3

1. "Phobia, What Is It?" Harvard Health Publishing, Harvard Medical School, December 2018, accessed September 23, 2019, https://www.health.harvard.edu/a_to_z/phobia-a-to-z.

2. "Phobia, What Is It?"

3. Dan Baker, *What Happy People* Know (New York: St. Martin's, 2003), 20.

4. Baker, *What Happy People Know*, 29.

5. "Subconscious (adjective)," *Oxford University Press (OUP)*, accessed September 2, 2019, https://www.lexico.com/definition/subconscious.

CHAPTER 4

1. Teresa J. Kennedy, "Language Learning and Its Impact on the Brain: Connecting Language Learning with the Mind through Content-Based Instruction," American Council on the Teaching of Foreign Languages, December 31, 2008, accessed November 10, 2019, https://doi.org/10.1111/j.1944-9720.2006.tb02900.x.

2. Andrew Shtulman and Rachel InKyung Yoo, "Children's Understanding of Physical Possibility Constrains Their Belief in Santa Claus," Elsevier, 2014, accessed May 2, 2019, https://doi.org/10.1016/j.cogdev.2014.12.006.

3. "Understanding Early Sexual Development," Rady Children's Hospital, 2014, accessed December 10, 2019, https://www.rchsd.org/health-articles/understanding-early-sexual-development/.

4. "8 Things to Remember about Child Development," Center on the Developing Child, Harvard University, 2016, accessed December 5, 2019, https://developingchild.harvard.edu/resources/8-things-remember-child-development/.

5. "Understanding Early Sexual Development," KidsHealth, Nemours Foundation, October 2014, accessed April 7, 2015, http://m.rossa-editorial.kidshealth.org/en/parents/development.html?WT.ac=m-p-ra.

6. "Healthy Gender Development and Young Children," Head Start—Early Childhood Learning and Knowledge Center, last updated October 2, 2018, accessed November 11, 2019, https://eclkc.ohs.acf.hhs.gov/publication/healthy-gender-development-young-children.

7. "Healthy Gender Development and Young Children."

8. Jason Rafferty, "Gender Identity Development in Children," *Healthy Children*, American Academy of Pediatrics, last updated September 18, 2018, accessed November 20, 2019, https://www.healthychildren.org/English/ages-

stages/gradeschool/Pages/Gender-Identity-and-Gender-Confusion-In-Children.aspx.

9. Gal Mayer and Hector Vargas, "GLMA Opposes Efforts to Eradicate Federal Recognition of Transgender Individuals," Health Professionals Advancing LGBTQ Equality (GLMA), October 2018, accessed November 16, 2019, http://glma.org/index.cfm?fuseaction=Feature.showFeature&CategoryID=1& FeatureID=840.

10. Rafferty, "Gender Identity Development in Children."

11. "Understanding Gender," Gender Spectrum, 2019, accessed September 6, 2019, https://www.genderspectrum.org/quick-links/understanding-gender/.

12. Amy Dickinson, "Gay Daughter Presents Sleepover Dilemma for Her Parents," *Arizona Daily Star*, November 4, 2019.

13. José A. Bauermeister et al., "Gender Policing During Childhood and the Psychological Well-Being of Young Adult Sexual Minority Men in the United States," *American Journal of Men's Health*, November 29, 2016, accessed November 30, 2019, https://doi.org/10.1177/1557988316680938.

14. José A. Bauermeister et al., "Gender Policing During Childhood."

15. "The Blue Eyes & Brown Eyes Exercise," Jane Elliot, 2019, accessed May 15, 2019, https://janeelliott.com.

CHAPTER 5

1. Matthew Robinson, "Hitler-Owned Book Hints at Plans for North American Holocaust," CNN, January 26, 2019, accessed January 26, 2019, https://edition.cnn.com/2019/01/25/americas/holocaust-canada-north-america-blueprint-scli-intl/index.html?no-st=1548452021.

2. Adrian Pei, *The Minority Experience* (Downers Grove, IL: InterVarsity Press, 2018), 4.

3. "Benign neglect (noun)," *Merriam-Webster Dictionary*, accessed July 19, 2019, https://www.merriam-webster.com/dictionary/benign%20neglect.

4. "Memorandum for the President," Nixon Library, January 16, 1970, accessed May 17, 2019, https://www.nixonlibrary.gov/sites/default/files/virtuallibrary/documents/jul10/53.pdf.

5. Sebastian Martinez, "Why We Need More Culturally Competent Therapists," National Alliance on Mental Health (NAMI), July 8, 2019, accessed July 8, 2019, https://www.nami.org/Blogs/NAMI-Blog/July-2019/Why-We-Need-More-Culturally-Competent-Therapists.

6. M. Scott Peck, *People of the Lie* (New York: Simon and Schuster, 1983), 62.

CHAPTER 6

1. "National Survey on LGBTQ Youth Mental Health," The Trevor Project, 2019, accessed September 5, 2019, https://www.thetrevorproject.org/wp-content/uploads/2019/06/The-Trevor-Project-National-Survey-Results-2019.pdf?ftag=MSF0951a18.

2. "National Survey on LGBTQ Youth Mental Health."

3. Brené Brown, "The Power of Vulnerability," *Sounds True*, November 15, 2012, accessed March 8, 2016, https://www.soundstrue.com/store/the-power-of-vulnerability-2917.html.

4. *Nanette*, directed by Jon Olb and Madeleine Parry, aired June 19, 2018, on Netflix.

5. "Introjection," *GoodTherapy*, last updated October 6, 2015, accessed June 7, 2019, https://www.goodtherapy.org/blog/psychpedia/introjection.

6. Helen Lucy and Ann Phoenix, "Introjection—Critical Social Psychology (18/30)," OpenLearn from The Open University, YouTube video, 2:20, July 26, 2011, accessed August 5, 2019, https://www.youtube.com/watch?v=Dv6BkKd1jNA.

7. Rory O'Neill (aka Panti Bliss), "Panti's Noble Call at the Abbey Theatre—With Subtitles," YouTube video, 10:47, February 2, 2014, accessed August 7, 2019, https://www.youtube.com/watch?v=WXayhUzWnl0.

8. Eric Larson, "Internalized Homophobia: The Next LGBT Movement after Same-Sex Marriage," *Mashable*, June 25, 2014, accessed May 7, 2015, https://mashable.com/2014/06/25/internalized-homophobia-lgbt/.

9. Oren Miron et al., "Suicide Rates Among Adolescents and Young Adults in the United States, 2000–2017," *JAMA*, June 18, 2019, accessed July 7, 2019, https://doi.org/10.1001/jama.2019.5054.

10. Alan Mozes, "Depression Rates Not Budging for Lesbian and Gay Teens," *US News & World Report*, October 22, 2019, accessed October 25, 2019, https://www.usnews.com/news/health-news/articles/2019-10-22/depression-rates-not-budging-for-lesbian-and-gay-teens.

11. Brené Brown, "The Cruelty Crisis: Bullying Isn't a School Problem, It's a National Pastime," *Psychology Today*, November 1, 2010, accessed October 25, 2019, https://www.psychologytoday.com/us/blog/ordinary-courage/201011/the-cruelty-crisis-bullying-isnt-school-problem-its-national-pastime.

12. "National Survey on LGBTQ Youth Mental Health."

13. "What Is Bullying?" *Bullying. No Way!*, 2019, accessed October 5, 2019, https://bullyingnoway.gov.au/WhatIsBullying.

CHAPTER 7

1. Bessel van der Kolk, *The Body Keeps the Score* (New York: Penguin Books, 2014), 67.

2. *One of Us*, directed by Heidi Ewing and Rachel Grady, (2017; Los Angeles: Loki Films, Netflix, 2017).

3. Jeremy Treat, "LGBT + Identity Formation: Trauma and Resilience," Presented at Penny Lane Center's 9th Annual EDGY Conference—Embracing Identities, Los Angeles, October 27, 2017).

4. "Anomie (noun)," *Merriam-Webster Dictionary*, accessed August 7, 2019, https://www.merriam-webster.com/dictionary/anomie.

5. Treat, "LGBT + Identity Formation."

6. Treat, "LGBT + Identity Formation."

7. Serene Jones, *Trauma and Grace* (Louisville, KY: Westminster John Knox Press, 2009), 15.

8. "Substance Use and SUDs in LGBTQ* Populations," National Institute on Drug Abuse, September 5, 2017, accessed July 23, 2019, https://www.drugabuse.gov/related-topics/substance-use-suds-in-lgbtq-populations.

9. V. J. Felitti et al., "Relationship of Childhood Abuse and Household Dysfunction to Many of the Leading Causes of Death in Adults. The Adverse Childhood Experiences (ACE) Study," National Center for Biotechnology Information, May 1998, accessed August 30, 2019, https://doi.org/10.1016/S0749-3797(98)00017-8.

10. "The Trevor Project Commends the FCC on Its Report on the National Suicide Hotline Improvement Act of 2018," The Trevor Project, August 15, 2019, accessed August 24, 2019, https://www.thetrevorproject.org/trvr_press/the-trevor-project-commends-the-fcc-on-its-report-on-the-national-suicide-hotline-improvement-act-of-2018/.

11. "The Trevor Project Commends the FCC."

12. Bianca D. M. Wilson et al., "Sexual and Gender Minority Youth in Foster Care: Assessing Disproportionality and Disparities in Los Angeles," Williams Institute, August 2014, accessed August 7, 2019, http://williamsinstitute.law.ucla.edu/wp-content/uploads/LAFYS_report_final-aug-2014.pdf.

13. Wilson et al., "Sexual and Gender Minority Youth in Foster Care."

14. Jeremy Treat, "LGBT + Identity Formation."

15. Elitsa Dermendzhiyska, "Rejection Kills," Aeon, April 30, 2019, accessed May 20, 2019, https://aeon.co/essays/health-warning-social-rejection-doesnt-only-hurt-it-kills.

16. Caitlin Ryan et al., "Family Rejection as a Predictor of Negative Health Outcomes in White and Latino Lesbian, Gay, and Bisexual Young Adults,"

American Academy of Pediatrics, January 2009, accessed May 14, 2019, https://doi.org/10.1542/peds.2007-3524.

17. City News Service, "L.A. County Will Track Suicide Data on LGBTQ Individuals," *Los Angeles Times*, September 3, 2019, accessed September 20, 2019, https://www.latimes.com/california/story/2019-09-03/la-county-track-suicide-data-lgbtq.

18. Mykhiel Deych, "On Behalf of Their Name," *Rethinking Schools* 33, no. 2 (Winter 2018–2019), accessed February 18, 2020, https://www.rethinking-schools.org/articles/on-behalf-of-their-name.

19. Kendra Cherry, "How Confirmation Bias Works," Verywell Mind, November 27, 2019, December 5, 2019, https://www.verywellmind.com/what-is-a-confirmation-bias-2795024.

20. Dan Allender, "Certificate in Narrative Focused Trauma Care Level I," presented at the Seattle School of Theology and Psychology's Allender Center Level I Training, Seattle, November 15–18, 2018).

CHAPTER 8

1. "Bullying Statistics," PACER's National Bullying Prevention Center, last updated December 27, 2017, accessed December 4, 2019, https://www.pacer.org/bullying/resources/stats.asp.

2. Susan Heitler, "Are You Good Enough?" *Psychology Today*, July 15, 2014, accessed June 3, 2019, https://www.psychologytoday.com/us/blog/resolution-not-conflict/201407/are-you-good-enough.

3. Tig Notaro, "R2 Where Are You," Podcast audio, 15:08, *The Moth Radio Hour*, December 5, 2012, accessed September 15, 2018, https://themoth.org/stories/r2-where-are-you.

4. Bessel van der Kolk, *The Body Keeps the Score* (New York: Penguin Books, 2014), 123.

5. van der Kolk, *The Body Keeps the Score*, 123.

6. Brené Brown, *I Thought It Was Just Me* (New York: Avery, 2007), 63.

7. "Preventing Suicide," The Trevor Project, 2020, accessed June 3, 2019, https://www.thetrevorproject.org/resources/preventing-suicide/facts-about-suicide/.

8. Sheree M. Schrager, Jeremy T. Goldbach, and Mary Rose Mamey, "Development of the Sexual Minority Adolescent Stress Inventory," *Frontiers in Psychology*, March 15, 2018, accessed June 3, 2019, https://doi.org/10.3389/fpsyg.2018.00319.

9. Jaime Veiga and Joshua Saxon, "Why Your Customers' Attention Is the Scarcest Resource in 2017, *Research World*, February 20, 2017, accessed June 16, 2019, https://www.researchworld.com/why-your-customers-attention-is-the-scarcest-resource-in-2017/.

10. Maria Millett, "Challenge Your Negative Thoughts," Michigan State University, March 31, 2017, accessed July 1, 2019, https://www.canr.msu.edu/news/challenge_your_negative_thoughts.

11. Robert Karen, *Becoming Attached* (New York: Oxford University Press, 1998), 378.

12. Sam Killermann, "Genderbread Person v4.0," The Genderbread Person, 2017, accessed November 2, 2018, https://www.genderbread.org/resource/genderbread-person-v4-0.

13. Talmud Yerushalmi, Tractate Sanhedrin (4:9).

14. van der Kolk, *The Body Keeps the Score*, 129.

CHAPTER 9

1. Elie Wiesel, *Night* (New York: Les Editions de Minuit, 1958), 48.

2. Lara Stemple, Andrew Flores, and Ilan H. Meyer, "Sexual Victimization Perpetrated by Women: Federal Data Reveal Surprising Prevalence," *Elsevier*, May 2017, accessed June 11, 2019, DOI: https://doi.org/10.1016/j.avb.2016.09.007.

3. Stemple, Flores, and Meyer, "Sexual Victimization Perpetrated by Women."

4. Brené Brown, "Listening to Ahame—Brené Brown," YouTube video, 20:38, July 19, 2013, accessed September 7, 2019, https://www.youtube.com/watch?v=7jtZdSRst94.

5. "Jeffrey Epstein Charged in Manhattan Federal Court with Sex Trafficking of Minors," United States Department of Justice, July 8, 2019, accessed February 3, 2020, https://www.justice.gov/usao-sdny/pr/jeffrey-epstein-charged-manhattan-federal-court-sex-trafficking-minors.

6. Samantha Joseph, "State Attorney Removed from Case as Florida Investigates Jeffrey Epstein's Sweetheart Deal," Law.com, August 6, 2019, accessed February 3, 2020, https://www.law.com/dailybusinessreview/2019/08/06/state-attorney-removed-from-case-as-florida-investigates-jeffrey-epsteins-sweetheart-deal/?slreturn=20200103191345.

7. Nadia Suleman, "Young Americans Are Increasingly 'Uncomfortable' With LGBTQ Community, GLAAD Study Shows," *Time*, June 25, 2019,

accessed June 30, 2019, https://time.com/5613276/glaad-acceptance-index-lgbtq-survey/.

8. Lauren Reiff, "Generation Z and the Rise of Conservatism," Medium, November 5, 2018, accessed June 25, 2019, https://medium.com/@laurennreiff/generation-z-and-the-rise-of-conservatism-677414f925d1.

CHAPTER 10

1. Ack M. Hamanova, "The Fish Baking Story," Rewriting Inner Scripts (RISE), accessed June 4, 2019, http://rewritinginnerscripts.com/index.html.

2. Dan Baker, *What Happy People Know* (New York: St. Martin's, 2003), 204.

3. Devika Desai, "Air Canada Drops 'Ladies and Gentlemen' Greeting on Planes for a Gender Neutral Welcome," *National Post*, October 15, 2019, accessed October 17, 2019, https://nationalpost.com/news/air-canada-drops-ladies-and-gentlemen-greeting-onboard-planes-for-a-gender-neutral-welcome.

4. "Healthy Gender Development and Young Children," Head Start—Early Childhood Learning and Knowledge Center, last updated October 2, 2018, accessed November 11, 2019, https://eclkc.ohs.acf.hhs.gov/publication/healthy-gender-development-young-children.

5. Justin Richardson and Peter Parnell, *And Tango Makes Three* (New York: Little Simon, 2005).

6. Marie-Sabine Roger and Anne Sol, *Of Course They Do!: Boys and Girls Can Do Anything* (Watertown, MA: Charlesbridge, 2014).

7. Munro Leaf, *The Story of Ferdinand* (New York: Viking Books, board book edition, 2017).

8. Robie H. Harris, *Who Has What? All About Girls' Bodies and Boys' Bodies* (Somerville, MA: Candlewick, 2011).

9. Jessica Herthel and Jazz Jennings, *I Am Jazz* (New York: Dial Books, 2014).

10. Sarah Hoffman and Ian Hoffman, *Jacob's New Dress* (Park Ridge, IL: Albert Whitman & Company, 2014).

11. Jeffrey Bone and Lisa Bone, *Not Every Princess* (Washington, DC: Magination Press, 2014).

12. Michael Hall, *Red: A Crayon's Story* (New York: Greenwillow Books, 2015).

13. Sophie Beer, *Love Makes a Family* (New York: Dial Books, 2018).

14. Bill Hathaway, "Doctors' Attitudes toward Lesbians and Gays Shaped Early in Medical School," *Yale News*, August 5, 2019, accessed August 14,

2019, https://news.yale.edu/2019/08/05/doctors-attitudes-toward-lesbians-and-gays-shaped-early-medical-school.

15. C. George Boeree, "Personality Theories—Carl Rogers." Psychology Department, Shippensburg University, last updated 2006, accessed August 11, 2019, https://webspace.ship.edu/cgboer/rogers.html.

CHAPTER 11

1. Harvey Milk, *Queer Past Becomes Present*, Permanent Exhibition, GLBT Historical Society Museum, San Francisco.

2. Brené Brown, *Daring Greatly* (New York: Avery, 2012).

3. Reuben Zellman, "The Holiness of Twilight," Transtorah, 2006, accessed November 3, 2019, http://www.transtorah.org/PDFs/Holiness_of_Twilight.pdf.

BIBLIOGRAPHY

"8 Things to Remember about Child Development." Center on the Developing Child, Harvard University, 2016. Accessed December 5, 2019. https://develop ingchild.harvard.edu/resources/8-things-remember-child-development/.

Allender, Dan. "Certificate in Narrative Focused Trauma Care Level I." Presented at the Seattle School of Theology and Psychology's Allender Center Level I Training, Seattle, November 15–18, 2018.

"America's Top Fears 2018: Chapman University Survey of American Fears." *Chapman University Blog*, October 16, 2018. Accessed September 15, 2019. https://blogs.chapman.edu/wilkinson/2018/10/16/americas-top -fears-2018/.

"APA Reiterates Strong Opposition to Conversion Therapy." American Psychiatric Association, November 15, 2018. Accessed June 20, 2019. https:// www.psychiatry.org/newsroom/news-releases/apa-reiterates-strong-opposi- tion-to-conversion-therapy.

Baker, Dan. *What Happy People Know*. New York: St. Martin's, 2003.

Bauermeister, José A., Daniel Connochie, Laura Jadwin-Cakmak, and Steven Meanley. "Gender Policing During Childhood and the Psychological Well- Being of Young Adult Sexual Minority Men in the United States." *American Journal of Men's Health*, November 29, 2016. Accessed November 30, 2019. https://doi.org/10.1177/1557988316680938.

Beer, Sophie. *Love Makes a Family*. New York: Dial Books, 2018.

"The Blue Eyes & Brown Eyes Exercise." Jane Elliot, 2019. Accessed May 15, 2019. https://janeelliott.com.

Boeree, C. George. "Personality Theories—Carl Rogers." Psychology Department, Shippensburg University, last updated 2006. Accessed August 11, 2019. https://webspace.ship.edu/cgboer/rogers.html.

Bone, Jeffrey, and Lisa Bone. *Not Every Princess*. Washington, DC: Magination Press, 2014.

Brown, Brené. "The Cruelty Crisis: Bullying Isn't a School Problem, It's a National Pastime." *Psychology Today*, November 1, 2010. Accessed October 25, 2019. https://www.psychologytoday.com/us/blog/ordinary-courage/201011/the-cruelty-crisis-bullying-isnt-school-problem-its-national-pastime.

———. *Daring Greatly*. New York: Avery, 2012.

———. *I Thought It Was Just Me*, New York: Avery, 2007.

———. "Listening to Shame—Brené Brown." YouTube video, 20:38. July 19, 2013. Accessed September 7, 2019. https://www.youtube.com/watch?v=7jtZdSRst94.

———. "The Power of Vulnerability." *Sounds True*, November 15, 2012. Accessed March 8, 2016. https://www.soundstrue.com/store/the-power-of-vulnerability-2917.html.

"Bullying Statistics." PACER's National Bullying Prevention Center, last updated December 27, 2017. Accessed December 4, 2019. https://www.pacer.org/bullying/resources/stats.asp.

Burton, Neel. "When Homosexuality Stopped Being a Mental Disorder." *Psychology Today*, September 18, 2015. Accessed June 25, 2019. https://www.psychologytoday.com/us/blog/hide-and-seek/201509/when-homosexuality-stopped-being-mental-disorder.

"Chapter 2: The Separation and the Atonement—Fear and Conflict." A Course in Miracles International. Accessed August 7, 2019. https://acimi.com/a-course-in-miracles/text/chapter-2/fear-and-conflict.

Cherry, Kendra. "How Confirmation Bias Works." *Verywell Mind*, November 27, 2019. Accessed December 5, 2019. https://www.verywellmind.com/what-is-a-confirmation-bias-2795024.

City News Service. "L.A. County Will Track Suicide Data on LGBTQ Individuals." *Los Angeles Times*, September 3, 2019. Accessed September 20, 2019. https://www.latimes.com/california/story/2019-09-03/la-county-track-suicide-data-lgbtq.

Daniel, H., and R. Bukus. "Lesbian, Gay, Bisexual, and Transgender Health Disparities: Executive Summary of a Policy Position Paper from the American College of Physicians." National Center for Biotechnology Information, July 21, 2015. Accessed August 5, 2019. https://doi.org/10.7326/M14-2482.

Datta, Vivek. "When Homosexuality Came Out (of the DSM)." *Mad in America*, December 1, 2014. Accessed June 25, 2019. https://www.madinamerica.com/2014/12/homosexuality-came-dsm/.

Dermendzhiyska, Elitsa. "Rejection Kills." *Aeon*, April 30, 2019. Accessed May 20, 2019. https://aeon.co/essays/health-warning-social-rejection-doesnt-only-hurt-it-kills.

Desai, Devika. "Air Canada Drops 'Ladies and Gentlemen' Greeting on Planes for a Gender Neutral Welcome." *National Post*, October 15, 2019. Accessed October 17, 2019. https://nationalpost.com/news/air-canada-drops-ladies-and-gentlemen-greeting-onboard-planes-for-a-gender-neutral-welcome.

Deych, Mykhiel. "On Behalf of Their Name." *Rethinking Schools* 33, no. 2 (Winter 2018–2019). Accessed February 18, 2020. https://www.rethinking-schools.org/articles/on-behalf-of-their-name.

Dickinson, Amy. "Gay Daughter Presents Sleepover Dilemma for Her Parents." *Arizona Daily Star*, November 4, 2019.

Donegan, Moira. "The Jeffrey Esptein-Victoria's Secret Connection." *Atlantic*, August 6, 2019. Accessed August 20, 2019. https://www.theatlantic.com/ideas/archive/2019/08/victorias-secret-epstein/595507/.

Drescher, Jack. "Science & Theology in Human Sexuality." Presentation on History, Science and Politics of Homosexuality, September 19, 2016. Accessed May 13, 2019. https://slideplayer.com/slide/11745908/.

"Egodystonic Sexual Orientation." PatientsLikeMe, last updated January 16, 2020. Accessed September 2, 2019. https://www.patientslikeme.com/conditions/egodystonic-sexual-orientation.

Ewing, Heidi, and Rachel Grady. *One of Us*. Los Gatos, CA: Netflix, 2017. Film.

Felitti, V. J., R. F. Anda, D. Nordenberg, D. F. Williamson, A. M. Spitz, M. P. Koss, and J. S. Marks. "Relationship of Childhood Abuse and Household Dysfunction to Many of the Leading Causes of Death in Adults. The Adverse Childhood Experiences (ACE) Study." National Center for Biotechnology Information, May 1998. Accessed August 30, 2019. https://doi.org/10.1016/S0749-3797(98)00017-8.

Goldstein, Joelle. "Conversion Therapy Founder Comes Out Publicly as Gay after 20 Years of Leading Homophobic Program." *People*, September 4, 2019. Accessed September 6, 2019. https://people.com/human-interest/conversion-therapy-founder-comes-out-as-gay/.

Gross, Terry. "'Fresh Air' Remembers 'Boyz n the Hood' Director John Singleton." NPR, May 3, 2019. Accessed May 5, 2019. https://www.npr.org/2019/05/03/719986809/fresh-air-remembers-boyz-n-the-hood-director-john-singleton.

Hall, Michael. *Red: A Crayon's Story*. New York: Greenwillow Books, 2015.

Hamanova, Ack M. "The Fish Baking Story." Rewriting Inner Scripts (RISE). Accessed June 4, 2019. http://rewritinginnerscripts.com/index.html.

Harris, Robie H. *Who Has What? All About Girls' Bodies and Boys' Bodies*. Somerville, MA: Candlewick, 2011.

Hathaway, Bill. "Doctors' Attitudes toward Lesbians and Gays Shaped Early in Medical School." *Yale News*, August 5, 2019. Accessed August 14, 2019. https://news.yale.edu/2019/08/05/doctors-attitudes-toward-lesbians-and-gays-shaped-early-medical-school.

"Healthy Gender Development and Young Children." Head Start—Early Childhood Learning and Knowledge Center, last updated October 2, 2018. Accessed November 11, 2019. https://eclkc.ohs.acf.hhs.gov/publication/healthy-gender-development-young-children.

Heitler, Susan. "Are You Good Enough?" *Psychology Today*, July 15, 2014. Accessed June 3, 2019. https://www.psychologytoday.com/us/blog/resolution-not-conflict/201407/are-you-good-enough.

Herthel, Jessica, and Jazz Jennings. *I Am Jazz*. New York: Dial Books, 2014.

Hoffman, Sarah, and Ian Hoffman. *Jacob's New Dress*. Park Ridge, IL: Albert Whitman & Company, 2014.

"Introjection." *GoodTherapy*, last updated October 6, 2015. Accessed June 7, 2019. https://www.goodtherapy.org/blog/psychpedia/introjection.

"Jeffrey Epstein Charged in Manhattan Federal Court with Sex Trafficking of Minors." United States Department of Justice, July 8, 2019. Accessed February 3, 2020. https://www.justice.gov/usao-sdny/pr/jeffrey-epstein-charged-manhattan-federal-court-sex-trafficking-minors.

Jones, Serene. *Trauma and Grace*. Louisville, KY: Westminster John Knox Press, 2009.

Joseph, Samantha. "State Attorney Removed from Case as Florida Investigates Jeffrey Epstein's Sweetheart Deal." Law.com, August 6, 2019. Accessed February 3, 2020. https://www.law.com/dailybusinessreview/2019/08/06/state-attorney-removed-from-case-as-florida-investigates-jeffrey-epsteins-sweetheart-deal/?slreturn=20200103191345.

Karen, Robert. *Becoming Attached*. New York: Oxford University Press, 1998.

Kennedy, Teresa J. "Language Learning and Its Impact on the Brain: Connecting Language Learning with the Mind through Content-Based Instruction." American Council on the Teaching of Foreign Languages, December 31, 2008. Accessed November 10, 2019. https://doi.org/10.1111/j.1944-9720.2006.tb02900.x.

Killermann, Sam. "Genderbread Person v4.0." The Genderbread Person, 2017. Accessed November 2, 2018. https://www.genderbread.org/resource/genderbread-person-v4-0.

Larson, Eric. "Internalized Homophobia: The Next LGBT Movement after Same-Sex Marriage." *Mashable*, June 25, 2014. Accessed May 7, 2015. https://mashable.com/2014/06/25/internalized-homophobia-lgbt/.

Leaf, Munro. *The Story of Ferdinand*. New York: Viking Books, Brdbk edition, 2017.

Lucy, Helen, and Ann Phoenix. "Introjection—Critical Social Psychology (18/30)." YouTube video, 2:20. July 26, 2011. Accessed August 5, 2019. https://www.youtube.com/watch?v=Dv6BkKd1jNA.

Mallory, Christy, Taylor N. T. Brown, and Kerith J. Conron. "Conversion Therapy and LGBT Youth." Williams Institute, January 2018. Accessed June 5, 2019. https://williamsinstitute.law.ucla.edu/wp-content/uploads/Conversion-Therapy-LGBT-Youth-Jan-2018.pdf.

———. "Conversion Therapy and LGBT Youth Update." Williams Institute, June 2019. Accessed June 5, 2019. https://williamsinstitute.law.ucla.edu/wp-content/uploads/Conversion-Therapy-LGBT-Youth-Update-June-2019. pdf.

Martinez, Sebastian. "Why We Need More Culturally Competent Therapists." *National Alliance on Mental Health (NAMI)*, July 8, 2019. Accessed July 8, 2019. https://www.nami.org/Blogs/NAMI-Blog/July-2019/Why-We-Need-More-Culturally-Competent-Therapists.

Maryfield, Bailey. "Implicit Racial Bias." Justice Research and Statistics Association, December 2018. Accessed August 8, 2019. https://www.jrsa.org/pubs/factsheets/jrsa-factsheet-implicit-racial-bias.pdf.

Mayer, Gal, and Hector Vargas. "GLMA Opposes Efforts to Eradicate Federal Recognition of Transgender Individuals." Health Professionals Advancing LGBTQ Equality (GLMA), October 2018. Accessed November 16, 2019. http://glma.org/index.cfm?fuseaction=Feature.showFeature&CategoryID=1 &FeatureID=840.

Mays, Jeffrey C. "New York City Is Ending a Ban on Gay Conversion Therapy. Here's Why." *New York Times*, September 12, 2019. Accessed September 18, 2019. https://www.nytimes.com/2019/09/12/nyregion/conversion-therapy-ban-nyc.html.

"Memorandum for the President." Nixon Library, January 16, 1970. Accessed May 17, 2019. https://www.nixonlibrary.gov/sites/default/files/virtualli-brary/documents/jul10/53.pdf.

Milk, Harvey. *Queer Past Becomes Present*. Permanent Exhibition. GLBT Historical Society Museum. San Francisco.

Millett, Maria. "Challenge Your Negative Thoughts." Michigan State University, March 31, 2017. Accessed July 1, 2019. https://www.canr.msu.edu/news/challenge_your_negative_thoughts.

Miron, Oren, Kun-Hsing Yu, Rachel Wilf-Miron, and Issac S. Kohane. "Suicide Rates among Adolescents and Young Adults in the United States,

2000–2017." *JAMA*, June 18, 2019. Accessed July 7, 2019. DOI: https://doi.org/10.1001/jama.2019.5054.

Morse, Brit. "The 7 Most Embarrassing Branding Mistakes of 2018." *Inc.*, November 28, 2018. Accessed September 2, 2019. https://www.inc.com/brit-morse/2018-biggest-marketing-branding-fails.html.

Mozes, Alan. "Depression Rates Not Budging for Lesbian and Gay Teens." *US News & World Report*, October 22, 2019. Accessed October 25, 2019. https://www.usnews.com/news/health-news/articles/2019-10-22/depression-rates-not-budging-for-lesbian-and-gay-teens.

Myss, Caroline. "Choices That Can Change Your Life—Caroline Myss—TEDx-FindhornSalon." YouTube video, 25:55. April 3, 2017. Accessed June 20, 2019. https://www.youtube.com/watch?v=-KysuBl2m_w&feature=emb_title.

"National Survey on LGBTQ Youth Mental Health." The Trevor Project, 2019. Accessed September 12, 2019. https://www.thetrevorproject.org/wp-content/uploads/2019/06/The-Trevor-Project-National-Survey-Results-2019.pdf?ftag=MSF0951a18.

Newport, Frank. "In U.S., Estimate of LGBT Population Rises to 4.5%." Gallup, May 22, 2018. Accessed September 15, 2019. https://news.gallup.com/poll/234863/estimate-lgbt-population-rises.aspx.

Notaro, Tig. "R2 Where Are You." Podcast audio, 15:08. *The Moth Radio Hour*, December 5, 2012. Accessed September 15, 2018. https://themoth.org/stories/r2-where-are-you.

Olb, Jon, and Madeleine Parry. *Nanette*. Los Gatos, CA: Netflix, June 2018. Film.

O'Neill, Rory (aka Panti Bliss). "Panti's Noble Call at the Abbey Theatre—With Subtitles." YouTube video, 10:47. February 2, 2014. Accessed August 7, 2019. https://www.youtube.com/watch?v=WXayhUzWnl0.

Pattanaik, Devdutt, and Jerry Johnson. *I Am Divine. So Are You: How Buddhism, Jainism, Sikhism and Hinduism Affirm the Dignity of Queer Identities and Sexualities*. New York: HarperCollins, 2017.

Peck, M. Scott. *People of the Lie*. New York: Simon and Schuster, 1983.

Pei, Adrian. *The Minority Experience*. Downers Grove, IL: InterVarsity Press, 2018.

"Phobia, What Is It?" Harvard Health Publishing, Harvard Medical School, December 2018. Accessed September 23, 2019. https://www.health.harvard.edu/a_to_z/phobia-a-to-z.

"Preventing Suicide." The Trevor Project. Accessed June 3, 2019. https://www.thetrevorproject.org/resources/preventing-suicide/facts-about-suicide/.

Rafferty, Jason. "Gender Identity Development in Children." *Healthy Children,* American Academy of Pediatrics, last updated September 18, 2018. Accessed November 20, 2019. https://www.healthychildren.org/English/ages-stages/gradeschool/Pages/Gender-Identity-and-Gender-Confusion-In-Children.aspx.

Reiff, Lauren. "Generation Z and the Rise of Conservatism." Medium, November 5, 2018. Accessed June 25, 2019. https://medium.com/@laurennreiff/generation-z-and-the-rise-of-conservatism-677414f925d1.

Reilly, Mollie. "The Criminal Justice System Disproportionately Targets LGBT People, Study Finds." *HuffPost,* February 25, 2016. Accessed July 7, 2019. https://www.huffpost.com/entry/lgbt-criminal-justice-system_n_56ce3108e4b03260bf756d5c.

Richardson, Justin, and Peter Parnell. *And Tango Makes Three.* New York: Little Simon, 2015.

Robinson, Matthew. "Hitler-Owned Book Hints at Plans for North American Holocaust." CNN, January 26, 2019. Accessed January 26, 2019. https://edition.cnn.com/2019/01/25/americas/holocaust-canada-north-america-blueprint-scli-intl/index.html?no-st=1548452021.

Roger, Marie-Sabine, and Anne Sol. *Of Course They Do!: Boys and Girls Can Do Anything.* Watertown, MA: Charlesbridge, 2014.

Russell, Stephen T., and Jessica N. Fish. "Mental Health in Lesbian, Gay, Bisexual, and Transgender (LGBT) Youth." National Center for Biotechnology Information, January 14, 2016. Accessed September 12, 2019. https://doi.org/10.1146/annurev-clinpsy-021815-093153.

Ryan, Caitlin, David Huebner, Rafael M. Diaz, and Jorge Sanchez. "Family Rejection as a Predictor of Negative Health Outcomes in White and Latino Lesbian, Gay, and Bisexual Young Adults." *Journal of the American Academy of Pediatrics,* January 2009. Accessed May 14, 2019. https://doi.org/10.1542/peds.2007-3524.

"Same-Sex Marriage Around the World." Pew Research Center, October 28, 2019. Accessed January 28, 2019. https://www.pewforum.org/fact-sheet/gay-marriage-around-the-world/.

"SB 1019: Amending Section 15-716, Arizona Revised Statutes; Relating to School Curriculum." State of Arizona Senate, 2019. Accessed February 5, 2019. https://www.azleg.gov/legtext/54leg/1r/laws/0086.htm.

Schimelpfening, Nancy. "'Not Otherwise Specified' (NOS) in the Diagnosis of Mental Disorders." *Verywell Mind.* Last Updated September 23, 2019. Accessed July 14, 2019. https://www.verywellmind.com/not-otherwise-specified-nos-1066918.

Schlanger, Zoe. "A Teen Health Survey Crucial to US Public Policy Is Finally Asking Kids about Their Sexual Orientation." *Quartz*, June 25, 2017. Accessed July 20, 2019. https://qz.com/1014142/a-teen-health-survey-crucial-to-us-public-policy-is-finally-asking-kids-about-their-sexual-orientation/.

Schrager, Sheree M., Jeremy T. Goldbach, and Mary Rose Mamey. "Development of the Sexual Minority Adolescent Stress Inventory." *Frontiers in Psychology*, March 15, 2018. Accessed June 3, 2019. https://doi.org/10.3389/fpsyg.2018.00319.

Shtulman, Andrew, and Rachel InKyung Yoo. "Children's Understanding of Physical Possibility Constrains Their Belief in Santa Claus." Elsevier, 2014. Accessed May 2, 2019. https://doi.org/10.1016/j.cogdev.2014.12.006.

Stemple, Lara, Andrew Flores, and Ilan H. Meyer. "Sexual Victimization Perpetrated by Women: Federal Data Reveal Surprising Prevalence." Elsevier, May 2017. Accessed June 11, 2019. https://doi.org/10.1016/j.avb.2016.09.007.

"Substance Use and SUDs in LGBTQ* Populations." National Institute on Drug Abuse, September 5, 2017. Accessed July 23, 2019. https://www.drugabuse.gov/related-topics/substance-use-suds-in-lgbtq-populations.

Suleman, Nadia. "Young Americans Are Increasingly 'Uncomfortable' with LGBTQ Community, GLAAD Study Shows." *Time*, June 25, 2019. Accessed June 30, 2019. https://time.com/5613276/glaad-acceptance-index-lgbtq-survey/.

Treat, Jeremy. "LGBT + Identity Formation: Trauma and Resilience." Presented at Penny Lane Center's 9th Annual EDGY Conference—Embracing Identities, Los Angeles, October 27, 2017.

"The Trevor Project Commends the FCC on Its Report on the National Suicide Hotline Improvement Act of 2018." The Trevor Project, August 15, 2019. Accessed August 24, 2019. https://www.thetrevorproject.org/trvr_press/the-trevor-project-commends-the-fcc-on-its-report-on-the-national-suicide-hotline-improvement-act-of-2018/.

"Understanding Early Sexual Development." KidsHealth, Nemours Foundation, October 2014. Accessed April 7, 2015. http://m.rossa-editorial.kidshealth.org/en/parents/development.html?WT.ac=m-p-ra.

"Understanding Early Sexual Development." Rady Children's Hospital, 2014. Accessed December 10, 2019. https://www.rchsd.org/health-articles/understanding-early-sexual-development/.

"Understanding Gender." Gender Spectrum, 2019. Accessed September 6, 2019. https://www.genderspectrum.org/quick-links/understanding-gender/.

"Unjust: How the Broken Criminal Justice System Fails LGBT People." Movement Advancement Project, February 2016. Accessed July 28, 2019. http://lgbtmap.org/lgbt-criminal-justice.

van der Kolk, Bessel. *The Body Keeps the Score*. New York: Penguin Books, 2014.

Veiga, Jaime, and Joshua Saxon. "Why Your Customers' Attention Is the Scarcest Resource in 2017, Research World, February 20, 2017. Accessed June 16, 2019. https://www.researchworld.com/why-your-customers-attention-is-the-scarcest-resource-in-2017/.

"What Is Bullying?" *Bullying. No Way!*, 2019. Accessed October 5, 2019. https://bullyingnoway.gov.au/WhatIsBullying.

Wiesel, Elie. *Night*. New York: Les Editions de Minuit, 1958.

Wilson, Bianca, Khush Cooper, Angel Kastanis, and Sheila Nezhad. "Sexual and Gender Minority Youth in Foster Care: Assessing Disproportionality and Disparities in Los Angeles." Williams Institute, August 2014. Accessed August 7, 2019. http://williamsinstitute.law.ucla.edu/wp-content/uploads/LAFYS_report_final-aug-2014.pdf.

Zellman, Reuben. "The Holiness of Twilight." Transtorah, 2006. Accessed November 3, 2019. http://www.transtorah.org/PDFs/Holiness_of_Twilight.pdf.

INDEX

ABOUT THE AUTHOR

Chris Tompkins is a teacher, TEDx speaker, spiritual life coach, and LGBTQ advocate based in Los Angeles, California. More importantly, he's an uncle of five. Chris believes *all* kids are the future and teaches social-emotional learning throughout Southern California.